Development Microeconomics

Development Microeconomics

PRANAB BARDHAN
and
CHRISTOPHER UDRY

OXFORD
UNIVERSITY PRESS

OXFORD
UNIVERSITY PRESS

Great Clarendon Street, Oxford OX2 6DP

Oxford University Press is a department of the University of Oxford
It furthers the University's objective of excellence in research, scholarship,
and education by publishing worldwide in

Oxford New York

Athens Auckland Bangkok Bogotá Buenos Aires Calcutta
Cape Town Chennai Dar es Salaam Delhi Florence Hong Kong Istanbul
Karachi Kuala Lumpur Madrid Melbourne Mexico City Mumbai
Nairobi Paris São Paulo Singapore Taipei Tokyo Toronto Warsaw

with associated companies in Berlin Ibadan

Oxford is a registered trade mark of Oxford University Press
in the UK and in certain other countries

Published in the United States
by Oxford University Press Inc., New York

British Library Cataloguing in Publication Data

Data available

Library of Congress Cataloging in Publication Data
Bardhan, Pranab K.
Development microeconomics / Pranab Bardhan and Christopher Udry.
p. cm.
Includes bibliographical references and index.
1. Microeconomics. 2. Economic development. I. Udry.
Christopher. II. Title.
HB172.B26   1999   338.5—dc21   99–20554

ISBN 0–19–877370–6 (hbk)
ISBN 0–19–877371–4 (pbk)

1 3 5 7 9 10 8 6 4 2

Typeset by Hope Services (Abingdon) Ltd.
Printed in Great Britain
on acid-free paper by
Bookcraft Ltd.,
Midsomer Norton, Somerset

Preface

Tolstoy begins *Anna Karenina* with the famous sentence: 'All happy families are alike but an unhappy family is unhappy after its own fashion.' Perhaps that is also the case in the world of economic misery and well-being. The diversity of experience of the poor countries in the world is much wider and sharper than that of the rich countries. This is partly because the number of people and countries that are poor is much larger (and, socially, geographically, and institutionally, far more heterogeneous) than that of rich countries. Under these circumstances, to aim at capturing even the broad contours of this diversity of development experience in a short textbook is hopeless. To any generalization about this experience that such a textbook may venture to suggest, one can easily cite many counter-examples from different parts of the world.

In this textbook we do not even attempt any comprehensive or broad representation of the issues of development and underdevelopment. Our intention is to be selective and illustrative, to give examples of analytical thinking on some of the major issues. In the choice of issues, our focus is on those that are more relevant to the very poor countries (not so much to the middle-income developing countries, or even, in the latter countries, on issues that are more relevant to the poorest sections of their population). Hence, for example, our frequent emphasis on the rural and the more unorganized or informal sectors of the economy.

The issue of relevance should not, however, be interpreted in the sense of immediate applicability in matters of practical policy. Our treatment of problems in this book is largely theoretical (though not technically at a highly sophisticated level). We do not try to capture the variety of empirical experience in different parts of the world that have accumulated over the last few decades (and the many careful econometric estimates that are now available on the basis of the data collected). We occasionally refer to some empirical work, but more as an example to highlight the theoretical point that we happen to be making. Even in the theoretical treatment we are highly selective, not comprehensive. While in our choice of issues we have to keep analytical tractability and ease of exposition in mind, we like to think that we have not done theory for theory's sake, but have chosen problems that have some, at least faint, resonance in the more complex, real world. (With our own background of empirical work in some of the poorest parts of the world—South Asia for one author, sub-Saharan Africa for the other—we are painfully aware of the difficulty of capturing the complexities of that real world.) In many chapters we briefly describe what we think are some of the major theoretical issues on a given problem, and then use a model or two to illustrate ways of deeper analytical probing, so that the student-readers get some experience of building models which they can then use to analyse other important problems in development. (We have presumed some familiarity with the tools and concepts of general microeconomic theory at the first-year graduate or the advanced undergraduate level.)

Lord Wavell entitled a book of poems *Other Men's Flowers*. In writing this textbook, we have essentially collected other men's and women's 'flowers', having freely borrowed their ideas and models; only the selection and the flower arrangement is ours. We express our general gratitude to all these authors (we attempt to refer to them individually in the chapters) for enriching the field of development economics and also to our respective students at Berkeley and Northwestern, the first visitors to our 'flower show', for encouraging us in this venture.

P.B.
C.U.

Contents

1

Introduction

In some sense, development economics used to be at the centre of all of economics. The classical economists of the seventeenth, eighteenth, and early nineteenth centuries were all development economists, as they were usually writing about a developing country (in many cases, Britain) going through a process of industrial transformation. Then, in the hundred years before the Second World War, development economics took the form primarily of protectionist arguments for industrialization in the rest of the world (List in Germany, Manoilescu in Eastern Europe, Ranade in India, and so on). In the third decade of this century it flourished briefly in the Soviet Union, dwelling on the problems of capital accumulation in a dual economy and of surplus mobilization from agriculture, and on the characteristics of the equilibrium of the family farm; the best products of this period—the dual economy model of Preobrazhenski (1926), the two-sector planning model of Feldman (1928), and the peasant economy model of Chayanov (1925)—came to be regarded as landmarks in the postwar literature when they were translated into English.

But it was only after 1940 that the subject of development economics really took off, beginning with the famous paper of Rosenstein-Rodan (1943) and the book by Mandelbaum (1945)—both, incidentally, written about the development problems of south-eastern Europe—and then with the works of Chenery, Hirschman, Kuznets, Lewis, Mahalanobis, Nurkse, Scitovsky, Sen, and others.[1] This, of course, coincided in some cases with the emergence of newly independent nation states under an anti-colonial leadership often suspicious of the historical impact of free markets and international trade and investment in their countries.

Much of this early postwar literature originated in a clear perception of the limited usefulness, in understanding underdevelopment, of orthodox

[1] For an introduction to this formative period of development economics as well as a retrospective view by some of the pioneers themselves, see Meier and Seers (1984).

economics, particularly in its standard Walrasian form with constant returns to scale, pure competition, perfect information, insignificant transaction costs and externalities, supposed institution neutrality, price-sensitive adjustments that unambiguously clear markets, and so on. Development thinking and practice on these lines sometimes led to iconoclastic excesses, for example in the form of indiscriminate state interventionism or autarkism; the failures and disasters of regulatory and autarkic states have now been widely documented. At the same time, the pillars of orthodox Walrasian economics have become much shakier today under the onslaught of a whole generation of mainstream economists, armed with their models of information asymmetry and strategic interaction of agents, imperfect and incomplete markets, dynamic externalities and increasing returns to scale, multiple equilibria and self-reinforcing mechanisms, models with which development economists of yesteryear would have been comfortable by and large, even though some of these were beyond their own model-making capacity.

Following thus on a respected tradition in development economics and recent advances in economic theory, we shall in some of the subsequent chapters explore issues of information-based market failures and fragmentation (particularly in factor markets), coordination failures and frequency-dependent equilibria (i.e. where the profitability of adopting a particular course depends on how many others are expected to do the same), and self-reinforcing mechanisms which govern the persistence of dysfunctional institutions so common in poor countries. In particular, we shall draw upon the pre-eminent breakthrough in economic theory that has taken the form of an explicit treatment of information in two ways: information in the sense of technical knowledge and human capital (this is germane to our discussion in Chapters 2, 10, 11, 12, and 14); and information in the sense of knowledge about the actions of others not being perfectly and freely available to everyone unlike in the standard model of perfect competition (this is prominent in Chapters 4, 6, 7, 8, and 9). Imperfect information underlies why markets operate (sometimes even fail to operate) in the way that they do and it generates coordination failures (this in different ways appears forcefully in Chapters 3, 13, 16, and 17).

At the same time, we have tried to avoid the preoccupation of the earlier development literature with blanket market failures and reflexive interventionism, and its serious underappreciation of the healthy disciplining effects of market rivalry (even when those markets work imperfectly), of the importance of price-guided allocative efficiency, and of limited government capacity and individual ingenuity in manipulating public programmes for private gain. We have also emphasized the dual relationship between equity and efficiency: while equitable policies in favour of the poor cannot be sustained for long if they seriously damage efficiency, there are also many cases where efficiency and equity go together, particularly when market failures (like those common in credit and insurance markets) block the escape routes out of poverty, suggesting that the famous equity–efficiency trade-off that is at the heart of much of mainstream economics may at times be false or exaggerated. Similarly, while studying the operation of some markets we have tried to keep a clear view of the institutional underpinnings of the market mechanism, at the same time, we have not taken the institutions as exogenous and have often tried to understand their economic rationale.

II

While the various models in subsequent chapters will illustrate our approach to markets and institutions, in the rest of this chapter we will discuss some general methodological issues relating to the principle of maximization that we have presumed throughout in these models, a principle that most economists take for granted, but one that is regarded with a great deal of suspicion by many other social scientists, particularly when talking about poor countries. Maximization, even by peasant households in traditional agriculture, is a basic presumption in development microeconomics, whereas sociologists and social anthropologists often emphasize the overwhelming importance of structural and cultural constraints, leaving little scope for freedom of action or rational choice. The economist often answers this with reference to a stylized biological model of natural selection:[2] not everybody is a maximizer, but the competitive process will tend to weed out the non-maximizers, so that we may assume that economic agents behave as if they met the conditions of maximization. However, when competition is lacking, when markets are 'thin' or highly segmented or inadequately formed, non-maximizers (e.g. large landowners in haciendas wastefully using their land) can survive for a prolonged period. The plausibility of the assumption of maximization is thus not entirely independent of the market structure or even of the mode of production.

A large empirical literature has now accumulated confirming intimations of peasant rationality, particularly when one is careful to take into account the insurance motivation underlying the pervasive uncertainty in the physical and social environment. In this empirical literature rationality has often been interpreted in the very narrow sense of price responsiveness. But even when a farmer is not very sensitive to market prices, or where the markets themselves

---

[2] In a survey of the recent literature on evolutionary dynamics in game theory, with the focus on understanding the extent to which evolutionary arguments can substitute rationality-based arguments as a foundation for Nash equilibrium and other non-cooperative solution concepts, Banerjee and Weibull (1992) conclude that there is an intimate connection between the attractors of evolutionary processes and Nash equilibrium even in environments that are much more general than the simple setting of the standard biological model.

are inadequately formed, there may still be ample evidence of a coherent pattern in a peasant's behaviour which indicates an attempt, by and large, to improve his or her condition under the given constraints. Even patron–client relations, which are often cited as a mark of a traditional custom-bound social system or a 'moral economy', may be viewed as a form of rational response to a situation of desperate need of subsistence insurance and protection on the part of the client, and of ready availability of cheap labour services on the part of the patron.

At the same time, there is no denying the fact that individual behaviour is socially embedded and mediated by social relations; individual tastes and expectations (about others' behaviour) are socially conditioned. Social norms can act as a selection procedure in choosing among several equilibria that are common, particularly in strategic situations. Self-esteem as a major driving force in individual behaviour (as well as frequently observed other-regarding tastes, such as a sense of fairness or the urge for revenge) often follows certain culturally specific codes of honour. This social embeddedness, which is important everywhere, is particularly deep in traditional societies; when uncertainties of the physical environment are more acute, or community bonds and sanctions are easier to enforce, or the lack of understanding of natural or social causality is more pervasive in the general population, people more often look to social norms for guidance in their actions. While in the evolution of social norms functionality of a particular norm may give it staying power, many norms are not ultimately reducible to pragmatic calculations, as Elster (1989) has emphasized.

Then there are systematic cognitive errors and biases in judgement (particularly under uncertainty) that arise in individual decision-making, as the mounting experimental evidence of psychologists and economists attests—for a succinct survey of this literature, see Rabin (1998). One ubiquitous example in choice under uncertainty is provided by 'loss aversion': in a wide variety of domains, people are more averse to losses than they are attracted to same-size gains.[3] Some of these systematic errors can be accommodated with a bit of stretching within the framework of expected utility maximization, but there are many cases (for example when people are not fully adept at evaluating their own preferences, or when their wishes influence their beliefs) in which it is clearly misleading to conceptualize people as attempting to maximize stable, well-defined utility functions. In situations of extreme poverty and deprivation, one particular kind of ambiguity in individual interest perception is salient: the poor often internalize the severe constraints they face (and which their earlier generations faced), and this internalization may manifest itself in the form of fatalism, low aspirations, low perception of needs, high rate of time discount,

---

[3] For a review of this problem, see Kahneman *et al.* (1991).

and so on. As Sen (1984) reminds us, 'many of the inequities of the world survive by making allies out of the deprived and the abused'.

In view of the empirical anomalies and the internal contradictions[4] of the model of the hyper-rational economic man, many economists follow Simon (1957) in assuming bounded rationality with full recognition of the costs of observation, communication, and computation. Others go beyond this and admit that economic agents' behaviour is sometimes difficult or impossible to rationalize in terms of any well-defined deductive model; they fall back upon inductive means of reasoning and learning.[5] People are supposed to have working hypotheses about the problems they are dealing with, and it is assumed that in their learning process they constantly update and adapt. Whether this process ultimately converges to rationality depends, even in the favourable case of the same situation repeated sufficiently often, on the characteristics of the decision problem or the game.

Keeping all this in mind, our adherence to the principle of maximization in the models of the subsequent chapters should be regarded more as a crude heuristic device than as a definitive statement on human behavioural regularity. In view of the considerable ingenuity that even the poor peasant in a traditional society often shows in responding to material incentives, the presumption of rationality may not be a bad working hypothesis or a benchmark to start with, even if one eventually finds it to be violated in many particular cases. As Elster (1979) comments, 'This presumption is a "principle of charity" similar to the one often used in textual interpretation. One should never take textual contradictions at their face value, but [should] consider whether the context might not give a clue to consistency. Similarly, one should always look very closely at apparently irrational behaviour to see whether there could not be some pattern there after all.' Development economics is full of examples of how apparently irrational behaviour may be successfully explained as an outcome of more complex exercises in rationality, particularly with deeper probes into the nature of the feasibility constraints or the preference patterns.

Similarly, our attempt in subsequent chapters to trace the microfoundations of development analysis in postulates of individual behaviour, i.e. our approach of what is called methodological individualism, should not be interpreted as a way to undervalue the substantive role of social interaction in influencing individual behaviour or in determining the rules of the game that individuals play. In giving explanatory priority to individuals, ours is, of course, a departure from some traditional theories of history or society which rely heavily on disembodied actors or collectivities (e.g. classes, kinship, or ethnic groups) rather than on actual persons. A class or a tribe or a caste does not act by itself, but

---

[4] In games with dynamic structure, the very notion of rationality becomes problematic and common knowledge of rationality may even lead to logical contradictions: see e.g. Binmore (1987).

[5] See e.g. Arthur (1994).

through individuals, however socially conditioned (or 'programmed') the latters' goals and belief systems may be. We may quote from Arrow (1994) on this; while he is convinced that 'social variables, not attached to particular individuals, are essential in studying the economy', he adds that 'it is a salutary check on any theory of the economy or any other part of society that the explanations make sense on the basis of the individuals involved'.

REFERENCES

Arrow, K. J. (1994), 'Methodological Individualism and Social Knowledge', *American Economic Review*, 84.

Arthur, B. (1994), 'Bounded Rationality and Inductive Reasoning', *American Economic Review*, 84.

Banerjee, A., and Weibull, J. W. (1992), 'Evolution and Rationality: Some Recent Game-Theoretic Results', Working Paper no. 345, Industrial Institute for Economic and Social Research, Stockholm.

Binmore, K. (1987), 'Modeling Rational Players: Part I', *Economics and Philosophy*, 3.

Chayanov, A. V. (1925), *The Theory of Peasant Economy*. Irwin, 1966 edn.

Elster, J. (1979), *Ulysses and the Sirens: Studies in Rationality and Irrationality*. Cambridge: Cambridge University Press.

—— (1989), 'Social Norms and Economic Theory', *Journal of Economic Perspectives*, 3.

Feldman, G. A. (1928), 'On the Theory of Growth Rates of National Income', in N. Spulber (ed.), *Foundations of Soviet Strategy for Economic Growth*. Bloomington, Ind.: Indiana University Press, 1964 edn.

Kahneman, D., Knetsch, J., and Thaler, R. (1991), 'Anomalies: The Endowment Effect, Loss Aversion, and Status Quo Bias', *Journal of Economic Perspectives*, 5.

Mandelbaum, K. (1945), *The Industrialization of Backward Areas*. Oxford: Basil Blackwell.

Meier, G.M., and Seers, D. (eds.) (1984), *Pioneers in Development*. Washington: World Bank.

Preobrazhenski, E. (1926), *The New Economics*. Oxford: Clarendon Press, 1965 edn.

Rabin, M. (1998), 'Psychology and Economics', *Journal of Economic Literature*, 36.

Rosenstein-Rodan, P. (1943), 'Problems of Industrialization of Eastern and Southeastern Europe', *Economic Journal*, 53.

Sen, A. K. (1984), *Resources, Values and Development*. Oxford: Basil Blackwell.

Simon, H. (1957), *Models of Man*. New York: John Wiley.

2
Household Economics

Most people in developing countries earn at least part of their livelihood through work in their own enterprises. Moreover, they often consume at least a portion of the output of their productive activities, and household labour is often an important input into the production process of the enterprise. Consequently, individuals make simultaneous decisions about production (the level of output, the demand for factors, and the choice of technology) and consumption (labour supply and commodity demand). This mixture of the economics of the firm and of the household is characteristic of the situation of most families in developing countries and provides the starting point for our analysis.

Most commonly, the enterprise that households operate is a farm. In the least-developed countries, about three-quarters of the labour force is involved in agriculture (United Nations 1994, table 17). A model of a household that is jointly engaged in production and consumption, therefore, is commonly called an 'agricultural household model' (AHM). We use this nomenclature, but it will be seen that the insights of the AHM apply as well to households that operate enterprises such as small-scale trading or petty manufacturing.

Section I provides an overview of the AHM when markets are complete. With complete markets, the production decisions of the household are *separable* from its consumption decisions. The household maximizes profit and then maximizes utility subject to a standard budget constraint which includes the value of these profits. The analysis of production decisions in this situation is greatly simplified. Section II discusses the AHM when markets are not complete. In this instance the separation property breaks down and production decisions depend on the preferences and endowments of the household. In Section III we briefly discuss the use of extensions of the AHM to examine issues of human resource development. In Section IV we briefly examine the strong assumptions that are required to treat the aggregate behaviour of a set of individuals in a household as if they were characterized by a single utility function and budget constraint.

I

The canonical model of an agricultural household includes a utility function, defined over consumption by each member of the household, and a budget constraint, which incorporates production on assets owned by the household.[1] Consider a household with two members, each of whom gets utility from consuming a good (c_1 and c_2) and from leisure (l_1 and l_2). The most simple agricultural household models assume that each household faces a complete set of competitive markets. (This includes, in more general models than the one presented here, a complete set of markets for time- and state-indexed commodities.) Let p be the price of the good, and w be the wage of labour. (We will assume, for simplicity, that the labour of the two family members is homogeneous.) The household can produce the good on its farm according to the concave production function $F(L, A)$, where A is the area of the farm cultivated by the household and L is the amount of labour used on the farm. Let E_i^L be person i's endowment of time, E^A the household's endowment of land, and r the price of one unit of land. The household's problem, then, is to solve

$$\text{Max } U(c_1, c_2, l_1, l_2) \tag{1}$$

subject to

$$p(c_1 + c_2) + wL^h + rA^h \leq F(L, A) + w(L_1^m + L_2^m) + rA^m \tag{2}$$

$$L = L_1^f + L_2^f + L^h \tag{3}$$

$$A = A^f + A^h \tag{4}$$

$$E^A = A^f + A^m, \; E_i^L = L_i^f + L_i^m + l_i, \; i \in \{1,2\} \tag{5}$$

$$c_i, l_i, L_i^f, L_i^m, A^f, A^m \geq 0, \; i \in \{1,2\}. \tag{6}$$

Equation (1) is a household utility function in which utility depends upon the consumption of goods and leisure by each individual. The maximization is with respect to consumption and leisure, hired labour and land, and household labour and land supplied to the market and used on the household farm: $\{c_i\}$, $\{l_i\}$, A^h, L^h, A^m, $\{L_i^m\}$, A^f, and $\{L_i^f\}$. Equation (2) is a conventional budget constraint: cash expenditures on consumption, hired labour, and rented land cannot exceed cash revenues from farming, market labour, and land rented out. Equations (3)–(5) define resource constraints: labour use on the farm is household labour used on the farm plus hired labour; land use on the farm is owned land used on the farm plus hired land; the household's land endowment is used on its own farm or rented out, and each individual's time endowment equals their labour use on the farm, plus market labour time, plus leisure time.

[1] The primary reference for the AHM is Singh *et al.* (1986).

Substituting (3)–(5) into (2), we find:

$$p(c_1 + c_2) + w(l_1 + l_2) \leq \Pi + w(E_1^L + E_2^L) + rE^A \tag{7}$$

$$\Pi = F(L, A) - wL - rA \tag{8}$$

$$c_i, l_i, L, A \geq 0, i \in \{1,2\}. \tag{9}$$

Equation (7) is called the 'full-income' constraint: the value of consumption cannot exceed the value of the household's endowment plus farm profits. The household's problem is now to maximize (1) (with respect to L, A, c_i and l_i) subject to (7)–(9).

The important fact to note is that the problem (1), (7)–(9) is recursive. As long as $U(\ )$ is characterized by local non-satiation, then (7) is binding at the solution and the maximized value of $U(\ )$ is increasing in Π. L and A do not appear in (1), hence (1) and (7) can be replaced with

$$\underset{\{c_i\},\{l_i\}}{\text{Max }} U(c_1, c_2, l_1, l_2) \tag{1'}$$

subject to

$$p(c_1 + c_2) + w(l_1 + l_2) \leq \Pi^*(w, r) + w(E_1^L + E_2^L) + rE^A, \tag{7'}$$

where

$$\Pi^*(w, r) = \underset{L, A}{\text{Max }} F(L, A) - wL - rA. \tag{8'}$$

Thus, an important simplification is possible. Equations (1)–(6) appear to be a joint problem in which production and consumption choices are intertwined, and in particular one in which the household's preferences over consumption and leisure might influence its choices regarding production. However, the transformation of the problem reveals the fact that the household's production decisions are characterized by a simple profit maximization condition— equation (8'). Households choose labour and land inputs so as to maximize profit. Production decisions made on any plot depend only on prices and the characteristics of that plot, not on the household's endowments or preferences. When markets are complete, therefore, the analysis of production is greatly simplified.

This result is often called the 'separation property' of the agricultural household model, because the production decisions of the household are separable from the household's consumption choices. Notice that the converse is not true. The consumption choices of the household do depend on the profit realized from production through the budget constraint (7'). To reiterate the logic, the existence of complete markets implies that a utility-maximizing household will choose to maximize profits in its production enterprise. Profit maximization (or, as it is commonly called in this literature, the separation property) is not an assumption: rather, it is derived from the twin assumptions of utility maximization and complete markets.

The separation property is robust to the non-existence of some markets. For example, if there is no land market, then replace A by E^A in (8') and set $r + 0$. The problem remains recursive, and the household chooses labour inputs to maximize profits given the household's endowment of land. This choice is independent of the household's preferences or endowment of labour. An analogous result is true if there is no labour market but land can be traded freely.

If we simplify the problem further (ignoring the fact that the household contains multiple members), then a graphical analysis becomes possible. Suppose that $U(\cdot)$ is such that at all prices and wages $c_1 = c_2 = c$ and $l_1 = l_2 = l$. Again, assuming that there is no market for land, the household chooses c, l, and L. The equilibrium is depicted in Figure 2.1. $F(L, E^A)$ is the production function on the household farm, given land endowment E^A. Given the real wage rate w/p, farm profits are maximized at $\Pi(w/p, E^A)$ using L^* units of labour on the farm (where $L^* = \operatorname*{argmax}_L F(L, E^A) - (w/p)L$). Then, given the budget constraint $pc = wE^L + \Pi(w/p, E^A) - wl$, household utility is maximized by choosing consumption c^* and leisure l^*. Thus, the household's decision-making process proceeds in two stages: first, farm profit is maximized, and then utility is maximized given the full income budget constraint.

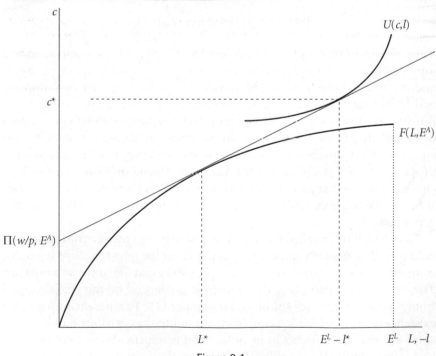

Figure 2.1

It might seem absurd to begin with the hypothesis of separation. It is difficult to argue on the basis of descriptions of economic conditions in the rural areas of developing countries that it is generally the case that markets are (nearly) complete. Therefore, it would seem appropriate to begin with the assumption that farmers do *not* maximize profits; that in fact their production decisions are related to their preferences and endowments. Indeed, in most developing countries where the hypothesis has been examined it is clear that the separation property does not hold. Everywhere in Africa, Latin America, and most of Asia where the hypothesis has been examined, it has decisively been rejected (Kevane 1994; Udry 1998; Barrett 1996; Collier 1983; Jacoby 1993; Carter 1984; Bardhan 1973). There is an interesting pair of papers, however, by Benjamin (1992, 1995) and another by Pitt and Rosenzweig (1986), which indicate that the separation property is not far from true in a large Indonesian data set. In most developing-country contexts, the separation property seems more useful as a benchmark for comparison rather than as a basis for empirical work.

II

If multiple markets are incomplete, the separation property no longer holds. The household no longer maximizes profit, and production decisions depend upon the preferences and endowments of the household. A classic example is the problem of a household that faces imperfections in both the land and labour markets. Suppose again that there is no market for land, but now add the possibility that there is some involuntary unemployment in the rural labour market. The household cultivates its endowment of land, and might face a binding constraint on the amount of labour it can supply off its own farm. The household problem (now assuming just one person in the household) is:

$$\underset{c,\, l,\, L^h,\, L^F \geq 0}{\text{Max}}\ U(c, l) \tag{10}$$

subject to

$$pc = F(L^f + L^h, E^A) - wL^h + wL^m \tag{11}$$

$$l + L^f + L^m = E^L \tag{12}$$

$$L^m \leq M, \tag{13}$$

where L^h is labour hired by the household to work on its farm, L^f is the household's own labour on its farm, L^m is the time spent by the household working for a wage, and M is the maximum amount of time the household can spend working for a wage as a result of some (here unmodelled) labour market rationing. If (13) is not binding, then (11) becomes $pc + wl = F(L, E^A) - wL + wE^L$, where L

is the amount of labour used on the farm. In this case, the household maximizes profits and the separation property holds.

If separation holds, and the production function has constant returns to scale (CRTS), then all farms look quite similar. With CRTS, we can write $F(L, E^A) = E^A f(L/E^A)$, and the first-order condition for labour use is $w = f'(L/E^A)$. All unconstrained farmers facing the same wage will use the same amount of labour per hectare, and achieve the same yield (output per unit of area) and output per unit of labour.

However, suppose (13) is binding, as it will be for small M, and when households desire to supply large amounts of labour to the market (perhaps because E^L is large relative to E^A). In this case $L^m = M$, $L^h = 0$ and the household's problem becomes

$$\underset{c,\, l \geq 0}{\text{Max}} \; U(c, l) \tag{14}$$

subject to

$$c = F(E^L - M - l, E^A) + wM. \tag{15}$$

The first-order conditions are (15) and $U_l/U_c = F_L$. The household's problem is illustrated in Figure 2.2 (which is similar to figure 2 in Benjamin 1992). The outer axes measure the household's consumption (goods consumption on the vertical axis, the time endowment minus leisure on the horizontal axis). The

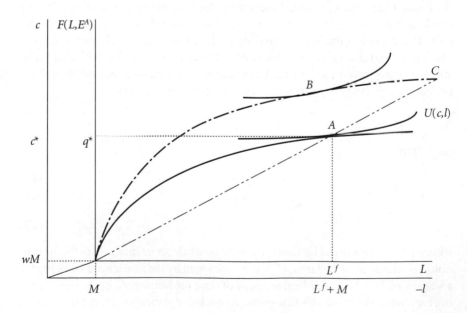

Figure 2.2

inner axes demonstrate production on the household's farm, with output on the vertical axis and labour input on the horizontal axis. M hours are spent working in the market, earning wM. The household's remaining labour time (L^f) is spent on the farm, producing q^*. So the household works $M + L^f$ hours and consumes $c^* = wM + F(L^f, E^A)$ units of the good. The household achieves a maximized utility of $U(c^*, l^*)$ at point A. The household's production choice clearly depends on its preferences and its endowment, and the separation property does not hold.

This sort of market structure could give rise to an oft-observed pattern in the rural areas of less developed countries. Many observers find that small farms are often cultivated more intensively than large farms. More labour per unit area is used on small farms, and yields are larger on these smaller farms. Consider a household with more land than the household consuming at point A in Figure 2.2, but facing the same wage and labour market constraint. If this household were to cultivate with the same intensity as household A, it would have to choose to produce and consume at point C in the figure. If leisure is a normal good, C will not be chosen. Instead, the household will choose to produce and consume at a point such as B, cultivating its larger farm less intensively than the smaller farm of household A. Formally, by implicitly differentiating the first-order condition, we find

$$\frac{\mathrm{d}L}{\mathrm{d}E^A} = \frac{L}{E^A} \frac{\dfrac{U_c f''}{E^A} - f'U_{cc}\left(\dfrac{E^A}{L}f - f'\right) + U_{lc}\left(\dfrac{E^A}{L}f - f'\right)}{\dfrac{U_c f''}{E^A} + U_{cc}f'f' + U_{ll} - 2U_{cl}f'} < \frac{L}{E^A} \text{ if } U_{cl} \geq 0 \quad (16)$$

(because $f'(L/E^A) < f$ for a concave CRTS function). As a household's endowment of land increases, the intensity with which it cultivates declines.

Labour and land market imperfections are perhaps the most straightforward rationale for an inverse relationship between farm size and cultivation intensity. Other market failures, however, could be associated with the same observation. For example, suppose that labour markets work well and the production function is CRTS but that production is risky, households are risk-averse, and insurance markets do not exist. To simplify this problem, suppose that households supply labour inelastically and that there is only a single good. The household's problem is to

$$\max_{L \geq 0} EU(c)$$

subject to $c = \theta E^A f\left(\dfrac{L}{E^A}\right) - wL + wE^L,$ (17)

where θ is a random variable with positive support and mean one. The household chooses labour so that

$$EU''(c)\left[\theta f'\left(\frac{L}{E^A}\right) - w\right] = 0.$$ (18)

The separation property, therefore, does not hold. Equation (18) can be rewritten as $f'E\theta U' = wEU'$ (where $U' \equiv U'(c)$ and $f' \equiv f'(L/E^A)$). Subtracting $f'EU'$ from both sides, we obtain $f'EU'(\theta - 1) = EU'(w - f')$. Recalling that $E\theta = 1$, we have $f'\mathrm{cov}(U', \theta) = (w - f')EU'$. Consumption increases with θ, so $\mathrm{cov}(U', \theta) < 0$; f' and EU' are both positive, so $w < f'$. This land is farmed less intensively than land that is cultivated under (expected) profit maximization.

We can now show that an inverse correlation between farm size and cultivation intensity is a consequence of this market imperfection. Apply the implicit function formula to (18) to find

$$\frac{\mathrm{d}L}{\mathrm{d}E^A} = \frac{L}{E^A} \frac{(f''/E^A)E\theta U' + f'E\theta(\theta f' - w)U''}{(f''/E^A)E\theta U' + E(\theta f' - w)^2 U''}.$$ (19)

Both terms in the denominator of the coefficient of L/E^A are negative, as of course is the first term in the numerator. The second term in the numerator is $f''(f'E\theta^2 U'' - wEU'') > 0$ because $f' > w$ and $E\theta^2 U'' < E\theta U'' < 0$. Thus $\mathrm{d}L/\mathrm{d}E^A < L/E^A$, and farm size is inversely correlated with cultivation intensity.

It is not possible, therefore, to conclude from the observation of an inverse farm size–productivity relationship that any particular market is malfunctioning. We have shown that a combination of labour, land, and/or insurance market failures could be associated with this observation; it is possible to construct simple models of financial market imperfections that lead to the same observation.

III

Simple extensions of the agricultural household model can be used to examine issues of human resource development in less developed countries. (See Strauss and Thomas, 1995, for a helpful and thorough review of the literature.) For example, households consume not only marketed goods, but also goods that are produced at home using household labour. One's utility might depend on a vector of consumption goods c, and on health, which depends on c and on time spent at home 'producing' health (e.g. by maintaining sanitation). This household's problem, in a simple one-period model with no uncertainty, is

$$\underset{c, l, L, L^c, \geq 0}{\mathrm{Max}} \quad U(c, H, l)$$ (20)

subject to

$$pc + wl + wL^c = F(L) - wL - wE^L \tag{21}$$

$$H = H(c, L^c), \tag{22}$$

where L^c is household labour devoted to producing health. The separation property is maintained with respect to production on the farm, but the production of health depends on preferences. The first-order condition for the allocation of labour to health is $\partial H / \partial L^c = w\lambda (\partial U / \partial H)^{-1}$. So the home production of health will depend on the prices of the goods that are used in maintaining health (p), and on the wage rate, but also on the parameters of the household utility function and on the household's endowments of labour and land. The use of models similar to this for the analysis of the determinants of human capital outcomes is discussed in more detail in Chapter 10.

IV

In setting up the problem of the household, we rather blithely wrote down a 'household utility function' in equation (1), which depended upon the leisure and consumption vector of each of the two individuals in the household. This approach, which (after Alderman *et al.* 1995) we called the *unitary household model*, seems at odds with the methodological individualism that is a basic premiss of microeconomic theory. Only in restricted circumstances can the collective actions of utility-maximizing individuals in a household be treated as if they were generated by the choices of a single utility-maximizing agent.

In order to represent the aggregate choices made by the individuals in a household as though they were made by a single optimizing agent, the preferences of these agents must be characterized by some form of transferable utility. Loosely speaking, transferable utility means that it is possible to find some utility representation of each individual's preferences such that, if one distribution of utilities within the household is feasible, then any other distribution of utilities such that the sum is constant is also feasible. Again loosely speaking, if utility is transferable, then household aggregate demand is not influenced by the distribution of utility within the household and the aggregate choices of the household would be consistent with the choices of a single individual who controls the household's aggregate income.[2]

The simplest case is that of a household that consumes only private goods and whose members have identical homothetic preferences. If this household always achieved a Pareto-efficient allocation of resources within the household, then by the second welfare theorem this allocation could be achieved through a

---

[2] Bergstrom (1997) is an excellent and comprehensive review of the literature on theories of the household.

competitive equilibrium within the household. Since the income-consumption paths of the members of the household are parallel lines, aggregate demand is independent of the distribution of income (and utility) within the household. Moreover, this aggregate consumption is what would be demanded by a single agent with these preferences endowed with the aggregate household income. The choices of this set of individuals, therefore, could be represented by a unitary household model (See Gorman 1953 for a fuller exposition.)

Slightly weaker assumptions on the preferences of members of the household are required for the validity of the unitary household representation if one makes strong assumptions regarding the allocation of resources within the household. For example, Becker's (1981) 'rotten kid theorem' relaxes the assumption of transferable utility to transferable utility conditional on the actions (e.g. labour supply decisions) of the household members. This relaxation comes at the cost of additional assumptions about the household allocation mechanism. In Becker's model, the allocation is not only efficient, but also driven by the presence of one household member (the altruist) who cares about the utility of each of the other household members and is rich enough, relative to the other members, to make positive transfers to each. As long as these gifts remain positive, a redistribution of income within the household has no effect on anyone's consumption, as the gift-giver simply reallocates the gifts to compensate for the changes. Conditional on the actions chosen by the household members, therefore, the household is indistinguishable from a unitary actor. More strikingly, as long as the utility of each household member is a normal good for the altruist, each member has an incentive to choose actions that shift out the household utility possibility frontier. The aggregate behaviour of the household, therefore, corresponds to that of a single utility-maximizing actor faced with the household's budget constraint.

There is no theoretical reason to presume the validity of any of the various combinations of assumptions required to make the aggregate behaviour of individuals in households correspond to the choices of a unitary optimizing agent. Nor is the available empirical evidence supportive of the unitary household model. In the unitary model, aggregate demand does not depend on the distribution of income within the household. However, a growing number of studies (see the review in Strauss and Thomas 1995) have found evidence that the budget shares of particular goods are significantly related to the shares of (arguably exogenous) income accruing to women in the household. For example, Thomas (1991) finds that in Brazil the unearned income of mothers has a much stronger positive effect on child health than the unearned income of fathers, contradicting the unitary household model.

To move beyond the unitary household model, it is necessary to model the interaction between the individuals who comprise the household. In seminal papers, Manser and Brown (1980) and McElroy and Horney (1981) proposed

Nash cooperative bargaining models of the allocation of household resources. These models assume that resources within the household are allocated efficiently, and that the particular Pareto-efficient allocation that is chosen is determined by the 'threat points' of the individual members of the household. The threat point of an individual is defined as the utility achieved by that person if the household does not come to an agreement regarding the distribution of resources. The higher an individual's threat point relative to those of the other individuals in the household, the higher the utility of that person in the equilibrium. Manser–Brown and McElroy–Horney proposed that the threat point of each person is determined by his or her utility in the event of a divorce; later authors (e.g. Lundberg and Pollak 1993) have assumed that the relevant threat point is determined by some sort of non-cooperative equilibrium within the household.

Chiappori (1988, 1992) and Browning and Chiappori (1994) argue that economists generally have little notion of the actual intra-household bargaining process. They argue, therefore, that any model of this process should make only very minimal assumptions. Of all the assumptions that underlie the bargaining models of earlier authors, they retain only that of the efficiency of household resource allocation. This 'efficient household' model makes minimal assumptions, but retains enough content to guide analysis in many cases. For example, if markets are complete, then the separation property holds for efficient households, just as it does for unitary households. To see this, replace equation (1) in the household's problem with (1'):

$$\text{Max} \sum_i \lambda_i \, U_i(\{c_i\}, \{l_i\}). \tag{1'}$$

Each individual i might care about the vector of consumption and leisure consumed by each other household member. A Pareto-efficient allocation of resources within the household is defined as the solution to the problem defined by (1') and the household resource constraints (equations (2)–(6)) for some choice if $\lambda_i > 0$. As was the case for the unitary household model with complete markets, decisions regarding production do not depend on the preferences or endowments of the individuals in the household, nor on the 'Pareto weights' λ_i assigned to each individual. Production decisions for the efficient household are guided by (8'), just as they were for the unitary household.

The assumption of household Pareto efficiency is weak relative to the assumptions required for the unitary household model, but it remains just that: an assumption that must be confronted with the actual behaviour of households. The demand patterns generated by an efficient household are different from those of a unitary household. Where tested (Browning *et al.* 1994; Browning and Chiappori 1994; Thomas and Chen 1994), the unitary model has been rejected in favour of the more general efficient household model. Udry (1996), however, finds that women's plots are cultivated much less intensively than their husbands' plots in parts of Burkina Faso, implying that total agricultural output within the household could be increased by reallocating factors of production across the plots cultivated by household members and contradicting the Pareto efficiency of resource allocation within the household.

The available empirical evidence casts serious doubt on the validity of the unitary model. While the available work is mostly supportive of the more general model of efficient households, there is some evidence, particularly in Africa, that calls even this weaker model into question. More research is required before the general validity of the efficient household model can be accepted. If the efficient household model cannot adequately account for the intra-household allocation of resources, it appears that it will be necessary to move towards more detailed, culturally and institutionally informed noncooperative models of the interaction between household members.

REFERENCES

Alderman, H., Chiappori, P.-A., Haddad, L., Hoddinott, J., and Kanbur, R. (1995), 'Unitary versus Collective Models of the Household: Time to Shift the Burden of Proof?' *World Bank Research Observer*, 10.

Bardhan, P. (1973), 'Size, Productivity and Returns to Scale: An Analysis of Farm-level Data in Indian Agriculture', *Journal of Political Economy*, 81.

Barrett, C. (1996), 'On Price Risk and the Inverse Farm Size–Productivity Relationship', *Journal of Development Economics*, 51.

Becker, G. (1981), *A Treatise on the Family*. Cambridge, Mass.: Harvard University Press.

Benjamin, D. (1992), 'Household Composition, Labor Markets, and Labor Demand: Testing for Separation in Agricultural Household Models', *Econometrica*, 60.

——(1995), 'Can Unobserved Land Quality Explain the Inverse Productivity Relationship?' *Journal of Development Economics*, 46.

Bergstrom, T. C. (1993), 'A Survey of Theories of the Family', unpublished paper, University of Michigan, Department of Economics.

——(1997), 'A Survey of Theories of the Family, in M. R. Rosenzweig and O. Stark (eds.), *Handbook of Population and Family Economics*, iA. Amsterdam: Elsevier.

Browning, M., and Chiappori, P.-A. (1994), 'Efficient Intra-household Allocations: A General Characterisation and Empirical Tests', Working Paper no. 94-07, McMaster University Department of Economics.

Browning, M., Bourguignon, F., Chiappori. P.-A., and Lechene, G. (1994), 'Incomes and Outcomes: A Structural Model of Intra-Household Allocation', *Journal of Political Economy*, 102.

Carter, M. (1984), 'Identification of the Inverse Relationship between Farm Size and Productivity: An Empirical Analysis of Peasant Agricultural Production', *Oxford Economic Papers*, 36.

Chiappori, P.-A. (1988), 'Rational Household Labor Supply', *Econometrica*, 56.

—— (1992), 'Collective Labor Supply and Welfare', *Journal of Political Economy*, 100.

Collier, P. (1983), 'Malfunctioning of African Rural Factor Markets: Theory and a Kenyan Example', *Oxford Bulletin of Economics and Statistics*, 45.

Gorman, W. M. (1953), 'Community Preference Fields', *Econometrica*, 21.

Jacoby, H. (1993), 'Shadow Wages and Peasant Family Labour Supply: An Econometric Application to the Peruvian Sierra', *Review of Economic Studies*, 60.

Kevane, M. (1994), 'Agrarian Structure and Agricultural Practice: Typology and Application to Western Sudan', unpublished paper, Harvard University Department of Economics.

Lundberg, S., and Pollak, R. (1993), 'Separate Spheres Bargaining and the Marriage Market', *Journal of Political Economy*, 101.

Manser, M., and Brown, M. (1980), 'Marriage and Household Decision-Making: A Bargaining Analysis', *International Economic Review*, 21.

McElroy, M., and Horney, M. (1981), 'Nash-Bargained Household Decisions: Towards a Generalization of the Theory of Demand', *International Economic Review*, 22.

Pitt, M., and Rosenzweig, M. (1986), 'Agricultural Prices, Food Consumption and the Health and Productivity of Indonesian Farmers', in I. Singh, L. Squire, and J. Strauss (eds.), *Agricultural Household Models: Extensions, Applications, and Policy*. Baltimore: Johns Hopkins University Press.

Singh, I., Squire, L., and Strauss, J. (1986), *Agricultural Household Models: Extensions, Applications and Policy*. Baltimore: Johns Hopkins University Press.

Strauss, J., and Thomas, D. (1995), 'Human Resources: Empirical Modeling of Household and Family Decisions', in J. Behrman and T. N. Srinivasan (eds.), *Handbook of Development Economics*, iii(A). Amsterdam: Elsevier Science.

Thomas, D. (1991), 'Intra-Household Resource Allocation: An Inferential Approach', *Journal of Human Resources*, 25.

—— and Chen, C.-L. (1994), 'Income Shares and Shares of Income: Empirical Tests of Models of Household Resource Allocations', RAND Labor and Population Working Paper 94-08.

Udry, C. (1996), 'Gender, Agricultural Productivity and the Theory of the Household', *Journal of Political Economy*, 104.

—— (1998), 'Efficiency and Market Structure: Testing for Profit Maximization in African Agriculture', unpublished paper.

United Nations (1994), *Human Development Report*. New York: Oxford University Press.

3
Population

I

The global rate of population growth over the past half century has been the highest in history. Most of this growth has occurred in poor countries. The rate of growth of the population in such countries currently is approximately 2 per cent per year, down from its 1960s peak of almost 2.5 per cent. This compares with an historical rate of population growth in Europe and North America of less than 1 per cent during the eighteenth and nineteenth centuries.

The current high rate of population growth has been driven by a large and sustained decline in mortality rates as a consequence of improved public health and rising incomes. Mortality rates in poor countries have fallen much faster over the past fifty years than was the case during the historical development of the industrial countries.[1] At the same time, fertility rates have also fallen at an historically unprecedented rate, but not fast enough to avoid a large increase in the population growth rate. Thus, the 'demographic transition'—the shift from a period of high mortality, high fertility, and relatively stable population through a period of lower mortality with still relatively high fertility and thus rapid population growth, to a period of low mortality and fertility and thus once again stable population—is still incomplete in most of the poor countries.

Simple Malthusian reasoning has proven incorrect. The rapid population growth of the past half-century has not brought falling real incomes and increasing mortality. Per capita income in poor countries has continued to rise (with the important exception of recent decades in sub-Saharan Africa). At the same time, there is a strong negative relationship (in both cross-sectional and time-series data) between national income *per capita* and aggregate fertility and population growth rates. On average, women in richer nations have one and a

---

[1] Birdsall (1988: 481) cites the case of India, which in 1982 had a life expectancy of 55 and a per capita income of under $300 (and a literacy rate below 40%). In contrast, life expectancy in England, Sweden, and the USA was below 50 years in 1900, while their per capita income was over $1,000 and literacy was above 80%.

half to two children over their lifetime, while women in poor countries average three and a half to four children over their lifetime. An average woman in Africa has between 6 and 7 children over the course of her life (Haab and Cornelius 1997). A similar regularity can be found in microeconomic data—richer women tend to have fewer children.

These simple correlations do not provide enough information to permit inference about the effect of population, or its growth, on income or its growth. Population growth and income growth influence each other; hence determining causality through statistical regularities is quite difficult. Nor does economic theory offer clear conclusions. To the extent that increasing returns to scale underlie growth, population growth can have a positive effect on growth. The existence of any fixed resources and diminishing returns, of course, tends to imply a negative effect of population on economic growth.

The remainder of this chapter examines the reproductive decisions of families in order to begin to unravel the connections between fertility, population, and income. In Section II we present a conventional model of household decision-making with respect to fertility and investment in the human capital of children. It will be seen that this household model provides a number of insights into the demographic transition. However, the assumption of a unitary household is particularly problematic in the context of fertility decisions. Explicit acknowledgement of the potentially divergent preferences of men and women is appropriate and opens up important areas of inquiry.

In the remainder of the chapter, we examine the interconnections between the fertility decisions of different families and the possibility that these interconnections give rise to multiple fertility equilibria. In Section III we argue that there may be important externalities associated with fertility decisions. People's notions of appropriate behaviour concerning the determinants of fertility are strongly influenced by cultural norms. Ideals concerning the age of marriage, births outside of marriage, birth spacing, breast feeding, and the use of modern methods of birth control are all strongly conditioned by the behaviour of other members of the community. Hence, a strategic complementarity arises in fertility decisions, and, using a model by Dasgupta (1993), we show that there may be multiple (Pareto-ranked) fertility equilibria. Finally, in Section IV we discuss another avenue through which fertility decisions are influenced by the choices of other households, even when there are no direct externalities. The link we explore (using a model by Basu and Van, 1998) is child labour. If fertility is low, labour is relatively scarce and adult wages are high; then families can afford to keep their children out of the labour force. On the other hand, an equilibrium might also exist in which families are large, wages are low, and impoverished families must send their children to work.

II

The conventional approach to understanding fertility decisions is based on the household model described in Chapter 2. The choices of a household with regard to fertility are treated in a manner analogous to all other decisions taken by the household. Most work by economists, following the seminal contributions by Becker (1960) and Becker and Lewis (1973), has focused on the trade-offs households face between the number of children, investment in these children, and current consumption of goods. Thus, let x be (parental) consumption and n be the number of children surviving (to an arbitrary, and for current purposes unspecified, age). For simplicity, we assume that each child is treated similarly, so let z be the level of human capital achieved by each child, known in this literature as 'child quality'. Household utility is described by the function $U(x, n, z; \alpha)$. We assume that $U(\cdot)$ is increasing in x and z, and increasing in n at least for small n. The human capital achieved by the household's children depends on their own consumption c and also on an input of time and effort by the parents t. Thus $z = Z(c, t; \beta)/n$. The opportunity cost of the time that the parents invest in children's human capital is the foregone wage that the parents would have earned. α and β are vectors incorporating exogenous factors that influence the preferences of the household and the technology for producing child human capital in the household. The household's problem, then, is to solve:

$$\max_{x, n, c, t} U(x, n, z; \alpha)$$

subject to

$$z = Z(c, t; \beta)/n$$

$$w(1 - t) = p_x x + p_c c, \tag{1}$$

where we have chosen units so that the time endowment of the parents is 1. Thus, parents face a trade-off between the human capital achieved by their children, the number of children they raise, and their own consumption.

This model provides a framework in which many of the features of the demographic transition can be understood. For example, as the wage (particularly the female wage) increases with economic growth, the opportunity cost of rearing children increases, sharpening the trade-off between adult consumption and both the number and human capital of the household's children. At the same time α is likely to be changing. Part of the utility derived from children and their human capital is the expected contribution that the children will make to the parents' consumption in the future. That is, children can be seen (at least in part) as investments. As economic growth occurs, the return to skilled labour increases relative to the return to unskilled labour. This change will be reflected in parental preferences over the number of children and the human capital embodied in each child. As a consequence, households move towards investing more resources into each of a smaller number of children. Similarly, β can change as a consequence of economic growth or government policy. The provision of free primary education would permit children to achieve higher levels of human capital at given inputs of c and t, and thus raise both z and n.

The conventional household model of fertility decisions also provides valuable guidance for empirical work. The household makes simultaneous and interdependent decisions regarding fertility, investment in child human capital, adult consumption, and labour market participation. It would be an error to treat any of these decisions as exogenous in an econometric exercise. Thus, for example, an analysis of the effect of household income on fertility has to be conducted with care. A simple regression in which fertility is the dependent variable and income an independent variable would be subject to simultaneity bias because income depends on the labour market decisions of the household. The household model provides a context for designing an appropriate empirical strategy; in this case it shows that the wage could serve as an instrument for the endogenous explanatory variable.

The household fertility model provides insight into the reproductive behaviour of families. Most importantly, it emphasizes the point of view that people evaluate the relative merits of their options regarding their family size and the health and education of their children. At the same time, the model is extremely incomplete and therefore can be misleading. On the one hand, this model of a unitary household obscures the potentially divergent goals of men and women regarding the number and treatment of children. On the other hand, the model neglects the potentially strong influence of the social context on fertility decisions. These comments are not mere cavils. Although it can be argued that they are true for all economic choices, they gain particular weight in the context of fertility decisions. Moreover, both lines of reasoning provide avenues through which the conventional model might be enriched to shed light on a crucial pair of questions: (1) Is the rate of population growth in the poorest countries too high? (2) Why has fertility responded so slowly to declining mortality in some areas, particularly in Africa?

The divergence between men and women in the costs and benefits of bearing and raising children is stark. Women bear all the physical risks of childbirth (which are very substantial in poor countries—1 in 100 births results in death for the mother in Africa (Haab and Cornelius 1997)). Most of the effort required to raise children is provided by women. Here, more than in virtually any other context, the fiction of 'household preferences' is inappropriate.

There is striking empirical evidence that men and women have divergent preferences with respect to fertility and investments in children's human capital. Men and women often express different targets for total fertility (Birdsall 1988). Much of the empirical evidence (reviewed in Strauss and Thomas 1995) that casts doubt on the unitary household model concerns investments in child human capital. In a number of countries, additional income in the hands of mothers leads to larger increases in child health and education than similar additional income in the hands of fathers.

Finally, there is strong evidence that more educated women have lower fertility and are more likely to use modern methods of birth control. It is likely that there are a number of different mechanisms through which female education affects fertility. Wages increase with education, so the opportunity cost of the time spent rearing children is higher for more educated women. More educated women tend to have healthier children, lower mortality among their children, and thus lower fertility. They may also place a higher value on education, or be more efficient at 'producing' child human capital, and thus prefer fewer children with higher investment in human capital in each child (see Behrman *et al.* 1997). Finally, it may be the case that more educated women are able to negotiate or bargain more effectively within the household, so that fertility outcomes are closer to their own preferences than is the case for women with less education.

If men and women have divergent preferences with regard to fertility and investment in children, then an understanding of fertility outcomes, and thus of the determinants of population growth, rests on an understanding of the process of household decision-making. It is apparent that the process of decision-making within households is quite variable across societies, and thus general lessons are difficult to draw. However, to the extent that decisions over fertility are made or influenced by individuals who do not bear the full cost of childbearing and raising, then there exists the potential for an equilibrium in which fertility is too high.

III

Fertility decisions are made through a process of negotiation within households, but they are not made in isolation.[2] Here, more obviously than is the case with most decisions, the behaviour of households depends upon the choices of their neighbours. The proximate determinants of fertility—the use of contraceptives, the timing of breast feeding, the frequency of intercourse—are actions that are strongly influenced by cultural patterns. Put most simply, it may be the case that imitation plays an important role in fertility decisions. As long as all or most other couples engage in practices that encourage high fertility, any

---

[2] This section draws extensively on the discussion in Dasgupta (1993: chs. 12 and *12).

individual couple might find it difficult to do otherwise. The same couple, however, might prefer a smaller household size in a different social context. If this is the case, then choices regarding fertility generate an externality: each household's child-bearing decision helps set a cultural pattern, and this affects the preferences of all other households.

The form of the externality generated by fertility decisions involves *strategic complementarities* (Cooper and John 1988). The marginal utility to a household of having an additional child is increasing in the number of children in other households. Following the notation in Dasgupta (1993), suppose that there are M households in a society, and let $X = (X_1, X_2, \ldots, X_M)$ be a vector describing the number of children in each household. Suppose that each household i has preferences over its own number of children, and also over the number of children in each other household. We ignore the obvious integer constraints, and assume that preferences can be summarized by the (twice continuously differentiable) utility function $U_i(X)$. For each household i, the externality we have described implies that $\partial^2 U_i(X)/\partial X_i \partial Xj > 0$ for $i \neq j$.

Strategic complementarities raise the possibility of multiple Nash equilibria. Suppose each household decides on the number of children taking the decisions of other households as given. Then household i solves a problem of the form: $\max_{X_i} U_i(X)$. Let $X_{-i} \equiv (X_1, \ldots, X_{i-1}, X_{i+1}, \ldots, X_M)$. If we make the conventional assumption of diminishing marginal utility over the number of the household's own children, then, for each vector X_{-i}, there is a unique value of X_i, say X^*, which solves household i's problems. The function $X^*(X_{-i})$ is the household's reaction function, describing its decision given the actions of all other households. The implicit function theorem implies that $\partial X^*(X_{-i})/\partial X_j > 0$. The number of children chosen by a household is an increasing function of the number of children in any other household.

Let's suppose that all households have identical preferences, and consider symmetrical Nash equilibria. Let Z be the number of children in all other households. Thus, $X_{-i} = (Z, Z, \ldots, Z) \equiv Z$. A symmetrical Nash equilibrium is a fixed point in which $X^*(Z) = Z$; that is if all other households have Z children, a representative household would also choose Z children. In Figure 3.1, the horizontal axis is Z, the number of children in each other household, and the vertical axis is X^*, the optimal choice of the representative household conditional on the choices of the other households. The number of children in a household must lie between 0 and X^{max}. We know that the reaction curve $X^*(Z)$ is upward-sloping—one example is drawn in the figure. Any intersection of the reaction function with the 45° line represents a symmetrical Nash equilibrium. We have drawn the reaction function so that there are three symmetric equilibria, corresponding to three different levels of fertility. Because the equilibria are symmetric and the households are identical, they can be Pareto-ranked—(generically) one is better than the others. There may be asymmetric equilibria as well, but

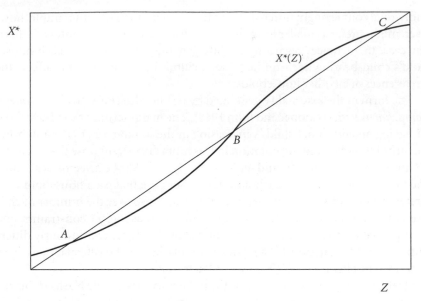

Figure 3.1

the general point has been made: when there are strategic complementarities, it is possible that there are multiple equilibria and that some of these equilibria are better than others.

Two similar societies (composed of households with similar preferences), therefore, might be found at different equilibria. Why should one society find itself in equilibrium at point A, while another is in equilibrium at the (say) Pareto-dominated point C? To answer this question, it is necessary to move outside the model as we have constructed it so far. The notion of Nash equilibrium rests on *expectations*. Given household i's expectation of the fertility choices of other households, it selects its preferred number of children. When this selection matches the expectations of all other households, and the same is true for each household's selection, then the society is at a Nash equilibrium.

In the context of fertility decisions, it is most useful to focus on the role of history in forming expectations. Suppose that a society is characterized by high fertility for conventional reasons (perhaps a high rate of infant mortality). Consequently, a set of practices (e.g. polygyny and a low age of marriage for women) that encourages high fertility is common. These practices are the empirical embodiment of the strategic complementarity that we have hypothesized, and they shape the expectations of each household. Even after infant mortality declines, these practices remain and as a consequence each household continues to choose high fertility. Thus, the type of externality that we have hypothesized to be important with respect to fertility decisions raises the possibility of a social equilibrium that is sub-optimal and requires coordinated effort to change.

IV

Household choices with regard to fertility are strongly conditioned by the social environment even when there is no direct interconnection between preferences and the choices of one's neighbours. The fertility decisions of households affect the demographic structure of the society, and this in turn can influence relative prices and thus other households' fertility decisions. In this section we present a simplified version of a model by Basu and Van (1998) which starkly illustrates the possibility of multiple fertility equilibria. In this model, if the economy is characterized by small families, labour is relatively scarce, adult wages are high, families can afford to keep children out of the labour force, and all families prefer to remain small. An alternative equilibrium might exist in which adult wages are low, families are so poor that all children must work, and each family decides to have many children (hence labour is abundant and wages are low).

The model is driven by three crucial assumptions. First, preferences are such that a family will send its children to work only if income from adult labour is very low; thus, child leisure is a luxury good. Second, technology is such that adult and child labour are substitutes. Third, children are capable of providing net economic benefits to the family; if children do work, they can contribute more than their consumption needs to the family. This final assumption is more likely to be valid in poor countries, where productivity is less tied to human capital than in rich countries. Children who work in poor countries are able to earn more than they consume at an earlier age than is the case in rich countries. (See Dasgupta 1993 for a discussion.)

These three assumptions are sufficient to generate the possibility of multiple fertility equilibria. For the remainder of this section, we will make a series of further (draconian) assumptions to simplify and clarify the analysis, but the general message that the interaction between fertility decisions and labour market outcomes might generate the possibility of multiple equilibria rests on these three core assumptions.

Suppose that there are N families, each of which has one adult and m children (the 'one adult', of course, could be interpreted as a husband–wife couple). There is one good, and we will not examine issues of intra-household distribution. Instead, we assume that, if the adult consumes c, then each child consumes βc with $\beta < 1$. Thus, β is an 'adult-equivalence' rating. Adult labour is supplied inelastically, but the household chooses child labour supply (e). Again abstracting from distributional issues within the household, we assume that all the family's children supply the same amount of labour. For simplicity, we restrict the available choices of child labour to 0 or 1. Continuing to assume away issues of negotiation and power within the household, let there be a household preference ordering over pairs of consumption (c) and child labour effort (e). These preferences exhibit a particularly strong form of the 'child labour as luxury good' assumption: the household prefers that children work only if consumption would fall below some exogenously specified subsistence level in the absence of income from child labour. Household preferences are defined over pairs (c, e) for $c \geq 0$ and $e \in \{0, 1\}$. (Recall that child consumption is simply βc.) Preferences are:

$$(c + \delta, e) > (c, e),$$
$$(c + \delta, 1) > (c, 0) \text{ if } c < s,$$
$$(c + \delta, 1) < (c, 0) \text{ if } c \geq s, \tag{2}$$

for $\delta = 0, c \geq 0, e \in \{0, 1\}$. Thus, preferences are such that higher (average) consumption is preferred to lower, but children work only if the family would be destitute in the absence of the income from their labour.

The household budget constraint is

$$c + m\beta c = mew_c + w_a, \tag{3}$$

where w_a is the adult wage and w_c is the child wage. The household chooses its preferred combination of m, c, and e subject to the budget constraint (3).

To begin with, consider the choice of c and e conditional on a given family size. Given m, children work only if the adult wage is too low to provide sufficient adult income for the family to avoid destitution. Thus,

$$c = \begin{bmatrix} \dfrac{w_a}{1 + m\beta} & \text{if } w_a \geq (1 + m\beta)s \\[3mm] \dfrac{w_a + mw_c}{1 + m\beta} & \text{if } w_a < (1 + m\beta)s, \end{bmatrix} \tag{4}$$

and

$$e = \begin{bmatrix} 0 \text{ if } w_a \geq (1 + m\beta)s \\ 1 \text{ if } w_a < (1 + m\beta)s. \end{bmatrix} \tag{5}$$

The aggregate supply of adult labour is $S_a = N$, and of child labour is $S_c = 0$ if $w_a \geq (1 + m\beta)s$, and $S_c = mN$ if $w_a < (1 + m\beta)s$.

Now we turn to our second assumption, regarding the demand for labour. We have assumed that child and adult labour are substitutes in production. Let us go further to assume that they are perfect substitutes, so that output in any firm i is determined by $f(A_i + \gamma c_i)$ where A_i is the amount of adult labour used in firm i, C_i is the amount of child labour used in firm i, and $\gamma < 1$. So $1/\gamma$ children can do the same work as 1 adult. Let there be n identical price-taking firms. If $\gamma w_a < w_c$, then adult labour is cheaper than child labour and no firm demands child labour. The aggregate demand for child labour $D_c = 0$, while the aggregate demand for adult labour D_a is determined implicitly by $f'(D_a/n) = w_a$. Similarly, if $\gamma w_a > w_c$, child labour is cheaper than adult labour and no firm demands adult labour. Thus, $D_a = 0$ and D_c is determined by $\gamma f'(\gamma D_c/n) = w_c$. Finally, if $\gamma w_a = w_c$, firms are indifferent between hiring adults or children. In this case, each firm only cares about the effective labour $(L_i \equiv A_i + \gamma C_i)$ it hires; the composition of L_i is a matter of indifference. Thus, in this case $D \equiv D_a + \gamma D_c$ is determined implicitly by $f'(D/n) = w_a = w_c/\gamma$.

Conditional on fertility choices (that is, given m), the labour market will clear if there is a pair of wages (w_a, w_c) such that at those wages $D_a = S_a$ and $D_c = S_c$. First, consider only wage pairs such that $\gamma w_a = w_c$, so that firms are indifferent between hiring adults or children. We set the level of fertility at $m = m^l$ for the purposes of this illustration. In Figure 3.2 we graph the the supply of effective labour $S^l \equiv S_a + \gamma S_c$ against the adult wage (remembering that, as the adult wage is changed, the child wage also changes to maintain $\gamma w_c = w_a$). If $w_a \geq (1 + m^l\beta)s$, the supply of effective labour is restricted to the adult labour force, so equals N. However, if the wage drops to $w_a < (1 + m^l\beta)s$, then families faced with destitution send their children to work and the labour supply increases to $(1 + \gamma m^l)N$. Our assumptions on preferences suffice to guarantee that this economy is characterized by a 'backward-bending' supply of labour. At higher wages, less labour is supplied. Obviously, we have made an extreme assumption for the sake of simplicity. Such stark behaviour is not required for

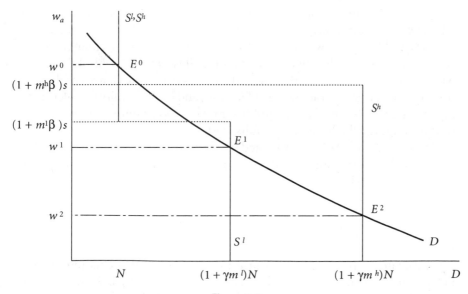

Figure 3.2

the conclusions we will draw. Any preferences that incorporate the assumption that child labour is withdrawn once adult wages are high enough, and that the rate at which child labour is withdrawn exceeds the rate at which adults increase their own supply of labour, will suffice to raise the possibility of multiple equilibria.

In Figure 3.2 we also graph the demand for effective labour (still restricting attention to the case in which $w_a = w_c/\gamma$), which is determined by $w_a = f'(D/n)$. We have drawn the supply of and demand for labour such that there are two equilibria. At E^0, adult wages are high, children do not work, and the demand for labour is met entirely by adults. At E^1 the adult wage is low, the child wage is very low ($w_c = \gamma w_a$), and both children and adults work. There are also equilibria at which $w_a \neq w_c/\gamma$. It cannot be the case that in equilibrium $w_a > w_c/\gamma$, for in that case the demand for adult labour is zero while its supply is positive. However, if $w_a = w^0$ (as at E^0), then any child wage such that $w_c \geq \gamma w^0$ is an equilibrium, for at those wage pairs both the demand for and the supply of child labour is zero.

Conditional on m, therefore, it is possible that there are multiple labour market equilibria. We now show that these multiple labour market equilibria might correspond to multiple equilibria with respect to the fertility choices of households. Suppose that households have a choice of two levels of fertility: $m \in \{m^h, m^l\}$, with $m^h > m^l$. We have drawn the labour market equilibria conditional on an assumed (low) level of fertility. We now ask the question: given these labour market outcomes, would the households voluntarily choose the assumed level of fertility?

In Figure 3.2, the supply function S^l is drawn with $m = m^l$. The supply of labour with m exogenously assumed to be m^h would be S^h. Now consider labour market equilibrium E^0, where $m = m^l$, the adult wage is w^0, and children do not work. Would households choose the level of fertility m^l? At E^0, with children not working, $c(m^l) = w^0/(1 + m^l\beta) > w^0(1 + m^h\beta) = c(m^h) > s$. Hence children do not work (regardless of the choice of fertility), and lower fertility is preferred to higher fertility. Hence E^0 is an equilibrium: households optimally choose low fertility, wages are high, and only adults work.

Now consider E^1. At E^1, we assumed that fertility is low (that is, $m = m^l$). The labour market clears with $w_a = w^1$, $w_c = \gamma w^1$, and children work. Consumption, therefore, is given by

$$c(m^l) = \frac{w^1(1 + m^l\gamma)}{1 + m^l\beta} < \frac{w^1(1 + m^h\gamma)}{1 + m^h\beta} = c(m^h).$$

The inequality is true because of our third assumption: that children provide net economic benefits to their families (that is, that $\gamma > \beta$). At E^1 children are working, and so families prefer high to low fertility in order to capture the economic benefits offered by the additional children. E^1, therefore, is not an equilibrium.

Instead, consider E^2, where it is assumed that fertility is high ($m = m^h$). The labour market is in equilibrium with $w_a = w^2$ and $w_c = \gamma w^2$, and children are supplying labour. In this case,

$$c(m^l) = \frac{w^1(1+m^l\gamma)}{1+m^l\beta} < \frac{w^2(1+m^h\gamma)}{1+m^h\beta} = c(m^h),$$

and high fertility is chosen by the household.

Thus, E^2 is an equilibrium, and this economy has multiple fertility equilibria. In E^0 there is low fertility, high adult wages, and a low supply of labour; in E^2 there is high fertility, low wages, and children work.

The high-fertility equilibrium is clearly inferior to the low-fertility equilibrium for each labouring household.[3] Yet it is individually optimal for each of these households to choose high fertility, given that the other households are each choosing high fertility. The demographic structure generated by the fertility choices of the rest of the population yields low wages, and drives households to send their children to work. Given this environment, it is individually optimal to have many children. The general point is that, once again, there is a possibility of a *coordination failure*, and thus a potentially valuable role for public policy. The design of appropriate policy, obviously, is not trivial. It could be easy to slip into the worst excesses of Indian or Chinese population policy using the argument that population has a natural tendency to be too large as a consequence of these and related coordination failures. Even focusing more carefully on particular mechanisms through which the coordination failure arises does not always lead to simple policy recommendations. Basu and Van (1998), for example, demonstrate the complexities of policy towards child labour in the model we have just described. Even in this model, a ban on child labour can have dramatically positive or negative effects on household welfare, and various forms of partial bans can raise or lower child welfare depending upon the specific characteristics of the economy.

REFERENCES

Basu, K., and Van, P.H. (1998), 'The Economics of Child Labor, *American Economic Review*, 88.

[3] It is not true that this equilibrium is Pareto-dominated by the low fertility equilibrium, however. We have not completely characterized this economy, as we have not described the consumption choices of the owners of the firms (which are making profits). If we assume that they are a separate population that consumes all the profits, then they are better off in the high-fertility equilibrium.

Becker, G. (1960), 'An Economic Analysis of Fertility', in G. Becker (ed.), *Demographic and Economic Change in Developed Countries*. Princeton: Princeton University Press.

—— and Lewis, H. G. (1973), 'Interaction between Quantity and Quality of Children', *Journal of Political Economy*, 81.

Behrman, J., Foster, A., Rosenzweig, M., and Vashishtha, P. (1997), 'Women's Schooling, Home Teaching, and Economic Growth', unpublished paper, University of Pennsylvania.

Birdsall, N. (1988), 'Economic Approaches to Population Growth', in H. Chenery and T. N. Srinivasan (eds.), *Handbook of Development Economics*, i. Amsterdam: North Holland.

Cooper, R., and John, A. (1988), 'Coordinating Coordination Failures in Keynesian Models', *Quarterly Journal of Economics*, 103.

Dasgupta, P. (1993), *An Inquiry into Well-Being and Destitution*. Oxford: Oxford University Press.

Haab, C., and Cornelius, D. (1997), *World Population Data Sheet*. Washington: Population Reference Bureau.

Strauss, J., and Thomas, D. (1995), 'Human Resources: Empirical Modeling of Household and Family Decisions', in J. Behrman and T. N. Srinivasan (eds.), *Handbook of Development Economics*, iii(A). Amsterdam: Elsevier Science.

4

Fragmented Markets: Labour

I

Following the lead from a famous paper by Arthur Lewis (1954), it has been a practice in economic theory to differentiate the modelling of less developed economies from that of industrially advanced economies primarily by referring to a different functioning of the labour markets. Until very recently, a distinguishing mark of models of the former set of economies was the assumption of a horizontal supply curve of labour at an exogenously given wage rate. While the empirical literature[1] has cast serious doubts on horizontal labour supply curves and on the exogeneity of the wage rate even in the densely populated agriculture of poor countries, the theoretical puzzle of explaining the coexistence of a significant positive and often (though not always) downwardly rigid wage, even under conditions of severe unemployment and underemployment, which exercised many development economists in the 1950s and 1960s, has not been completely resolved. When in recent years high and persistent unemployment in developed countries became a focus of serious attention, macroeconomists and labour economists in search of the micro foundations of this disturbing phenomenon again turned their attention to the paradox. The puzzle, of course, is particularly striking for the densely populated agriculture of poor countries, where trade unions (and unemployment benefits) are weak or non-existent and minimum wage legislation is hardly enforced.

One early attempt to tackle the puzzle theoretically was made independently by Leibenstein (1957) and Mazumdar (1959), building on a presumed link between nutrition intake and work efficiency, and exploring the effects of this link on wages and involuntary unemployment: at too low a wage, the productivity of a worker may also be too low for the employer to be interested in hiring him or her. This is the earliest version of the efficiency wage theory, which was generalized later to the case of industrially advanced countries.

---

[1] See e.g. Hansen (1969), Bardhan (1984), and Rosenzweig (1984).

Suppose the production function is given by:

$$Q = F(n\lambda(W)), \; F' > 0, \; F'' < 0, \text{ and } \lambda'(W) > 0, \tag{1}$$

where Q is quantity produced, n is the number of standard units (say, hours) of labour employed, W is the time wage rate, and λ is a measure of labour efficiency. We shall take the $\lambda(W)$ function to be given by Figure 4.1. Maximizing the employer's profits, $F - nW$, with respect to n and W respectively, we get:

$$F'(n\lambda(W)) \, \lambda(W) - W = 0 \tag{2}$$

and

$$F'(n\lambda(W)) \, \lambda'(W) - 1 = 0. \tag{3}$$

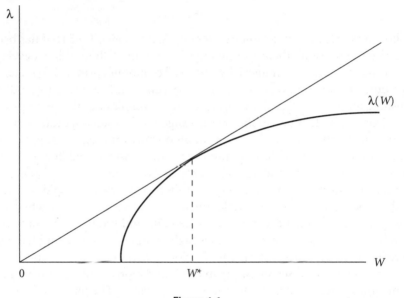

Figure 4.1

Equations (2) and (3) determine W^*, the efficiency wage. $W/\lambda(W)$ is the cost of buying one efficiency unit of labour, and the efficiency wage, W^*, minimizes this cost. If all employers are identical, Figure 4.2 shows the aggregate demand curve for labour, $D(W)$. Note that the employers will not hire any extra worker even if the wage rate offered by the worker is below W^*. On the other hand, the demand for labour is downward-sloping for all W exceeding W^*. This is because, as W rises above W^*, $W/\lambda(W)$ also rises (as can be checked from Figure 4.1). From (2) and (3), this implies a rise in $F'(n\lambda(W))$, which in turn implies a lower n. If now the aggregate supply curve $S(W)$ is as in Figure 4.2, then there is involuntary unemployment in equilibrium at the efficiency wage W^*.

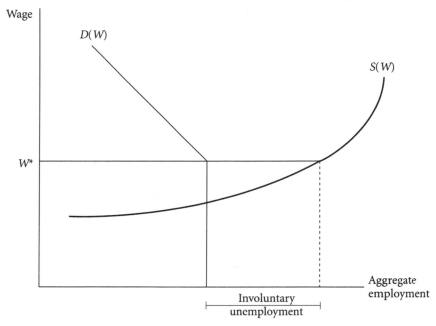

Figure 4.2

An interesting extension of this basic model to the case where workers have differential access to alternative income (say, from ownership of land or other assets) was carried out by Dasgupta and Ray (1986), and again in Dasgupta (1993). The main argument is that the minimum cost of buying an efficiency unit of labour—let us call it μ—is relatively high for labour supplied by the landless (compared with that by the landed small peasants, who have access to some income from cultivation or rentals), so that the latter may undercut the former in the labour market; μ is also high for large landowners whose alternative sources of income keep the opportunity costs of their labour high. In Figure 4.3, the horizontal axis represents a continuum of workers along the unit interval $[0, 1]$, each with a landownership label, m, in a land-scarce economy; the higher is the m-value of a worker, the larger is the amount of land owned by him or her. The μ curve traces out the minimum cost of buying an efficiency unit of labour across workers from different land classes. For the landless, μ is given by what we have described above as the efficiency wage. It is higher than the corresponding μ for small landed peasants, and so the curve dips down, only to rise again for the wealthy landowners. Now superimpose on Figure 4.3 a horizontal line for $\bar{\mu}$ representing the aggregate marginal product of effective labour, so that for workers whose μ exceeds $\bar{\mu}$ there is no demand for them in the labour market. If the $\bar{\mu}$ line is as in Figure 4.3, clearly workers with land labels in the

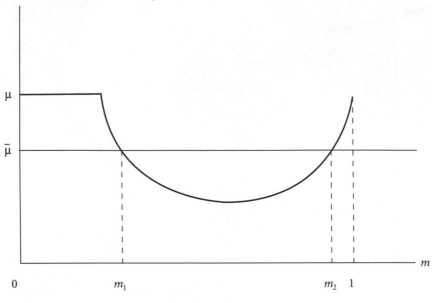

Figure 4.3

range 0 to m_1 (the landless plus some marginal farmers) are rationed out of the labour market, because they are too costly to hire in terms of efficiency units (even if they are prepared to work for a low hourly or daily wage rate). These are the involuntarily unemployed. The workers (the 'gentry' is a more appropriate term) in the land range m_2 to 1 are also unemployed in agriculture, but voluntarily so. An important policy conclusion of Dasgupta and Ray (1986) is that land reform can lower parts of the μ curve in Figure 4.3 and thus can add to aggregate output. (Some of the previously unemployed may become employable now, the employed small peasants may become more productive than before with better nourishment, and even some of the gentry may now work.)

While the nutrition-based efficiency theory of wages is one of the more elegant theories of wages and unemployment in the rural sector of poor countries, some of its testable implications run counter to the limited evidence that is available. For example, the evidence on employment probabilities (see Datt 1989) is not at all consistent with the idea suggested in the preceding paragraph that the landed labourers enjoy an employment advantage over the landless. Furthermore, even at very low levels of nutrition intake (when the efficiency wage should be binding), the observed variations in agricultural wage rates in response to variations in supply and demand parameters run quite contrary to the wage rigidity suggested by the stability in the physiological nutrition–

productivity relationship of the theory.[2] This applies not just to the wage rates of casual labourers, but also to the case of long-term contract labour where the employer has time to capture the benefits of higher productivity of the better-fed workers (see e.g. Bardhan 1984: ch. 4). The prediction of the theory on wage diversity for labourers belonging to different asset groups is also often belied by the evidence.[3]

In the context of labour markets in developed countries, the link between wage and efficiency has been generalized to cases where paying wages above market-clearing levels is justified on the grounds of boosting worker morale, loyalty, and effort-intensity, of reducing the incentive to shirk (when direct monitoring is costly), of improving the average quality of the pool of job applicants, of raising norms of gift-exchange between employers and employees, and so on. The standard papers modelling these grounds are collected in Akerlof and Yellen (1986). These grounds are valid to some extent in developing countries as well, although in the small neighbourhood community of the village or the urban informal sector, efficiency wage stories based on screening (for unobserved ability) or shirking (for unmonitored effort) are sometimes less compelling.[4]

In the context of a developing country a particularly important variant of the efficiency–wage story may be related to the problem of ensuring a steady work-force with low turnover and absenteeism (as the growing industrial sector tries to shape a disciplined work-force out of a ragtag army of peasant migrants), or even, in the agricultural sector, to the problem of reducing the costs and risks of delay in labour recruitment when weather dependence in the crop cycle makes the employer place a high premium on quick and ready availability of labour in some operations.[5]

In a highly simplified version of this model, let us suppose that the profits of the employer are given by $[F(L) - WL - AR(W)L]$, where F is output which depends only on labour employed, L, W is the wage rate, R is the cost of recruiting labour and A is a shift parameter. We shall assume that a higher wage paid by the employer makes recruitment easier, so that $R'(W) < 0$. This is to capture the idea of the wage premium the employer is prepared to pay for readily

---

[2] Dasgupta (1993) attempts to explain variations in wages by extending the model to incorporate a case where there are differences in the productivity of the village common property which the landless workers fall back upon. This is, however, too tenuous a base to support variations in efficiency wages in response to general changes in demand or productivity parameters.

[3] For a discussion of the evidence, see Bardhan (1984) and Rosenzweig (1988).

[4] Esfahani and Mookherjee (1995) show in a theoretical model that in poor countries with a relative abundance of labour and high effective time discount rates it may not be worthwhile for firms even in the formal sector to pay the 'informational rents' (i.e. premiums in excess of the reservation wage) required for creating strong performance incentives or offering high-powered incentive contracts.

[5] A labour turnover model can be found in Stiglitz (1974), and a recruitment cost model in Bardhan (1984: ch. 4).

available or steady labour. Maximizing the employer's profits with respect to L and W, we get:

$$F'(L) - W - AR(W) = 0 \tag{4}$$

$$1 + AR'(W) = 0. \tag{5}$$

Equation (5) determines the efficiency wage W^*, and putting that into (4) we determine L. If all employers are identical, and if the recruitment cost function is convex (i.e. if $R'' > 0$)—just as we assumed convexity of the nutrition–productivity set in Figure 4.1—we get a demand and a supply curve exactly as in Figure 4.2, and again there can be involuntary unemployment in equilibrium at the efficiency wage W^*.

Now suppose the shift parameter A depends on the tightness or slackness of the market in general (over and above the particular labour market under consideration), so that, for example, a larger general unemployment rate, u, in the surrounding area shifts the parameter A of the recruitment cost function downward, i.e., $A'(u) < 0$. In this case, it is easy to show that W^* is higher the tighter is the general labour market (or the lower is u). In this way we can introduce some sensitivity to the general market conditions into the efficiency wage.

II

One implication of all variants of the efficiency theory of wages is that it is the employer who resists the possible undercutting of the wage by the involuntarily unemployed. This is not adequate to account for the frequently observed phenomenon, both in urban and rural labour markets, that attempts to undercut wages on the part of unemployed or underemployed labourers are not as common as one would expect from their desperate conditions. The social norm that forbids such undercutting is part of what Solow (1990) describes as the social institutions in the labour market. The persistence of such a norm against Hobbesian competition in the labour market is explained in terms of an individualistic rationale for implicit cooperation among workers, in the context of industrially advanced countries, by Solow (1990) and in terms of rural labour markets of poor countries by Osmani (1990). We shall follow here the latter model of self-enforcing cooperation in an infinitely repeated non-cooperative game situation, even when formal institutions of collective bargaining are absent.

Each worker takes a decision on which wage rate to bid, and in doing so takes into account what he or she expects the others to do. A Nash equilibrium is established when each worker finds that it does not pay to revise his or her bid. Suppose a perceived wage vector $w = (W_1, \ldots, W_i, \ldots, W_N)$ for a worker i (when there are N such workers) consists of his or her own bid W_i as well as the expected bids of others. On the basis of w, the worker estimates his or her probability of employment, $p_i(w)$, which goes down (up) as own (others') wage bid increases. His or her expected pay-off P_i is given by:

$$P_i(w) = p_i(w)W_i + (1 - p_i(w))W_0, \tag{6}$$

where W_0 is the reservation wage.

If all workers have the same reservation wage and the competitive market-clearing wage rate is also given by W_0, any wage rate above W_0 is collectively superior to W_0 for positive p. Such a collectively superior outcome is feasible if each worker could make sure that no one will resort to undercutting. This is possible if in a repeated game one can punish deviant behaviour by imposing a much bigger future loss on the deviant. One such strategy for a self-enforcing cooperative outcome is the well-known 'trigger-strategy' in the context of an infinitely repeated game. A trigger-strategy equilibrium will be established if everybody continues to bid a wage rate $W^* > W_0$ every day as long as everybody else is seen to bid W^*; however, if anyone ever bids a lower wage, everybody else will bid W_0 in the next period and continue to do so for ever. The threat of this punitive action is credible, since, if everybody other than i is bidding W_0, then i can do no better than bid W_0 and the wage rate is actually forced down to that level. For the deviant, whether this is too costly or not depends on the time discount rate that is used to balance the immediate gain and the future loss. If $\rho < 1$ is the discount factor, then the discounted value of all payoffs from the trigger-strategy wage rate W^* is given by

$$\pi(W^*) = P(W^*)(1 + \rho + \rho^2 + \dots) = \frac{P(W^*)}{1 - \rho}, \tag{7}$$

where $P(W^*) = p(W^*)W^* + [1 - p(W^*)]W_0$. Any worker contemplating deviation on day t by bidding a wage rate $W' < W^*$ can calculate that his or her discounted income stream will be:

$$\left[\frac{1 - \rho^t}{1 - \rho} P(W^*) + \rho^t W' + \frac{\rho^{t+1}}{1 - \rho} W_0 \right].$$

If this value is less than or equal to $\pi(W^*)$ in (7) for all workers at all t, then W^* is a viable trigger-strategy. This defines a feasible range for the wage rate W^*, depending on the time discount rate. It can be shown that the greater the impatience for present consumption (i.e. the lower is ρ), as is more likely in the case of extreme poverty, the lower is the limit of the viable trigger-strategy wage. Within this feasible range, one can get an interior-maximum equilibrium wage by maximizing $\pi(W^*)$ in (7) with respect to W^*. Measuring $p(W^*)$, the probability of employment, by the fraction of the labour supplied that is actually demanded, one can easily show from the first-order condition of this maximum that, the higher is the elasticity of labour demand, the lower is the equilibrium W^*.

As Osmani (1990) points out, this model presumes 'common knowledge', particularly about the factors determining the choice of W^*. While this presumption is generally constricting, as in most game-theoretic models, it may be somewhat less so in the context of the small closed community of a village labour market with settled technology. For the same reason, common knowledge may break down in transitional periods after some technical change or migration of outsiders.

There are two other problems with this model. (1) The threat to bid W_0 for ever once someone defects is implausible, and there are subtle issues of the possibility of renegotiation (and its attendant incentive effects) here. (2) It is not clear what prevents an employer and a worker from entering into personalized relations instead of going through the daily job lottery, the employer assuring the worker job security (converting p into unity) in exchange for the latter accepting (slightly above) the market-clearing wage rate.

Besides, the model attempts to formalize implicit cooperation only among workers, i.e. on the supply side of the labour market. There are reasons to believe that the collective action problem for cooperation among employers may often be less acute. Allowing for some cooperation on both sides of the labour market, Datt (1989) has characterized the outcomes in the (agricultural and, a fortiori, non-agricultural) labour market in terms of the asymmetric version of the well-known two-party Nash bargaining solution. It is assumed that the two parties bargain only over the wage rate, leaving the employers free to determine employment at the bargained wage. (This is not implausible when formal unions are weak or non-existent.) The disagreement payoff of the employers is taken to be zero profit (foregoing production), and that of the workers is taken to be equal to the reservation wage. Maximizing the usual Nash product of the surplus of the profits and wage incomes over the respective disagreement payoffs (with the coefficients of bargaining power as exponents), one can get from the first-order condition the standard result that the workers' wage earnings relative to the employers' profits depend on the ratio of the coefficients of bargaining power, the wage elasticity of labour demand, and the workers' reservation wage. This model is consistent with the existence of involuntary unemployment as an equilibrium phenomenon (as the rent-sharing[6] between the employer and the employees rations out other potential workers), along with some sensitivity of the bargained wage rate to changes in demand and supply parameters. An extended (three-party) wage bargaining model,

---

[6] In the literature on inter-industry wage structure, rent-sharing is an obvious candidate for explaining the widely observed correlation between industry wage premiums and industry profitability.

where male and female labour are imperfectly substitutable inputs in production, can be used to explain the prevalence of gender disparities in wages as a possible outcome of differences in bargaining powers, in disagreement payoffs, and in wage elasticities of demand for male and female labour.

It may be also important to consider an implication of the labour market as a social institution in the context of gender disparity in wages and occupational segmentation of women. In a patriarchal society, standards of 'fairness' in wages and jobs and the nature of expected collusive behaviour, the social sanctions on wage undercutting, and the domain of enforcement of social norms in general may be gender-specific. Both men and women internalize these and help to perpetuate the disparities.

While distinctions by visible group characteristics like gender (or in some cases ethnicity or caste) are more easily accepted, employer-made distinctions in wage payment on the basis of unobserved individual-specific characteristics such as ability are likely to be more controversial. For a given task, the spread in wage rates is thus often narrower than that in ability of workers.[7] Employers may be unwilling to create invidious distinctions among their workers which may lead to problems of morale and tension. Workers may also use a uniform wage as a focal point in their efforts at implicit cooperation to raise wages. (In the case of explicit collusion, this has been observed in a much enhanced form in solidaristic wage bargaining in Scandinavia.)

Another example of how labour market transactions are often embedded in the social processes of poor countries relates to the domain of the localized or segmented labour market. Village employers sometimes (though not always) preferentially hire local labourers even when cheaper labour by 'outsiders' is available: in hiring 'outsiders', they may not be able to draw upon the considerable reservoir of village loyalty and goodwill they utilize in maintaining their social control over the labour process. Urban labour contractors and 'jobbers' often recruit from certain communities and neighbourhoods in preference over others, as they have developed over the years a network of territorial affinities and social control over the dependability characteristics of the workers. The workers on their part look up to their local employers or recruitment agents (even when the wages offered are not competitive) as providers of sustained job opportunities, an information network, regular credit, and emergency help over the years. The daily or monthly wage rate in the labour market (on which the usual supply–demand models concentrate) is only one aspect of a complex social and economic transaction that takes place.[8]

---

[7] Foster and Rosenzweig (1996) have argued, on the basis of data from the Philippines, that productivity differences of different workers are not fully reflected in different wages on account of information asymmetry, except in the case of certain visible group characteristics (like gender, where there is evidence of 'statistical discrimination', i.e. wage based on perceived *average* productivity of the group as a whole).

[8] For a discussion of labour mobility in the context of 'the boundaries of the village moral economy'

The particularistic modes of recruitment sometimes turn the factory labour market in poor countries, even with weak trade unions, into an 'insider–outsider' mould (although in a somewhat different sense compared with the way the term is used in the unionized labour world of industrially advanced countries: see e.g. Lindbeck and Snower 1988). Employers sometimes informally use their long-term employees to recommend and screen new recruits and hold them responsible for any subsequent 'misbehaviour' on the part of the latter. In this system, the employer gets 'dependable' hires at a low recruitment and monitoring cost and the 'insider' employees establish a network of patronage and influence in their community and kinship groups; the unconnected 'outsiders' face formidable barriers to entry, and their possible attempts at wage undercutting can be rendered largely irrelevant by the system.

III

In this section we discuss different aspects of a multi-tiered labour market. One way of distinguishing the tiers is in terms of differences in the duration of contract: the terms of contract may vary between long-term (say, annual in the case of agriculture) contract labourers and daily casual labourers, even when they are of similar ability and carry out similar tasks.[9] In the industrial sector, protective labour legislation often creates small pockets of tenured factory workers surrounded by a 'floating mass' of temporary or casual labourers. Over time, of course, the former accumulate firm-specific skills which then differentiate them from their casual cohorts and offer them opportunities for rent-sharing and promotion in the 'internal labour market' of the firm. In the smaller-scale agricultural sector, where the reach of such labour legislation is tenuous, a two-tiered labour market for similar tasks is often the outcome of sharp seasonality in the crop cycle. Let us explore three kinds of rationale for the phenomenon of labour-tying in agriculture, all following from seasonality.

First, we have noted in Section I that the employer often puts a high premium on quick and ready availability of labour for some operations in the peak season: weather dependence not only makes the timing of these operations somewhat unpredictable, it also means that when the time comes the job has to be done very quickly, and there are various risks and costs of delay. This is a reason why the employer may be prepared to enter into contracts with labourers in the

in India, see Bardhan and Rudra (1986); for a discussion of how 'non-market' institutions for allocating labour such as the communal work party in Africa embody networks and clientage relations that mediate access to resources, reciprocity, and outside employment opportunities, see Kevane (1994).

[9] For examples of finer variations in the duration (and exclusiveness) of labour contracts in agriculture, see Bardhan and Rudra (1981).

lean season (even if they were to be paid a wage rate higher than their marginal product in that season) in exchange for a commitment to providing ready labour in the peak season as soon as the employer needs it. The residual labour need in the peak season is supplied by casual labourers involving a recruitment cost on the part of the employer. (For a simple model of this, see Bardhan 1984: ch. 4, sec. V.)

A second rationale for labour tying in agriculture, provided in Bardhan (1984: ch. 5), is in terms of insurance against wage fluctuations and implicit contract theory, taking labourers to be more risk-averse than employers. Suppose there is no work to be done in the lean season and the peak-season labour requirement per unit of output is given by a fixed coefficient β. Mean output level is given by F, while the actual yield is θF, where θ is a random factor (representing weather and other production uncertainties) with an expected value of unity. If the total labour requirement in the peak season, $\beta\theta F$, exceeds the amount of tied labour, L_t, hired in the lean season, the employer then enters the spot or casual market, hiring the additional labour at the uncertain wage rate $W(\theta)$ of that time. If the employer is risk-neutral and the labourers risk-averse, then optimal risk-sharing will imply a smoothing of worker consumption across seasons at a given consumption level $\bar{c}$, which is what the tied labourers get paid in each season. Ignoring across-season time discounting, the employer's expected profits are then given by

$$E\pi = F - 2\bar{c}L_t - \int_z^{\bar{z}}(\beta\theta F - L_t)\,W(\theta)\,f(\theta)\,d\theta, \qquad (8)$$

where $z = L_t/\beta F$, $\bar{z}$ is the maximum value taken by θ, and $f(\theta)$ is a density distribution of θ.

The first-order condition of maximizing (8) with respect to L_t gives demand for tied labour which in equilibrium is equal to supply. Casual labour exists in this model because 'labour-hoarding' is costly.

In both of the rationales for labour-tying mentioned above, casual labour is a residual category with its extent depending on the state of labour demand in the peak season. Mukherjee and Ray (1995) modify this implicit contract model by introducing an incentive constraint which makes labour-tying optimal if and only if seasonal fluctuations in the labour market exceed a certain threshold level. The smoothing of wage across seasons implies that in situations where the spot wage exceeds the tied wage the tied labourer may be tempted to breach the contract, which will then incur a punishment in terms of contract termination by the employer. If the worker can return to the tied labour market in the next period relatively unscarred by this incident, incentive compatibility requires that the employer offers a premium in the tied contract to discourage such reneging by the tied worker. This is costly to the employer, but in equilibrium this cost is balanced against the gain to the employer from the insurance contract in the face of seasonal fluctuations. In equilibrium, there will always be an active casual labour market in this model.

A third kind of rationale for labour tying, again depending on seasonality, but now in terms of the efficiency theory of wages, is provided by Guha (1989). Suppose again there is no work in the lean season and there is also a one-period lag with which the nutrition–efficiency link that we have discussed in Section I works. So only in the peak season can the employer capture the higher productivity effect of paying an efficiency wage to the tied labourer in the lean season. This, of course, requires costly labour-hoarding on the part of the employer. Casual labourers need to be paid only in the peak season, and they have to survive the lean season scrounging in the village commons (where their income depends on the pressure of the casual working population on the commons for that season). The working efficiency of tied and casual labourers differs according to their different consumption histories in the lean season. The coexistence of tied and casual labour is thus brought about by a trade-off between the positive effects of tied contracts on productivity and the costly seasonal idleness of tied labour.

The three kinds of rationale for labour-tying in agriculture all refer to cases where tied and casual labourers differ in the duration of their labour contract but not in the tasks they carry out. Now let us refer to some cases where the rationale involves different tasks and functions. Take, for example, the model of Eswaran and Kotwal (1985). They also have a two-season model, but there is work of different kinds in the two periods. The work in the first period requires a lot of discretion and responsibility (e.g. in crop choice, water management, animal care) and is inherently difficult to monitor (although bad decisions and irresponsibilities in the first period become discernible by the end of the second period, i.e. at the completion of the crop cycle). The work in the second period involves more mechanical or repetitive work (like weeding, harvesting, or threshing) that is less difficult to monitor. Tied labour works for the employer in both periods, but casual labour is hired only for the second period. A tied labourer risks contract termination at the end of the second period if he or she has been lax in the first period. The threat is *real* if the tied labourer is rendered worse off by the contract termination; this will be the case if the tied labour contract includes an incentive premium over and above his or her opportunity income. (This is akin to the incentive compatibility constraint in shirking models in the efficiency theory of wages: the employer has to make sure that the discounted stream of expected utility of the shirker is not more than that of the honest worker.) The threat of termination is *credible* because the employer, with a relatively easy access to a pool of workers at the beginning of the crop cycle, is usually made no worse off. In fact, on account of the incentive premium (or what is sometimes called the informational rent in models of imperfect information) there will be an excess supply of workers in the tied labour market who will not succeed in bidding it away. The excess supply may be absorbed in the casual labour market, the analog of involuntary unemployment in the usual shirking model.

Another case of task differential between the two types of worker takes place when the employer finds it useful to mobilize the services of a small band of tied labourers in overseeing the work of the more numerous casual labourers working on the farm and reporting on cases of delinquency or rebelliousness. The two-tiered labour system with its policy of selective exclusion in one tier can be an effective divide-and-rule device on the part of the employer.

Once the equilibrium in these various models of labour-tying is described, some interesting comparative-static questions may be answered. For example, does agricultural development and commercialization tend to increase or decrease the incidence of tied labour? This depends on the interplay of a conflicting set of forces. If development is associated with tighter labour markets in the peak season (raising recruitment costs), with a larger interseasonal fluctuation in the spot wages, with a larger number of crops raised in the year (thus reducing seasonal underutilization of tied labour and the cost of labour-hoarding), and with an increase in the number of tasks that are more complex and require more responsible decision-taking on the part of the workers and are less monitorable on the part of the employer, then the models discussed above suggest an increase in the incidence of labour-tying. On the other hand, if it is associated with increased mobility and outside opportunity for workers (raising the necessary incentive premium for tied labour) and with a reduction in personalized information regarding worker history (making worker default easier), or if technological progress is labour-saving, or if it is associated with better access to financial markets (making it less necessary for the worker to use labour-tying contracts as a consumption-smoothing device), then development may reduce labour-tying in terms of those models. Also, the models above have assumed homogeneity of tied and casual labourers. If, as is usually the case, the employer also looks for some behavioural traits like docility in a tied labourer, with the increased opportunities for 'voice' as well as 'exit' that modernization may bring about, such traits may be less easily available (particularly if some people act docile when they have no alternatives), lowering the incidence of labour-tying.

It should also be noted that in the discussion above we have assumed that the tied labourer voluntarily enters long-duration contracts with the employer and reserves the right to leave unconditionally at the end of the specified period. Historically, of course, agrarian labour-tying brings to mind the blatant cases of obligatory service by the tenant-serf to the lord of the manor (as in the classic instances of European feudalism), or of debt–paeonage to moneylender-cum-landlord as observed in many parts of the world. These are clearly cases in which tying involves a continuing lack of freedom on the part of the labourer and the sanctions underlying the employer's authority are based primarily on social or legal compulsion or what is sometimes called *extra-economic* coercion. Although circumstances obviously vary from country to country, it is probably correct to say that today in most parts of the world labour-tying in the sense of bonded and unfree labour is quantitatively not very important and/or is on the decline. Yet there are many cases where the current so-called voluntary long-duration contract is an evolution from older unfree arrangements and to this day may contain some lingering traces of degrees of unfreedom which are not openly or formally coercive but are socially embedded in the form of norm-guided context-specific rules of behaviour.

In the non-agricultural sector, the multi-tiered nature of the labour market is particularly salient in view of the 'closed shop' practices of unions, which some-times create an island of privileged 'labour aristocracy', with job security and relatively high wages, in an ocean of unorganized, job-insecure, and low-paid workers. But, as Freeman (1992) points out, the empirical case of negative effects of unions and other 'distortions' in the labour market is rather weak, and the positive effects associated with collective bargaining in terms of higher pro-ductivity, lower labour turnover, workplace safety, and job training are not insignificant. Besides, as we noted at the end of the last section, the particularis-tic models of labour recruitment and internal promotion systems imply that a 'closed shop' often operates even without unions.

Another way in which the urban (non-manual) labour market gets splin-tered into non-competing groups is through the widespread practice in the dominant public sector, and also in some large private firms, of using minimum educational qualifications as a rationing criterion when there is an over-supply of job applicants.[10] Not only does this practice of 'education credentialism' block chances of upward mobility for workers with low education (but possibly high ability), but the latter also get 'bumped' or crowded out of their existing jobs as the employers respond to the excess supply by raising the minimum edu-cational qualifications for those jobs when the salary levels are not flexible. Under these circumstances, if the uneducated have very few places to go, inequality may increase as a paradoxical result of educational expansion.

REFERENCES

Akerlof, G. and Yellen, J. (eds.) (1986), *Efficiency Wage Models of the Labor Market.* Cambridge: Cambridge University Press.

Bardhan, P. (1984), *Land, Labor and Rural Poverty.* New York: Columbia University Press.

[10] See the useful discussion on education and the labour market in Mazumdar (1989).

—— and Rudra, A. (1981), 'Terms and Conditions of Labor Contracts in Agriculture: Results of a Survey in West Bengal', *Oxford Bulletin of Economics and Statistics*, 43.

—— and —— (1986), 'Labor Mobility and the Boundaries of the Village Moral Economy', *Journal of Peasant Studies*, 13.

Dasgupta, P. (1993), *An Inquiry into Well-being and Destitution*. Oxford: Clarendon Press.

—— and Ray, D. (1986), 'Inequality as a Determinant of Malnutrition and Unemployment: Theory', *Economic Journal*, 96.

Datt, G. (1989), *Wage and Employment Determination in Agricultural Labor Markets in India*, Ph.D. thesis, Australian National University.

Esfahani, H. and Mookherjee, D. (1995) 'Productivity, Contracting Modes, and Development', *Journal of Development Economics*, 46.

Eswaran, M., and Kotwal, A. (1985), 'A Theory of Two-tiered Labor Markets in Agrarian Economies', *American Economic Review*, 75.

Foster, A. and Rosenzweig, M. (1996), 'Comparative Advantage, Information, and the Allocation of Workers to Tasks: Evidence from an Agricultural Labor Market', *Review of Economic Studies*, 63.

Freeman, R. (1992), 'Labor Market Institutions and Policies: Help or Hindrance to Economic Development', *Proceedings of the World Bank Annual Conference on Development Economics*. Washington: World Bank.

Guha, A. (1989), 'Consumption, Efficiency, and Surplus Labor', *Journal of Development Economics*, 31.

Hansen, B. (1969), 'Employment and Wages in Rural Egypt', *American Economic Review*, 59.

Kevane, M. (1994), 'Village Labor Markets in Sheikan District, Sudan', *World Development*, 22.

Leibenstein, H. (1957), *Economic Backwardness and Economic Growth*. New York: John Wiley.

Lewis, W. A. (1954), 'Economic Development with Unlimited Supplies of Labour', *Manchester School*, 28.

Lindbeck, A., and Snower, D. (1988), *The Insider-Outsider Theory of Employment and Unemployment*. Cambridge, Mass.: MIT Press.

Mazumdar, D. (1959), 'The Marginal Productivity Theory of Wages and Disguised Unemployment', *Review of Economic Studies*, 26.

—— (1989), 'Microeconomic Issues of Labor Markets in Developing Countries: Analysis and Policy Implications', EDI Seminar Paper no. 40, World Bank.

Mukherjee, A., and Ray, D. (1995) 'Labor Tying', *Journal of Development Economics*, 47.

Osmani, S. (1990), 'Wage Determination in Rural Labor Markets: The Theory of Implicit Cooperation', *Journal of Development Economics*, 34.

Rosenzweig, M. (1984), 'Determinants of Wage Rates and Labor Supply Behavior in the Rural Sector of a Developing Country', in H. Binswanger and M. Rosenzweig (eds.), *Contractual Arrangements, Employment, and Wages in Rural Labor Markets in Asia*. New Haven: Yale University Press.

Rosenzweig, M. (1988), 'Labor Markets in Low-Income Countries', in H. B. Chenery and T. N. Srinivasan (eds.), *Handbook of Development Economics*, i, Amsterdam: North-Holland.

Solow, R. (1990), *The Labor Market as a Social Institution*. Oxford: Basil Blackwell.

Stiglitz, J. (1974), 'Alternative Theories of Wage Determination and Unemployment in LDCs: The Labor Turnover Model', *Quarterly Journal of Economics*, 88.

5

Migration

Development involves the transformation of the spatial organization of a society. From a dispersed, rural, mostly agrarian, society, a nation in the process of development becomes a more concentrated urban and industrial economy. A fundamental part of this transformation is the movement of a large number of individuals via migration from the rural areas to the cities. The pace of urban growth in many poor countries is extremely rapid: many cities in Africa are growing at more than 7 per cent per year, while several of the giant cities of Asia and Latin America are growing at more than 5 per cent per year.

The driving force behind this transformation is the different technical requirements of agricultural and industrial production. Most obviously, agricultural production is land-intensive, thus requiring a labour force dispersed over a large area, while industrial production requires relatively little land; it is possible, therefore, for the industrial labour force to be concentrated. The possibility of concentration, however, does not provide a sufficient explanation for the emergence of large cities as industrial production expands in the course of development. Why is it that industrial production tends to become concentrated in a few small areas, rather than being dispersed throughout the nation?

One important set of explanations relies on preferences. There may be consumption externalities associated with city life. Individuals might prefer living near many other people, and this positive externality might outweigh the familiar negative congestion externalities associated with population concentration. Given the opportunity to concentrate afforded by the minimal land requirements of industrial production, therefore, cities form.

Economists have tended to focus on the possibility that externalities in production underlie the impetus for population to agglomerate into large urban centres. Marshall (1920) provides the classic account. The concentration of manufacturing firms offers: (1) a pool of skilled industrial workers, and thus lower search costs associated with changes in employment; (2) the possibility of benefiting from positive externalities generated by the production of nontraded goods by neighbouring firms; and (3) the information externality generated by being able to observe neighbouring firms' technological choices. (See chapter 12 for a full discussion of this last externality.) To these, Krugman (1991) (relying on Pred 1966 and Meyer 1983) adds a fourth: industrial production is characterized by increasing returns to scale. This implies that production of manufactures will occur at only a limited number of sites. To minimize transportation costs, production should be located near major markets. Since industrial workers can generate demand for manufacturing output, it is possible that cities can begin to form: manufacturing concentrates in the city to take advantage of the large urban market, and the large market is brought into existence by the large, localized industrial labour force. The process is limited by the strength of increasing returns in industry and by the magnitude of transportation costs. Less strong increasing returns and higher transportation costs imply more dispersed industrial production. But with strongly increasing returns and relatively low transportation costs, industrial production can fully concentrate in large cities, and the 'bright lights' of the large cities (cheaply available consumer goods) can attract a large urban population.

I

Central to this process of urbanization and industrialization is the mass movement of population from the rural areas to the cities. A model of migration, therefore, is required for an understanding of this structural transformation. Few models have been as dominant in their subject area within development economics as that of migration introduced by Todaro (1969) and Harris and Todaro (1970) (HT). The HT model combines simple and uncontroversial assumptions about migrant behaviour (potential migrants compare the expected utility of migrating with the expected utility of remaining in the countryside) with assumptions regarding the structure of urban and rural labour markets which accord well with many highly visible features of some developing countries. The key institutional assumptions of the model include the following:

1. The rural labour market is competitive.
2. Modern firms hire labour in the city, and the wage they pay is fixed above the market-clearing level, either by restrictive union activity or by governmental policy on wages.
3. Only urban residents can apply for jobs in modern firms, and if modern firms are faced with more applicants than they have jobs, jobs are allocated by lottery.
4. There is an 'informal sector' in which urban residents not otherwise employed can eke out a subsistence living using their labour power alone.

In a moment we will examine the implications of combining these institutional assumptions with the behavioural assumption that potential migrants move to the sector in which their expected utility is highest. First, however, let us briefly consider the empirical foundation of these institutional assumptions.

The most controversial of the institutional assumptions is that regarding the informal sector. In the HT formulation, this sector is viewed as an unproductive holding ground in which workers denied access to the modern industrial sector (merely) survive until they are lucky enough to find a job. This conception of the informal sector is clearly inadequate. In many poor countries there is a large urban population engaged in an extremely diverse set of activities outside the direct scrutiny of the state, and not covered by labour unions. One important literature views this sector as the domain of small-scale entrepreneurs who choose to remain outside the regulatory reach of the state.[1] It is not well established that the wages of comparably skilled individuals in this sector are significantly different from those in the formal sector. Certainly the productivity of individuals in the informal sector is not zero (as we shall assume below).

Second, the evidence on wage rigidity in the urban formal sector is mixed. The conventional view of the source of the rigidity is labour union activism in this sector, or, alternatively, binding minimum wage legislation. While it is correct that most developing countries have minimum wages, that these are more likely to apply to (or to be enforced in) the urban formal sector, and that unions are much more powerful in this sector, the quantitative importance of these institutions in wage determination is only poorly documented (see Williamson 1988). In Section II we present a simple model which addresses this concern, modifying the HT model by endogenizing the wage in the urban formal sector, but retaining many of the features of HT as a consequence of information imperfections.

Finally, the migration decision is surely more complex than the HT scheme. Migrants do not lose all contact with the rural sector when they move to the city. Many authors have documented the importance of ongoing economic interactions between migrants and their communities of origin.[2] One important consequence is that the geographical dispersion of family members can be seen, at least in part, as one component of a strategy for dealing with spatially correlated risk (Paulson 1993). By spreading individuals (who remain economically linked either through altruism or via implicit risk-sharing contracts) across different agroclimatic zones or different economic sectors, families can diversify their incomes and protect themselves against risks that cannot be insured locally (see Chapter 8). Nor do migrants simply move to a city to join an

---

[1] See Maloney (1996) for evidence that the informal sector in Mexico is better characterized in this manner. Hart (1973) is an important early statement of this point of view.

[2] See e.g. Lucas and Stark (1985), Katz and Stark (1986), Rosenzweig (1988), Rosenzweig and Stark (1989).

undifferentiated mass of migrants. Migrants use connections based at least in part on social networks formed in their communities of origin to improve their prospects of obtaining formal-sector employment and to smooth their transition into the city. In Section III we look more closely at the migration process than is possible in the simple HT model.

With these caveats in mind, the HT model remains a simple and powerful model of some aspects of structural transformation in at least some poor countries. Let L_r be the rural population, which is employed in agriculture on a fixed amount of land. Agricultural output is determined by the production function $g(L_r)$, and is sold on a world market at a price normalized to unity. (The small open economy assumption is made to abstract from changes in the relative prices of food and manufactures as the structure of the economy changes.) The rural labour market is competitive, so rural wages are

$$w_r = g'(L_r), \tag{1}$$

as shown in Figure 5.1. The urban population is either employed in manufacturing (L_m) or is unemployed (working in the informal sector) (L_u). Normalize the population to 1, so that $L_r + L_m + L_u = 1$. The urban unemployed live by their wits in this model, scratching out a subsistence existence by engaging in petty trade, craft production, or urban agriculture. We normalize their wage to zero. w_m is the institutionally fixed manufacturing wage. Thus, manufacturing employment L_m is implicitly defined as a function of this fixed wage to satisfy

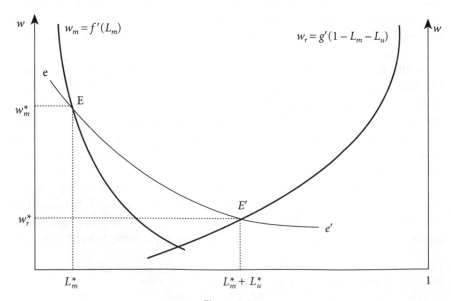

Figure 5.1

$$w_m = f'(L_m). \tag{2}$$

Equation (2) defines the manufacturing demand for labour $L_m(w_m)$, which is drawn in Figure 5.1. Only urban residents can apply for manufacturing employment, and the probability of employment is simply the number of jobs divided by the number of urban residents. The expected wage of an urban resident, therefore, is $[L_m/(L_m + L_u)]w_m$—i.e. the probability of finding a job times the urban wage.

Migration occurs to equalize the expected wage of an urban resident with the wage that the resident could earn in the rural areas:

$$w_r = \frac{L_m(w_m)}{L_u + L_m(w_m)} w_m. \tag{3}$$

Equation (3) defines the size of the urban informal sector as a function of the urban wage. Migration takes place until the size of the urban informal sector is large enough (and the rural population small enough) to equalize the rural wage with the expected wage earned in the city. The equilibrium is depicted in Figure 5.1, which is based on Corden and Findlay (1975). The exogenously fixed manufacturing wage w_m^* determines manufacturing employment L_m^*.

Rewriting equation (3), we see that equilibrium requires that $w_r(L_u + L_m) = w_m L_m$. The curve ee' is the locus of points such that the wage times the amount of labour is equal to $w_m^* L_m^*$ (it's a rectangular hyperbola). At points E and E' there is an urban informal sector of size L_u^*, a rural population of $1 - L_m^* L_u^*$, and thus a rural wage of w_r^*. Because E and E' are on ee', $w_r^*(L_u^* + L_m^*) = w_m^* L_m^*$ and expected wages are equalized in the urban and rural sectors.

The urban informal sector characterized by very low living standards serves to equilibrate the migration process. If the exogenously fixed manufacturing wage w_m is high, then the proportion of population employed in the manufacturing sector is relatively small. If there were no urban informal sector ($L_u = 0$), the remainder of the population ($1 - L_m$) would be employed in agriculture. The marginal product of labour in agriculture and hence the rural wage would be very low. At the same time, the probability of employment $L_m/(L_u + L_m)$ would be one, and hence the expected urban wage would be high. Labour market equilibrium is achieved through migration, as people move out of agriculture (raising the rural wage) and into the city. This creates a pool of unemployed workers which makes up the urban informal sector, lowers the probability of finding a job in the city, and thus lowers the expected urban wage.

Migration slows to a halt with rural wages still a fraction $[L_m/(L_u + L_m)]$ of the wages earned by manufacturing employees. Thus, the model is consistent with a persistent gap in living standards between rural residents and those employed in the urban formal sector.

II

In some economies, it is not plausible that the manufacturing wage is fixed exogenously, either by government regulation or by the political strength of unions. In these circumstances, is the HT model irrelevant? It has been argued that (relatively) high manufacturing wages and an urban informal sector can emerge endogenously as a consequence of information asymmetries between employers and employees. Here we present a simple model of adverse selection which maintains much of the flavour of the HT model without assuming an exogenously set manufacturing wage. (We follow Bencivenga and Smith 1997, who use a similar model as the foundation of their study of the dynamics of migration in a growing economy. See Esfahani and Salehi-Isfahani (1989) for a model in which moral hazard gives rise to a similar equilibrium.)

As in the basic HT model, we assume that agents choose to locate in the rural or urban sector on the basis of expected income. Suppose that there are two types of agent, indexed by $i = 1, 2$. Individuals know their own type, but this is not known by anyone else. In the rural areas, production takes place using only labour, and agents work as independent producers. The fact that agents do not know each other's types, therefore, is of no consequence in this sector. An agent of type i can produce π_i in agriculture, with $\pi_2 > \pi_1 > 0$. We maintain the small open economy assumption, so the relative price of agricultural and manufactured products is fixed (at unity).

In the city, firms produce using the technology $f(L)$, where L is the number of type 2 workers employed. Type 1 workers do not contribute to industrial output. The same good can also be produced by effort alone in the city. (This is the 'informal sector'.) A type i worker can produce β_i units of the good, with $\beta_2 > \beta_1 = 0$.

We are going to describe an equilibrium in which type 1 agents remain in the countryside, and some type 2 agents come to work in the city. There is a problem of adverse selection—type 2 agents are more productive in firms than type 1 agents, but firms cannot distinguish between them *a priori*. We will see that this adverse selection problem leads to a labour market equilibrium and migration process quite similar to that discussed by HT.

Let u be the fraction of the urban population that is unemployed (employed in the informal sector). In keeping with the assumption of the HT model, $(1 - u)$ will be the probability of any city resident being employed in manufacturing. In order for the type 1 agents to choose to remain in the rural area, it must be the case that

$$\pi_1 \geq (1 - u)w_m, \tag{4}$$

where w_m is the manufacturing wage. The left-hand side of (4) is the rural income of type 1 agents, and the right-hand side is their expected income in the city. If some, but not all, type 2 agents choose to move to the city, then their expected income must be the same in the two locations:

$$\pi_2 = (1-u)w_m + u\beta_2. \tag{5}$$

Each manufacturing firm offers a wage (w_m) and a probability of employment ($1-u$) with the offers of other firms taken as given, and then hires labour to maximize profits. The expected urban incomes of type 1 and 2 agents satisfy the single crossing property; hence (4) will be binding in any Nash equilibrium. To see this, note that

$$\left.\frac{dw_m}{du}\right|_{\text{type 1 income constant}} = \frac{w}{1-u} > \frac{w-\beta}{1-u} = \left.\frac{dw_m}{du}\right|_{\text{type 2 income constant}}.$$

Suppose that other firms offer a wage and probability of employment such that (4) is not binding. Any single firm could then offer a lower wage and lower probability of employment such that (5) remains true and (4) remains a strict inequality. This firm would still attract no type 1 workers (because these workers prefer to stay in the rural sector), would remain acceptable to type 2 workers (because (5) is satisfied), but would achieve higher profit. Therefore (4) is binding in any equilibrium.

Solving (4) and (5), we find

$$u^* = \frac{\pi_2 - \pi_1}{\beta_2}, \tag{6}$$

and

$$w_m^* = \frac{\beta_2 \pi_1}{\beta_2 - (\pi_2 - \pi_1)}. \tag{7}$$

The migration equilibrium looks much the same as with the conventional HT model. The manufacturing wage is higher than the rural wage ($w_m^* > \pi_2 > \pi_1$), but the existence of a pool of unemployed (or, more properly, *under*employed) workers in the urban informal sector serves to equalize urban and rural expected wages. (Equations (4) and (5) both hold with equality.) The overall size of the urban population is determined by manufacturing demand. Manufacturers hire labour until $f'(L) = w_m^*$. If the marginal product of manufacturing labour increases (perhaps because of an increase in the quantity of manufacturing capital), the number of manufacturing workers and the number of workers in the informal sector increase in equal proportion.

III

The models we have examined thus far contain strikingly simple accounts of the migration process. Among the more important aspects of migration that are ignored are the search for employment in the city by migrants, the fact that the migration decision is forward-looking, and the selectivity of the migration process. A simple model based on Carrington *et al.* (1996) enables us to examine these three attributes of the migration process.

First, migration involves forward-looking behaviour: people make locational decisions based on their expectations regarding their future prospects in the city and the countryside. Second, migration involves selection. Not everyone simultaneously finds it optimal to move to the city. Most dramatically, young adults and the well educated are heavily over-represented among migrants moving from rural areas to the city. For these individuals, the discounted expected wage differential between the city and the village is particularly high, and it is likely that the same individuals find the moving process less costly. It is this last difference that is modelled by Carrington *et al.*

Finally, migration involves a search for employment. Crucially, both the cost of moving and the difficulty of finding employment in the new location can be mitigated by the presence in the city of previous migrants. These migrants are a vital source of information about housing and job prospects for potential migrants in their communities of origin. They also provide a social environment in the city which eases the transition to a new kind of living for those newly arrived from the countryside. Finally, communities of established migrants in the city often provide introductions to potential employers, landlords, and creditors. Migrants to a city often concentrate within specific areas where they can best take advantage of this support.

Suppose that individuals can choose to live either in the city or in the countryside. Normalize the time zero population in each area to be 1. M_t is the number of (originally) rural workers who live in the city at time t, so the rural population at t is $1 - M_t$. Let π_t be the profit per worker from agricultural production time t, which depends on the rural population:

$$\pi_t = \gamma^r(M_t). \tag{8}$$

Let E_t be the number of the migrants who are employed in industry at time t ($E_t \leq M_t$, because migrants need to search for employment), and w_t be the industrial wage. The inverse labour demand function in manufacturing is

$$w_t = \gamma^m(E_t). \tag{9}$$

γ^r is increasing in M_t and γ^m is decreasing in E_t, and $\gamma^m(0) > \gamma^r(0)$, so that the manufacturing wage is higher than the rural wage before any migration occurs.

Migration from the rural area to the city at time t involves a cost of $c(M_{t-1}, h)$. Thus, the cost of moving depends upon the presence in the city of previous migrants and on h, a measure of the personal characteristics (for example the age or education) of the potential migrant. We assume that $\partial c/\partial M < 0$ and $\partial c/\partial h > 0$. (For simplicity, we will also assume that $\partial^2 c/\partial M \partial h = 0$.) Let $F(h)$ be a measure of (originally) rural workers of type less than or equal to h. We assume that workers live for ever, and that they choose their location to maximize the expected discounted value of income (net of migration cost).

A move to the city does not guarantee employment. New migrants have to search for jobs, and they are helped in this search by the presence in the city of former migrants who are themselves employed. Let $p(E_{t-1})$ be the probability of a migrant to the city finding employment at time t. The externality through which previously employed migrants help currently unemployed migrants find jobs is reflected in the assumption that $p'(\cdot) > 0$. (We also assume that $p(0) > 0$.) For simplicity, we assume that anyone born in the city or who has ever found a job in the city is employed with certainty.

Let $V^m(M_t, E_{t-1}, h, u)$ be the expected discounted value of future income for a (previously rural) worker of type h who is unemployed in the city at time t. $V^m(M_t, E_{t-1}, h, e)$ is the similar value for an employed worker, and $V^r(M_t, E_{t-1}, h)$ is the value of staying in the rural area at time t. It can be shown (Carrington *et al.* 1996: lemma 1) that there will never be reverse migration from the city to the countryside.[3] Without reverse migration, the future expected income of individuals in the city does not depend on their type (h), because h affects only the cost of moving to the city. Thus, the expected discounted income of an unemployed migrant to the city with discount rate is (we take the wage to be zero if a manufacturing job is not found)

$$V^m(M_t, E_{t-1}, u) = p(E_{t-1}) \, V^m(M_t, E_{t-1}, e) + \delta[1 - p(E_{t-1})] \, V^m(M_{t+1}, E_t, u). \tag{10}$$

The expected income of an employed urban resident is

$$V^m(M_t, E_{t-1}, e) = \gamma^m(E_t) + \delta V^m(M_{t+1}, E_t, e), \tag{11}$$

while the expected income of someone remaining in the countryside is

$$
\begin{aligned}
V^r(M_t, E_{t-1}, h) = \gamma^r(M_t) + \delta \mathrm{Max}\,\{ & V^m(M_{t+1}, E_t, h, u) \\
& - c(M_t, h), V^r(M_{t+1}, E_t, h)\}.
\end{aligned} \tag{12}
$$

Now consider the migration decision of someone of type h currently living in a rural area. She will move to the city if

---

[3] The cost of migrating to the city ensures that there will be no overshooting, provided that expected wages for new migrants are increasing in E_t. An increase in E_t increases the probability of new migrants finding a job, but decreases the wage (through (8)). As long as the former effect is stronger, there can never be reverse migration back to the countryside.

$$V^m(M_t, E_{t-1}, u) \geq V^r(M_t, E_{t-1}, h,) + c(M_{t-1}, h). \tag{13}$$

The right-hand side of (13) is strictly increasing in h, so if type h prefers to migrate at time t, so do all types $h' \leq h$. As migration proceeds and the stock of migrants increases, the cost of migrating falls. At the same time, the number of employed migrants increases, and with that the probability of a new migrant locating a job also increases. For both reasons, rural residents of increasingly higher type find it profitable to migrate. The process finally halts when the wage gap has diminished sufficiently that there are no further incentives to move. In this steady-state, $M_t = M_{t+1} = M$, so that there is no further migration. All who have migrated find employment (as $t \to \infty$), so that $M = E$. Let $H \equiv F^{-1}(M)$ be the marginal type of rural worker, just indifferent between locating in the city and staying in the rural area at the steady state. In the steady state, there must be no incentive for urban workers to move back to the countryside, so

$$V^m(M, M, e) = \gamma^m(M)/(1 - \delta) \geq V^r(M, M, h) \; \forall \, h \leqslant H, \tag{14}$$

and there must be no incentive for those in the rural areas to move to the city:

$$V^r(M,M,h) \geq V^m(M,M,u) - c(M,h) = \frac{p(M)V^m(M,M,e)}{1 - \delta(1 - p(M))} - c(M,h) \forall h \geq H. \tag{15}$$

The steady-state equilibrium level of migration satisfies (15) with equality for the marginal H. Thus, $V^r(M, M, h) = \gamma^r(M)/(1 - \delta)$ (from (12)). Recalling that $V^m(M, M, e) = \gamma^m(M)/(1 - \delta)$ and substituting into (15) with $h = H$, we see

$$\frac{\gamma^m(M) - \gamma^r(M)}{1 - \delta} = c(M, H) + \frac{\gamma^m(M)(1 - p(M))}{1 - \delta(1 - p(M))}. \tag{16}$$

For the marginal rural potential migrant in the steady-state equilibrium, the present discounted value of the urban–rural wage gap is just equal to the cost of migrating (c), plus the expected present value of the lost income during her period searching for a job in the city.

This enriched model contains interesting implications for the migration process. Early migrants generate an externality by easing the transition of later migrants from their low productivity rural employment to higher-productivity industrial work. In this model this benefit comes in two distinct forms: reducing the moving costs associated with migration, and reducing the expected loss of income resulting from job search. In reality, of course, these two effects are intertwined—migrant communities that are more densely interconnected are likely to be more effective, both in providing employment to new migrants and in supporting them in their adjustment to new living conditions in the city. Migrants from particular rural origin communities congregate in particular cities, and even in particular neighbourhoods of cities, in order to capture as fully as possible the benefits provided by earlier migrants.

REFERENCES

Bencivenga, V. R., and Smith, B. D. (1997), 'Unemployment, Migration and Growth', *Journal of Political Economy*, 105.

Carrington, J., Detragiache, E., and Vishwanath, T. (1996), 'Migration with Endogenous Moving Costs, *American Economic Review*, 86.

Corden, W., and Findlay, R. (1975), 'Urban Unemployment, Intersectoral Capital Mobility and Development Policy', *Economica*, 42.

Esfahani, H., and Salehi-Isfahani, D. (1989), 'Effort Observability and Worker Productivity: Towards an Explanation of Economic Dualism', *Economic Journal*, 99.

Harris, J. R., and Todaro, M. (1970), 'Mining, Unemployment and Development: A Two-Sector Analysis', *American Economic Review*, 60.

Hart, K. (1973), 'Informal Income Opportunities and Urban Employment in Ghana', *Journal of Modern African Studies*, 11.

Katz, E., and Stark, O. (1986), 'Labor Migration and Risk Aversion in Less-Developed Countries', *Journal of Labor Economics*, 4.

Krugman, P. (1991), 'Increasing Returns and Economic Geography', *Journal of Political Economy*, 99.

Lucas, R. E. B., and Stark, O. (1985), 'Motivations to Remit: Evidence from Botswana', *Journal of Political Economy*, 93.

Maloncy, W. (1996), 'Labor Market Structure in Developing Countries: Time Series Evidence on Competing Views', CIBER Working Paper no. 96-105, University of Illinois College of Commerce and Business Administration.

Marshall, A. (1920), *Principles of Economics*. London: Macmillan.

Meyer, D. R. (1983), 'Emergence of the American Manufacturing Belt: An Interpretation', *Journal of Historical Geography*, 9.

Paulson, A. (1993), 'Insurance Motives for Migration: Evidence from Thailand', unpublished paper, University of Chicago Department of Economics.

Pred, A. R. (1966), *The Spatial Dynamics of US Urban–Industrial Growth, 1800–1914: Interpretive and Theoretical Essays*. Cambridge, Mass.: MIT Press.

Rosenzweig, M. R. (1988), 'Risk, Implicit Contracts and the Family in Rural Areas of Low-Income Countries', *Economic Journal*, 98.

—— and Stark, O. (1989), 'Consumption Smoothing, Migration, and Marriage: Evidence from Rural India', *Journal of Political Economy*, 97.

Todaro, M. (1969), 'A Model of Labor, Migration and Urban Unemployment in Less-Developed Countries', *American Economic Review*, 59.

Williamson, J. (1988), 'Migration and Urbanization', in H. Chenery and T. N. Srinivasan (eds.), *Handbook of Development Economics*, i. Amsterdam: North Holland.

6

The Rural Land Market

I

In poor countries land, particularly agricultural land, plays a special role in the daily livelihood and the general social structure of the vast majority of the people. But compared with the massive influence of the distribution of land on economic and social activities, the extent of actual transactions in the land market in a given year is relatively low. The market *flow* is a trickle compared with the weighty *stock*, and even the market is often more active in land-lease than in the buying and selling of land. In this chapter we shall start with some comments on the evolution of property rights in land and on the relative inactivity of the land market, and then we shall discuss some features of agricultural tenancy in terms of a principal–agent model.

The history of land rights is quite complex and context-specific in most parts of the world. But there may be some general patterns decipherable in the evolution of land rights. For example, with demographic changes (say, rising population pressure on arable land) or commercial and technological advances increasing the productivity and value of land, there is a tendency to move from the earlier communal patterns of landholding to more well-defined private property rights on land. Even when land belonged to the community, individuals often had heritable use rights[1] (giving them incentives to take care of the land), but not the right to sell it or transfer the use right to outsiders. Over time, however, as inequalities in labour and other productive assets among households increased along with outside opportunities and mobility, and as community cohesion eroded and land disputes multiplied, transferable property rights on land evolved. The individualization of tenure and transferability rights enforced on the basis of public records and cadastral surveys can reduce uncer-

---

[1] As Feder and Feeny (1991) point out, sometimes the individual and community rights may be mixed: in medieval England and contemporary South India, rights to the crop are private, whereas rights to the stubble after harvesting are communal; similarly, in many parts of sub-Saharan Africa the domain of individual rights are different between land and tree tenure.

tainties and thus encourage investment and allow for a more efficient reallocation of land. Investment may also be encouraged by the easier convertibility of
land into liquid assets, and the emergence of a credit market may be helped by
land rendered collateralizable.

In reality, however, the process is fraught with problems that may harm both
equity and efficiency. The public records and the court systems are woefully
inadequate in most poor countries, and the process is easily manipulated by the
powerful and the well connected. As a result, the evolution of private property
rights in land has often been associated with the dispossession of the traditional
use rights of the poor farmers (or women, as in the case of the land titling programmes in parts of Africa), with heightened social tensions and the creation of
new uncertainties, and in general with a proliferation of litigation and other
transaction costs. As Boserup (1965) comments for many of the African cases,
'each new step on the road to private property in land may well create less and
not more security of tenure, and a vast amount of litigation is the obvious
result'. In addition, marketability of land, particularly to outsiders, may undermine long-term implicit contracts among the traditional producers on the land
and discourage relation-specific investments in land preservation and cultivation.

As for the function of the land market in reallocating land in favour of
more efficient cultivators, an important theoretical puzzle is why the land
market does not always function that way. In many poor countries the empirical evidence[2] suggests that economies of scale in farm production are insignificant (except in some plantation crops, and that more in processing and
marketing than in production), and the small family farm is often the most
efficient unit of production. The puzzle is then why the large landlords do not
voluntarily sell their land to small family farmers and exercise their power by
grabbing much of the surplus arising from this efficient reallocation.

First, land as an asset serves some special functions for the rich which the
poor are less capable of using and which therefore are not reflected in the prices
offered by the latter. For example, holding land may offer some tax advantages
or speculative opportunities or be a generally safe investment vehicle (particularly when non-agricultural investment opportunities are limited or too risky)
for the rich which are not particularly relevant for the small farmer. Similarly,
large landholdings may give their owner special social status or political power
in a lumpy way (so that the status effect derived from owning 100 hectares is
larger than the combined status effect accruing to 50 new buyers owning 2
hectares each). Binswanger et al. (1995) point out that land is often used as a
preferred collateral in the credit market and thus serves more than just as a productive asset; so the asking price for land may be above the capitalized value of

---

[2] For a brief summary of the evidence and the methodological shortcomings of the empirical exercises, see Binswanger et al. (1995).

the agricultural income stream for even the more productive small farmer, rendering mortgaged sales uncommon (since mortgaged land cannot be used as collateral to raise working capital for the buyer).

With low household savings and severely imperfect credit markets, the more efficient small farmer may thus be incapable of affording the going market price of land. Mookherjee (1995), in a complete contracting model with the presence of incentive-based informational rents, provides additional reasons why there will be no scope for mutually profitable land sales from landlords to tenants (or farm labourers), as the latter will be unable to borrow enough to finance the purchase. This is because there is an inherent moral hazard problem associated with loan repayment out of output produced on the land. The wealth-constrained farmer has a 'limited liability': in a bad state of nature he cannot be made to repay more than a given amount, while in a good state he must repay a larger amount. This 'debt overhang' reduces the farmer's incentive to exert effort on the farm after purchasing it. Anticipating this, lenders may assess a default risk high enough that they are unwilling to advance the loan. We pursue the implications of limited liability in more detail in our discussion of land tenancy in Section III.

For all these reasons, land ownership does not pass from the large to the small farmer and, accordingly, the land market is very thin. In rich countries a large part of land transactions may be related to the life-cycle: old people sell land to buyers at an accumulating stage in their life-cycle. In the more intergenerationally close-knit families in poor countries, such life-cycle-related land transactions are rare. More often, in poor countries land sales go the opposite way to what is suggested by the evidence of the more efficient small farmer: land passes from distressed small farmers to landlords and money-lenders. This increases as the traditional reciprocity-based risk-coping mechanisms get weaker and farmers may have to depend more on land sales in times of crisis. Thus, in general, imperfections of the insurance or credit market may prevent the land market from bringing about Pareto-improving trades, which is an example of the theorem of the second best (whereby correcting imperfections in one market need not improve welfare in the presence of imperfections in other markets).

II

The land-lease market is usually more active than that of buying and selling land, unless land legislation restricts or prohibits tenancy (often driving it underground) or tenancy reforms make the landlord worry that the tenant will acquire occupancy rights on the land. There is a large literature on tenancy,[3]

---

[3] For surveys of the literature, see Singh (1989) and Hayami and Otsuka (1993).

particularly on sharecropping, which is an ancient institution in most parts of the world. The standard rationale for sharecropping used to be in terms of risk-sharing. But with constant returns to scale it can easily be shown that share-cropping has no extra risk-sharing advantage over a suitable mix of fixed-rent tenancy and wage labour contracts. To see this, let us suppose that output is given by a production function $F(A, e, \theta)$, with constant returns to scale for any θ, where A is area leased in and cultivated, e is labour effort, and θ is a random parameter (say, representing weather fluctuations). Suppose α is the share of the production the sharecropper receives, and the rest goes to the landlord.

Let W be the given wage rate and R the (fixed) rental rate. Suppose the landlord gives out α fraction of the land on fixed rent and cultivates the rest with wage labour; and suppose, instead of being a sharecropper, the peasant allocates a fraction α of her effort e to fixed-rent tenancy and a fraction $(1 - \alpha)$ to working on a wage contract. The peasant's income is then given by

$$Y = W(1 - \alpha)e + F(\alpha A, \alpha e, \theta) - R\alpha A \lesseqgtr \alpha F(A, e, \theta),$$
$$\text{as } R\alpha A \gtreqless W(1 - \alpha)e \tag{1}$$

and the landlord's income by

$$\pi = R\alpha A + F[(1 - \alpha)A, (1 - \alpha)e, \theta] - W(1 - \alpha)e$$
$$\gtreqless (1 - \alpha)F(A, e, \theta), \text{ as } R\alpha A \gtreqless W(1 - \alpha)e. \tag{2}$$

Clearly, if $R\alpha A > W(1 - \alpha)e$, the landlord's income is higher under this mixed contract than under sharecropping and he will reject the sharecropping contract. Similarly, if $R\alpha A < W(1 - \alpha)e$, the peasant will reject the sharecropping contract. So the sharecropping contract will survive only if $R\alpha A = W(1 - \alpha)e$, but under that condition both Y and π are the same as the (random) income under sharecropping, and thus the latter does not have any extra risk-sharing advantage.[4]

Stiglitz (1974) was the first to formalize sharecropping as a compromise between risk-sharing and work incentives. When the peasant's work effort is not observable (as in the case of the 'rep', or travelling salesman, who is often on a percentage commission system), the higher is α, the more is the work incentive, reaching a maximum when α is one (as in the case of the owner–cultivator or fixed-rent tenant), but then the more is the brunt of the risk borne by the peasant. Stiglitz introduced the first principal–agent model in the literature to study the moral hazard problem[5] with respect to unobservable (and therefore non-contractible) work effort.[6]

[4] Newbery (1977) shows that sharecropping may still have some advantage if, apart from production uncertainty, factor markets are also risky.
[5] There are some models of tenancy where the problem of adverse selection rather than moral hazard is emphasized. For example, Hallagan (1978) was one of the first to introduce a screening model of tenancy. The peasant's ability is private information and his or her choice of contract is to reveal something of this ability. The most productive workers will self-select themselves by choosing fixed-rent contracts;

Let us assume that there is one landlord and one tenant, and the former is risk-neutral and the latter risk-averse. Suppose the latter has a simple utility function of the form $U(Y) - e$, where Y is the tenant's income and e is the unobserved labour effort. The tenant's reservation utility is given by $\underline{U}$. The amount of land leased out is fixed and so is suppressed in the model. The tenant's output is given by the production function $\theta F(e)$, where θ is a multiplicative random parameter with mean value of one, and F has the usual properties of positive but diminishing marginal productivity. Y is a function of output, as determined by the contract offered by the landlord. For a pure fixed-rent contract, $Y = \theta F(e) - R$, where R is the rental payment. For a pure share contract, $Y = \alpha\theta F(e)$, where α is the tenant's share. If there is a side payment as well (which can be negative), $Y = \alpha\theta F(e) + S$ for the more general case, of which the fixed-rent and the pure share contracts are special cases.

The landlord maximizes his expected profits,

$$(1 - \alpha)\theta F(e) - S, \tag{3}$$

subject to the tenant's participation constraint (PC),

$$E[U\{\alpha\theta F(e) + S\}] - e \geq \underline{U}, \tag{4}$$

and the tenant's incentive compatibility constraint (ICC), given by the first-order condition for the choice of labour effort, given the contract parameters

$$E\{U'[\alpha\theta F(e) + S]\alpha\theta F'(e)\} - 1 = 0. \tag{5}$$

The landlord can drive the tenant down to her reservation utility level. So the two constraints may be solved for $e(\alpha, \underline{U})$ and $S(\alpha, \underline{U})$; and, substituting these in the landlord's maximand, we get the first-order condition (omitting arguments, using subscripts for partial derivatives, and rearranging) as

$$\alpha = 1 - (F + S_\alpha)/F'e_\alpha. \tag{6}$$

One can show from the constraints that $S_\alpha = -FE(U'\theta)/E(U')$, which is negative and less than F in magnitude with risk aversion. If e_α is positive, α is then less than unity (thus ruling out the pure fixed-rent case under risk aversion). One can show that e_α is positive for the standard case of decreasing absolute risk aversion.

In this principal–agent model, the agent has only one decision variable: that relating to her labour effort. But the tenant may control more than one decision variable (particularly when there are several inputs), and the terms of the share-

---

those who are least productive will work for wages; and those of intermediate ability will opt for share tenancy. It is doubtful how important this role of tenancy contract as a screening device is in the small closed world of a traditional village, where the landlord usually has a fairly good idea of the ability of the different members of the village work force.

[6] We follow here a version of the Stiglitz model described in Singh (1989).

cropping contract may reflect this. Take, for example, the decision about the use of an input like fertilizers. If only the tenant has to pay for its costs, there will in general be an underapplication of this input. The presumption in the literature has been that, if the landlord shares in the cost of fertilizers in the same proportion as in the output, efficient application of this input will follow. Braverman and Stiglitz (1986) have shown that this 'equal share' rule breaks down when one introduces uncertainty and information asymmetry. Without fully developing this model, we shall give some hints for this result and then point to some problems we have to be wary about in a model of cost-sharing with moral hazard.

The tenant's income is now given by

$$Y = \alpha \theta F(e, x) - \beta px, \tag{7}$$

where the production function now includes the fertilizer input x, the price of which is p, and β is the share of the fertilizer costs borne by the tenant. The landlord's expected profits is given by

$$\pi = (1 - \alpha)F(e, x) - (1 - \beta)px. \tag{8}$$

The risk-averse tenant's maximand is $[E\,U(Y) - e]$, and the first-order conditions with respect to the tenant's choice of x and e define two implicit functions $e(\alpha, \beta)$ and $x(\alpha, \beta)$. The landlord chooses the terms of the sharecropping contract subject to the two constraints, (PC) and (ICC). The latter is given by these two implicit functions, and the former by $E\,U(\alpha, \beta) \geq \underline{U}$. With (PC) binding, one can express α as a function of β. So we can now rephrase the landlord's problem as that of maximizing with respect to β:

$$\pi(\beta) = [1 - \alpha(\beta)]\,F(e(\alpha(\beta), \beta], x(\alpha(\beta), \beta)] - (1 - \beta)\,px[\alpha(\beta), \beta]. \tag{9}$$

In the general solution of this problem, $\alpha \neq \beta$. If fertilizers increase the marginal product of labour effort, the landlord may seek to increase e by lowering β, the tenant's cost share of fertilizers. Then again, changing β will lead to a change in α, the tenant's output share, which changes the amount of risks faced by the tenant. Under the 'equal share' rule of $\alpha = \beta$, the tenant still underapplies fertilizers because of risk aversion (she will equalize the marginal product of fertilizers discounted by a risk premium to its price); as the landlord is risk-neutral, he will encourage the tenant to use more fertilizers by charging a lower β.

In one significant way, the above formulation of the problem of cost-sharing under uncertainty and moral hazard is unsatisfactory. If the landlord cannot observe the tenant's use of x, how can he pay a share of its costs? Following an alternative formulation of the problem, suggested in Bardhan and Singh (1987), let us suppose the landlord chooses the amount of fertilizers to be bought, z, but the tenant may not use all of it and may secretly sell or use some of it elsewhere. So we may reformulate (7) and (8) as

$$Y = F(e, x) - \beta pz + p(z - x) \tag{10}$$

and

$$\pi = (1 - \alpha)F(e, x) - (1 - \beta)pz. \tag{11}$$

The tenant chooses e and x, given α, β, and z. Taking this behaviour into account the landlord decides on α, β, and z.

We can rewrite (10) and (11) as

$$Y = \alpha\theta F(e, x) - px + K \tag{12}$$

and

$$\pi = (1 - \alpha)F(e, x) - K, \tag{13}$$

where $K = (1 - \beta)pz$ is a fixed cost to the tenant. So now the tenant's marginal cost of fertilizer is simply p. Since the landlord does not manipulate the tenant's marginal cost of fertilizer, he effectively pays the tenant a fixed sum, and the latter decides how much fertilizer to use. There is thus cost-sharing, but not at the margin.

Hayami and Otsuka (1993) suggest that the prevalence of the 'equal share' rule in many parts of the world may be due to the common practice of the landlord deciding and enforcing the amount of purchased non-labour inputs. An alternative perspective, they suggest, is to look upon the landlord-supplied inputs as a *de facto* production loan and treat the matter as part of an interlinked tenancy-cum-credit contract.

Among the major unresolved problems in the theory of sharecropping to date, two are salient. First, any general theory of agency implies that the payments received by the landlord and the tenant should depend on all observable and verifiable information that is correlated with the unobserved random variable that affects outcomes; yet we do not see many sharecropping contracts in which the return to the tenant depends upon the yields of other farms in the area, or the weather. Second, there is still no convincing theory that explains the virtually universal linearity of share contracts, or the fact that often share contracts are uniform across plots in a village. Young (1996) in this context has a plausible model of boundedly rational players with limited information who come to bargain with their expectations shaped by precedent (i.e. what they and others like them have received in recent bargains); they settle on some distributive norms (like 50–50) that are focal points as the outcome of an evolutionary process of expectations formation, and the equilibrium (or one class of equilibria) may be stochastically stable (i.e. robust under small, persistent random shocks).

III

We now consider a somewhat different principal–agent model which emphasizes, along with moral hazard, a limited liability constraint, i.e., the tenant is liable up to his own wealth level w. (This reflects a credit market imperfection.[7]) We abstract from risk-sharing issues and assume both the tenant and the landlord to be risk-neutral. There is one landlord and a large pool of tenants, and we go back to the single variable input case. We shall use this model to discuss the static inefficiency associated with tenancy and also to point to the possibility of a 'tenancy ladder' for tenants facing different wealth constraints.

The tenant's effort e is now assumed $\in [0,1]$ and is a source of disutility $d(e)$, an increasing, convex function with $d(0) = 0$. Output takes only two non-negative values, a high value H and a low value L, with probability e and $1 - e$ respectively. The landlord offers the tenant a contract (h, l), which pays h when H is realized and l when L is realized. The limited liability constraint implies that $h + w \geq 0$ and $l + w \geq 0$; only the latter inequality matters since $h \geq l$. The amounts of rent the contract specifies the tenant has to pay are $(H - h)$ and $(L - l)$ in the two states of nature. Since output takes only two values in this model, all contracts could be expressed as linear contracts.

Let us start with the benchmark case where e is fully observable. Given the convexity of $d(e)$, there exists a unique value of e that maximizes the combined payoff of the landlord and the tenant, $eH + (1 - e)L - d(e)$. Let us denote this first-best e as e^*, and $d'(e^*) = H - L$. If e is fully observable, the landlord can offer the tenant a take-it-or-leave-it contract, which pays the latter her reservation income m when e is observed to be e^*, and 0 if e is observed to be anything else.

When e is not fully observable, the landlord will offer a contract based on the output level. In order to induce an effort level e, the landlord needs to design a contract that satisfies the incentive compatibility (ICC) and the participation (PC) constraints, i.e., given the contract, the tenant chooses e as a best response, and receives an income no lower than m. So the landlord now has to

$$\text{Max } [e(H - h) + (1 - e)(L - l)], \tag{14}$$

subject to

$$\text{(PC)} \quad eh + (1 - e)l - d(e) \geq m, \tag{15}$$

and

---

[7] The first theoretical model in the literature with the limited liability constraint is that of Shetty (1988). In a more recent paper Laffont and Matoussi (1995) use a data set from the region of El Oulja in Tunisia to support their theoretical result that financial constraints have a significant impact on the type of tenancy contract chosen, and hence on productive efficiency.

(ICC) $e \in \text{Argmax}_e \, eh + (1 - e)l - d(e)$. (16)

Equivalently, the landlord solves the following two-stage problem. In stage 1, the landlord finds the least-cost contract (h, l) to induce e by solving

$$C(e; m) = \text{Min}_{h,l} \, eh + (1 - e)l,$$

subject to (ICC) and (PC). This gives solutions for $h^*(e) = m + d(e) + (1 - e)d'(e)$ and $l^*(e) = m + d(e) - ed'(e)$. Thus, $C(e; m) = eh^*(e) + (1 - e)l^*(e) = d(e) + m$. In stage 2, the optimal level of e for the landlord to induce is thus calculated from $\text{Max}_e \, eH + (1 - e)L - C(e; m)$. The solution of e that satisfies $H - L = d'(e)$ is the same as our first-best solution e^*. Thus, in this case the unobservability of e does not pose a problem for the landlord, who can induce the first-best effort level and capture all the surplus. The intuitive reason is that the landlord rewards the tenant highly for a good outcome, and penalizes strongly when a bad outcome occurs. There is no problem with the strong penalty, since the tenant does not face a liquidity constraint.

Now let us introduce the limited liability constraint (LLC), $l + w \geq 0$. If $l(e^*) + w \geq 0$, then the landlord can still induce e with the same contract as above. But if $l(e^*) + w < 0$, then LLC is binding and the landlord has to design a new contract. In the new contract, for all $e \geq e_0$ (where e_0 is defined by $l(e_0) = -w$, $l^{**}(e) = -w$, $h^{**}(e) = d'(e) - w$), and the expected cost of inducing e is $C^{**}(e) = ed'(e) - w$. LLC does not bind for all $e \leq e_0$, and in that case $C(e) = m + d(e)$. Figure 6.1 depicts the corresponding marginal cost $C'(e)$ of inducing e for different values of e.

Given $C^{**}(e)$, the landlord chooses e to maximize expected profits:

$$\text{Max}_e \, eH + (1 - e)L - C^{**}(e),$$

which yields

$$H - L = C^{**'}(e). \tag{17}$$

We shall assume $C^{**}(e)$ to be convex in e, so that the second-order condition in (17) is satisfied. Figures 6.2, 6.3, and 6.4 depict three different cases (a), (b) and (c) to determine the optimal value of e, e^{**}. Figure 6.2 is for case (a), when $(H - L) < d'(e_0)$; in this case we show $e^{**} = e^* < e_0$. Figure 6.3 is for case (b), when $d'(e_0) \leq H - L \leq d'(e_0) + e_0 \, d''(e_0)$; in this case the landlord chooses $e^* = e_0$. Figure 6.4 is for case (c), when $(H - L) > d'(e_0) + e_0 \, d''(e_0)$; in this case the landlord chooses e^{**}, which solves

$$H - L = d'(e) + ed''(e). \tag{18}$$

One can thus see that, for cases (b) and (c), the e^{**} chosen with limited liability constraint is less than the first-best e^*. This indicates the allocational inefficiency of tenancy. The intuition is that with limited liability the landlord would prefer a contract in which the tenant pays more when the output is high than

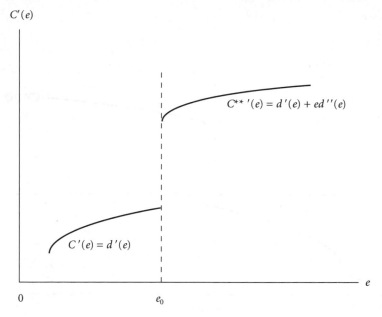

Figure 6.1

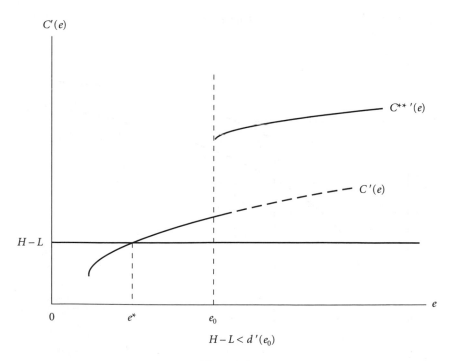

Figure 6.2

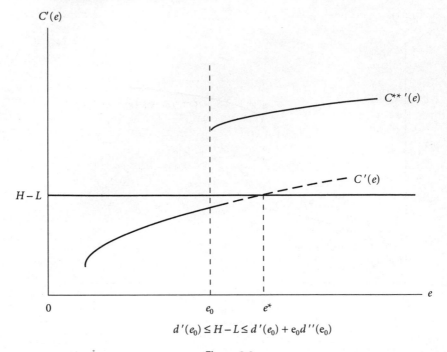

$$d'(e_0) \leq H - L \leq d'(e_0) + e_0 d''(e_0)$$

Figure 6.3

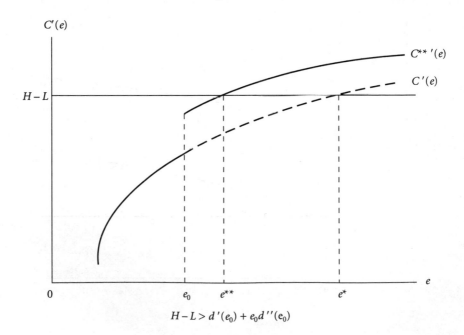

$$H - L > d'(e_0) + e_0 d''(e_0)$$

Figure 6.4

when it is low; but then the tenant will earn less than her marginal product and this will reduce her incentive to produce high outputs, and thus her effort level will be below the first-best level.

We shall now discuss the effects of parametric changes in the initial wealth levels of the tenants, with differential wealth giving rise to a heterogeneity of contracts.[8] Most of the literature on tenancy with limited liability assumes that the tenant's reservation income m and the wealth level w are unrelated. We shall assume a more general and plausible case, where m positively depends on w; i.e., $m'(w) > 0$.

Going back to cases (a), (b), and (c) above, we can see that there are two critical points: $d'(e_0(w))$, and $d'(e_0(w)) + e_0(w)d''(e_0(w))$. Both of these increase in w, since from its definition one can check that e_0 is an increasing function of w, and we apply the second-order condition from the landlord's maximization. We can now define two critical levels of w:

$$H - L = d'(e_0(w_1))\tag{19}$$

and

$$H - L = d'(e_0(w_2)) + e_0(w_2)d''(e_0(w_2)).\tag{20}$$

From Figure 6.5 it is now possible to distinguish the three wealth ranges for cases (a), (b), and (c). Case (a) corresponds to $w > w_1$, where the optimal e^{**} is equal to the first-best e^*. Case (b) corresponds to $w \in [w_2, w_1]$, where the optimal e^{**} is equal to $e_0(w)$ which is increasing in w. Case (c) corresponds to $w < w_2$, where the optimal e^{**} is equal to $e_0(w_2)$. Figure 6.6 summarizes these results, showing the relation between the allocational inefficiency of tenancy and the wealth level of the tenant.

The landlord's profit from leasing out to a tenant with w is

$$\pi(w) = e^*(w)H + (1 - e^*(w))L - C^{**}(e^{**}(w)),\tag{21}$$

where $e^{**}(w)$ is as above, and

$$C^{**}(e^{**}(w)) = m(w) + d(e), \text{ if } e^{**}(w) = e^*, \text{ i.e. } w > w_1\tag{22}$$

$$= e^{**}(w)d'(e^{**}(w)) - w = e_0(w)d'(e_0(w)) - w \text{ if } w \in [w_2, w_1],\tag{23}$$

$$= e_0(w_2)d'(e_0(w_2)) - w \text{ if } w < w_2.\tag{24}$$

For $w < w_2$ it is easy to check that $\pi(w)$ is an increasing function of w, so that the landlord would prefer less asset-poor tenants. For $w > w_1$, π is invariant with respect to w. For the intermediate range of $w \in [w_2, w_1]$, $\pi'(w)$ is difficult to sign

[8] For a model with unobserved work effort and unequal access to credit endogenously determining heterogeneous agrarian classes and the resultant production inefficiency, see Eswaran and Kotwal (1986).

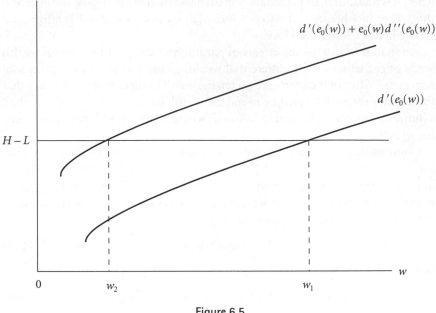

Figure 6.5

in general; but if, as in much of the relevant literature, m does not depend on w, then $\pi'(w)$ is positive, suggesting again a kind of 'tenancy ladder' with more wealthy tenants preferred.

In the model here as well as that in the preceding section, we have discussed only the one-period game. In a multi-period model there are interesting extra dimensions of the incentive effects under tenancy. The landlord may mitigate the problem of underapplication of the non-contractible input by using a threat of eviction when output is low.[9] The threat can be effective in the model of this section with limited liability, since the tenant earns some rent over and above her reservation income m, which she would lose if evicted (unlike in the 'utility-equivalent contract' model of the preceding section, where the tenant is pressed down to the minimum reservation utility in any case). In a multi-period model, apart from labour effort and other current input choice, the incentive to invest may also be affected by the eviction threat. Such a threat may discourage long-term improvements on the land[10] (which are often non-contractible). One may add that the removal of the threat (say, through a land reform programme that

---

[9] This observation goes back to Johnson (1950) and has been formalized in Bardhan (1984) and Dutta *et al.* (1989).

[10] Classical economists have emphasized this adverse effect of tenurial insecurity on investment. John Stuart Mill, for example, regarded this as the major defect of *metayage* in France. This effect is formalized in Bardhan (1984) and Banerjee and Ghatak (1996).

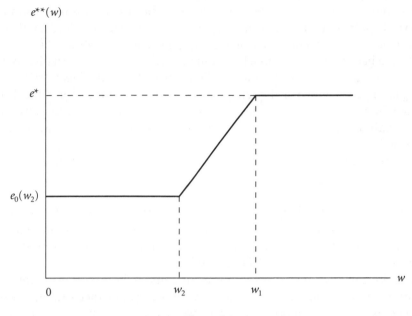

Figure 6.6

provides tenurial security) may also improve the bargaining power of the tenant, and investment may be encouraged because the tenant now expects to get a higher share of the additional output generated by that investment.

But, as Banerjee and Ghatak (1996) point out, there are two ways in which eviction threats may also have a positive effect on the incentive to invest. First, just as eviction threats raise current labour effort because the tenant cares about the expected value of future rents from the work and the prospect of losing them induces her to work harder, similarly, investment today raises the chances of doing well tomorrow and hence of retaining the job the day after tomorrow; thus, the tenant may respond positively to eviction threats. Second, if eviction threats raise current effort, that then raises the chance of the tenant being around in the next period, and this effect too is favourable to investment. All these put together make the net effect of eviction threats on investment rather ambiguous. The empirical evidence of Banerjee and Ghatak from a tenancy reform programme in West Bengal suggests that the net effect of the programme on the rate of growth of agricultural productivity is positive.

One major limitation of limited liability models in the context of rural areas in poor countries is that some of the main results are driven by the assumption that the asset-poor cannot be penalized enough by the landlord for rent default in bad times. In long-term relationships of closed village communities, landlords can sometimes get around this problem with a weather-dependent side-payment (credit) to the tenant, to be paid back in better times. It should also be kept in mind that in a traditional village context the landlord has access to various non-economic forms of punishing a defaulting poor tenant.

Going back to the static model without limited liability, an alternative to the principal–agent model of tenancy has been provided in the literature by the bargaining model. When the tenant owns some non-traded (or difficult to trade) factors or skills,[11] both the landlord and the tenant stand to gain from cooperation on a bargained lease contract. Bell and Zusman (1976) have looked at equilibrium contracts as an outcome of a two-person Nash bargaining problem. The tenant's share α is now determined by bargaining as a solution to

$$\text{Max}_\alpha \, [(1 - \alpha)F(e(\alpha)) - \underline{\pi}][EU(Y(\alpha) - \underline{U}], \qquad (25)$$

where $\underline{\pi}$ and $\underline{U}$ are the disagreement payoffs of the risk-neutral landlord and the risk-averse tenant, respectively. At the disagreement payoff point the landlord leaves the land fallow and the tenant falls back on wage labour, and thus does not get to utilize the nontraded factors and skills.[12]

In this chapter we started with some comments on the evolution of property rights in land and on the relative inactivity of the land market. The land-lease market is somewhat more active, and we discussed it first in terms of a principal–agent model with a focus on the trade-off between risk-sharing and incentives: sharecropping is often a compromise between these two objectives. We then discussed another type of principal–agent model, with a limited liability constraint, to capture the effect of credit market imperfection and the consequent impact of the tenant's wealth level on the nature and efficiency implications of the tenancy contract.

REFERENCES

Banerjee, A. V., and Ghatak, M. (1996), 'Empowerment and Efficiency: The Economics of Tenancy Reform', unpublished paper, MIT.

Bardhan, P. (1984), *Land, Labour and Rural Poverty: Essays in Development Economics*. New York: Columbia University Press.

——(ed.) (1989), *The Economic Theory of Agrarian Institutions*. Oxford: Clarendon Press.

[11] These may refer to the underutilized but indivisible managerial and husbandry skills of tenant cultivators, underemployed family labourers (particularly women and children for whom there may be constraints on participating in the wage labour market), and underutlilized animal labour (the rental market in which is partly hampered by a moral hazard problem: the possible misuse and damage of the rented animals that may not be immediately traceable by the owner and attributable to any particular user).

[12] For a detailed comparison of the solutions yielded by the principal–agent (with 'utility-equivalent contracts') and bargaining formulations of tenancy, see Bell (1989).

—— and Singh, N. (1987), 'A Note on Moral Hazard and Cost Sharing in Sharecropping', *American Journal of Agricultural Economics*, 69.

Bell, C. (1989), 'A Comparison of Principal–Agent and Bargaining Solutions: the Case of Tenancy Contracts', in Bardhan (1989).

—— and Zusman, P. (1976), 'A Bargaining Theoretic Approach to Cropsharing Contracts', *American Economic Review*, 66.

Binswanger, H. P., Deininger, K., and Feder, G. (1995), 'Power, Distortions, Revolt and Reform in Agricultural and Land Relations', in J. Behrman and T. N. Srinivasan (eds.), *Handbook of Development Economics*, iiiB. Amsterdam: North-Holland.

Boserup, E. (1965), *The Conditions of Agricultural Growth: The Economics of Agrarian Change under Population Pressure.* London: Allen & Unwin.

Braverman, A., and Stiglitz, J. E. (1986), 'Cost-sharing Arrangements under Sharecropping: Moral Hazard, Incentive Flexibility, and Risk', *American Journal of Agricultural Economics*, 68.

Dutta, B., Ray, D., and Sengupta, K. (1989), 'Contracts with Eviction in Infinitely Repeated Principal–Agent Relationships', in Bardhan (1989).

Eswaran, M., and Kotwal, A. (1986), 'Access to Capital and Agrarian Production Organization', *Economic Journal*, 96.

Feder, G., and Feeny, D. (1991), 'Land Tenure and Property Rights: Theory and Implications for Development Policy', *World Bank Economic Review*, 5.

Hallagan, W. (1978), 'Self-selection by Contractual Choice and the Theory of Sharecropping', *Bell Journal of Economics*, 9.

Hayami, Y., and Otsuka, K. (1993), *The Economics of Contract Choice.* Oxford: Clarendon Press.

Johnson, D. G. (1950), 'Resource Allocation under Share Contracts', *Journal of Political Economy*, 58.

Laffont, J. J., and Matoussi, M. S. (1995), 'Moral Hazard, Financial Constraints, and Share Cropping in El Oulja', *Review of Economic Studies*, 62.

Mookherjee, D. (1995), 'Informational Rents and Property Rights in Land', IED Discussion Paper, Boston University, April.

Newbery, D. M. G. (1977),'Risk-sharing, Sharecropping, and Uncertain Labour Markets', *Review of Economic Studies*, 44.

Shetty, S. (1988), 'Limited Liability, Wealth Differences, and the Tenancy Ladder in Agrarian Economies', *Journal of Development Economics*, 29.

Singh, N. (1989), 'Theories of Sharecropping', in Bardhan (1989).

Stiglitz, J. E. (1974), 'Incentives and Risk-sharing in Sharecropping', *Review of Economic Studies*, 41.

Young, H. P. (1996), 'The Economics of Convention', *Journal of Economic Perspectives*, 10.

7

Fragmented Credit Markets

I

Agricultural production takes time. The lag between the start of production and the realization of output ranges from a few months to several years. In this environment, credit transactions serve to finance production and to permit farmers to consume before harvest. Moreover, the agricultural production process depends on a host of external factors, many of which are not under the control of the farmer. When production is risky and insurance markets are incomplete, credit transactions serve a valuable role by permitting people to smooth consumption in the face of a randomly fluctuating stream of income. Where farmers are poorer, these motivations for credit transactions are stronger—liquidity constraints are more likely to be binding so that production and consumption cannot be financed from savings, and the costs (in terms of utility, health, and even survival) or fluctuations in an already low level of consumption are very high.

Seasonal credit transactions, therefore, are found in virtually all poor agricultural economies. The institutional arrangements through which these transactions are effected are varied and often complex. There are formal financial institutions, including banks, credit cooperatives, and group lending schemes. Many financial transactions, however, occur outside the boundaries of the formal financial system. There are specialist moneylenders, informal loans among family and friends, loans tied to purchases, labour transactions or land rental arrangements, and a variety of informal financial groups. Often, in rural areas of poor countries, several of these different institutional forms coexist and interact.

The terms and conditions under which credit is transacted may vary substantially across different transactions, depending upon the characteristics of the borrower and lender and the relationship between them. Credit transactions occurring over a short period in a single village might include: extremely informal zero interest loans between friends; formal-sector loans backed by documentation and collateral; commercial loans between a moneylender and his clients, some of which are backed by collateral; lending from a trader to the farmers who supply him with their harvests, backed only by the promise to sell this year's harvest to that trader; consumption loans from an employer to her long-term employees; group loans from a micro finance institution to self-selected groups of borrowers lacking collateral; and a potentially large number of variations on these themes.

An important determinant of the structure and terms of credit contracts available in any particular area is the nature of government regulation and intervention in financial markets in that area. Common policies have included interest rate ceilings, regulations requiring financial institutions to direct a certain proportion of their loans to particular sectors or types of business, and subsidized credit programmes. There seem to have been two main types of motivation for such interventions. On the one hand credit (particularly agricultural credit) was conceptualized as a factor of production; as with any other factor of production, an increase in supply of credit would lead to an increase in production and income. On the other hand, informal financial transactions have often been characterized as exploitative and immoral; government action has been deemed necessary, therefore, to raise rural incomes by providing access to a necessary factor of production and to protect borrowers from monopolistic lenders. Over the past few decades, however, there has been an increased consensus on the need for financial market liberalization. The recommendation that credit markets be liberalized is based on simple economic logic: interest rate ceilings and similar policies lower the supply and raise the demand for credit, leading to administrative rationing and associated rent-seeking behaviour, while discouraging saving mobilization.[1]

The argument for the liberalization of financial markets is compelling, yet it is also incomplete. A loan involves the exchange of current resources for future resources. It therefore involves a promise. If a loan transaction occurs in a risky environment, and if a complete set of markets for contingent commodities does not exist, then the promised transfer of future resources may not be certain. The character of the loan transaction will then be influenced by the risks faced by the parties involved, and by their knowledge of each other and the activities they undertake.

Thus, the contractual arrangements through which financial transactions occur in the rural areas of poor countries have been influenced by institutional adaptations to the problems of information asymmetries and contract enforcement, as well as by government intervention. The simple model of a smoothly operating market with complete information and perfect contract enforcement which underlies the conventional argument for liberalization, therefore, is

---

[1] For a classic statement of this argument, see Adams *et al.* (1984).

potentially misleading. Our goal in this chapter is to develop some basic models of rural credit markets, and to use these models to outline some of the consequences of asymmetric information and imperfect competition on the characteristics of loan transactions within these markets.

The organizing theme of this chapter is information. In separate sections, lessons are drawn from the relevant literature concerning the effects on credit transactions of adverse selection and moral hazard. We are especially interested in the effects of specific information asymmetries on the structure of the rural credit market. In particular, can monopolists in a particular area, say a village, extract rents using their superior information concerning local borrowers? How is the answer to this question affected by the presence of competition from relatively less well-informed outside lenders?

In each section, contractual mechanisms that can mitigate the difficulties caused by specific information asymmetries are described. We should note that it is artificial to treat separately the issues of adverse selection and moral hazard because most economic environments are characterized by a mixture of the two. However, for the sake of clarity, in this chapter we write as though a clean distinction can be made between moral hazard and adverse selection.

We will be concerned with four alternative market situations. To provide a benchmark case, we will first examine a competitive market for loans with complete information. Second (perhaps more realistically), we will develop a model of a rural credit market in competitive equilibrium, but with imperfect information. Here we imagine a situation in which villagers borrow from non-resident commercial lenders, banks, or government agencies which compete with one another for borrowers. We assume that the lenders cannot monitor actions of the borrowers, which might affect the returns from loans (moral hazard), or that the lenders cannot distinguish between borrowers with different characteristics, which might affect returns on loans (adverse selection). Third, as an alternative, we construct a model of a rural credit market dominated by a local monopolistic moneylender who has perfect information concerning the characteristics and activities of village borrowers. Finally, we examine the case of a fragmented national market, in which residents of a village have the option of borrowing from one of a set of relatively uninformed, competitive non-resident lenders or from a local omniscient moneylender. In this last case, the rents that accrue to the local moneylender through his control of local information become apparent.

We focus on rural credit markets to provide a concrete setting for the models, and because of the central importance of such markets to the development process. However, many of the lessons that can be drawn from the models developed below can be applied to firms borrowing in an urban centre, to sovereign governments in the international credit market, or to students borrowing to finance their education.

II

To begin our simplifications, we will assume that all borrowers and lenders are risk-neutral. This eliminates an important motivation for borrowing: the desire to smooth consumption in the face of fluctuating income. We discuss the use of credit markets as a mechanism for coping with risk in Chapter 8. For now, we focus exclusively on credit as a source of working capital for productive activities that take time. We suppose that each individual in a village has access to the same amount of land, and can farm this land for a certain fixed cost (which we normalize to 1). The farm yields 0 if there is a harvest failure, and $R > 1$ otherwise. The probability of a successful farming season is $\pi(a)$, where $a \in [0, 1]$ is an index of (say) the effort the farmer puts into her land. $\pi(a)$ is strictly increasing and concave. There is a utility cost to the farmers of working; we denote this cost as $D(a)$. $D(a)$ is increasing and strictly convex, so that the marginal utility cost of effort is increasing in effort. We also suppose that the farmers have no wealth of their own (there is no land market). Therefore, if these farmers are to engage in cultivation, they must borrow the necessary working capital. If a lender offers an interest factor (which is 1 plus the rate of interest) of $i \le R$, the returns to the farmer and lender are as follows:

	Borrower	Lender
Success	$R - i - D(a)$	i
Failure	$D(a)$	0

We assume that lenders have access to a risk-free capital market with a return of ρ ($R > \rho \ge 1$). We also assume that, if the borrower does not involve herself in farming, she can receive a return of $W(R > W \ge 0)$ in alternative employment.[2] Therefore, the expected utility of a borrower is $U(i, a) = \pi(a)(R - i) - D(a)$, and the expected return of a lender is $\Pi(i, a) = \pi(a)i$.

In compiling the above table, we have made two extremely important assumptions. The first is that the loan contract has limited liability: if the borrower's harvest fails, she has no funds to repay the loan and the lender receives nothing. The second is that we have assumed there are no problems of enforcement: if the harvest is successful, the borrower has the resources to repay and the loan is repaid. In this model, the borrower cannot renege on her commitment to repay the loan if the project is successful.

Both of these assumptions are oversimplifications of reality. First, faced with a harvest failure, borrowers often request that loans be rescheduled, or make partial repayments. Second, rural financial transactions in many areas are

---

[2] Now it is clear why we impose the restriction $i \le R$. If $i > R$, then the borrower receives a negative return in any state of nature. She would do better to take her reservation income of W.

characterized by imperfect formal legal enforcement mechanisms. Why, then, do borrowers repay? Theorists have focused on two mechanisms that might serve to provide repayment incentives. The first is the 'self-enforcing contract'. The idea is that borrowers repay because they fear losing access to future loans if they were to default. In fact, this is the explanation often provided by borrowers when asked why they repay loans. The second is the existence of social sanctions to punish defaulters. This idea is that defaulters are penalized broadly by the community as a whole, in addition to being denied access to future loans. Theorists (see e.g. Kandori 1992) have only recently begun to model the process through which such sanctions arise and persist.

It is clear that both loss of future access to credit and general social sanctions play an important role in sustaining many rural credit markets. To simplify our analysis and to focus attention on the role of information asymmetries, however, we abstract from problems of enforcement in this chapter.

(a) Moral Hazard

(i) Competitive equilibrium with complete information
First, we assume that there are a large number of competitive lenders. We initially assume that the lenders can observe the borrowers' choice of a. Therefore, they can write contracts that specify both the interest factor i and the effort level a. We define an equilibrium to be a pair (i_1, a_1) such that: (a) $U(i_1, a_1) \geq W$; (b) $\Pi(i_1, a_1) \geq \rho$; and (c) there is no other pair (i, a) that yields a return greater than or equal to ρ to a lender and which a borrower would prefer to (i_1, a_1).[3] If there is an equilibrium with lending, it is characterized by the solution to

$$\underset{i,a}{\text{Max}} \quad \pi(a)(R - i) - D(a)$$

subject to $$\pi(a)i \geq \rho$$

and $$\pi(a)(R - i) - D(a) \geq W.$$

There may be no solution to this problem. If there is no (i, a) such that both constraints are satisfied, then there is no lending in equilibrium. For any fixed ρ, there is a W low enough so that both constraints may be satisfied.

The equilibrium is depicted in Figure 7.1. The $\Pi(\cdot) = \rho$ contour is downward-sloping and strictly convex. (You should be able to show this.) The $U(\cdot) = W$ contour is strictly concave (and, given our assumptions on $\pi(\ )$ and $D(\ )$, will reach a maximum with $0 < a < 1$). As long as there is an interior point in the constraint set, there will be lending in equilibrium with terms (i_1, a_1) as at

---

[3] This corresponds to T1 competition in Chan and Thakor (1987).

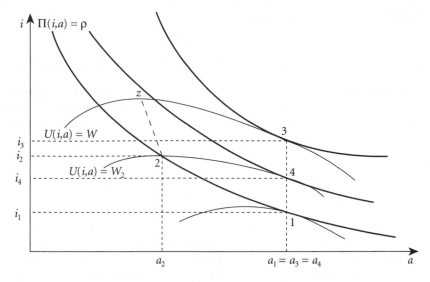

Figure 7.1

point 1 in Figure 7.1. In this equilibrium, the required input of effort a_1 is set by $\pi'(a_1)R = D'(a_1)$, so that the expected marginal return to additional effort is set equal to its marginal cost. The allocation of effort is efficient. The contractual interest rate i_1 is set so that $\pi(a_1)i_1 = \rho$ and lenders make zero profits. Borrowers achieve an expected utility $U(i_1, a_1) = \pi(a_1)R - D(a_1) - \rho > W$.

(ii) Competitive equilibrium and moral hazard

Now consider the possibility that a lender cannot observe the input of effort by the borrower, so the lender cannot directly control the borrower's choice of a. The borrower will choose the action that maximizes her utility given the credit contract offered to her. A lender's return from a loan still depends on the choice of a by the borrower, so this is an example of moral hazard. We retain the assumption that the lenders operate in a competitive market. As before, an equilibrium pair of interest charged and effort exerted (i_2, a_2) must satisfy (a) $U(i_2, a_2) \geq W$, and (b) $\Pi(i_2, a_2) \geq \rho$; and furthermore (c) there is no other pair (i, a) that yields a return greater than or equal to ρ to a lender and which a borrower would prefer to (i_2, a_2). Now, however, because the lender cannot monitor the borrower's choice of a, we must add the condition (d), that the lender can only offer contracts such that the borrower *wants* to choose a_2, given i_2. The equilibrium loan contract will be characterized by the solution to:

$$\underset{a,i}{\text{Max}} \qquad \pi(a)(R - i) - D(a)$$

subject to $\qquad\qquad \pi(a)i \geq \rho$

$$\pi(a)(R-i) - D(a) \geq W$$

and $\qquad\qquad \pi(a)(R-i) - D(a) \geq \pi(a')(r-i) - D(a') \ \forall \ a' \in [0,1].$

The problem is identical to that of subsection (i) above, except for the third set of constraints, which are added as a result of moral hazard. The first implication of this analysis is that, for a given set of 'primitives' (the functions $\pi(\ )$ and $D(\ )$ and the values of R, ρ, and W), if an equilibrium with lending exists in the case of moral hazard, then there must also be an equilibrium with lending in the case of perfect information. The converse is not true. In a competitive situation in which lending would be possible with complete information, the additional incentive compatibility constraints may result in there being no contract (i, a) that satisfies all the constraints, so no equilibrium with lending need exist.

The borrower's utility function is differentiable and strictly concave for all $i \leq R$, so the condition $\pi'(a)(R-i) - D'(a) = 0$ is necessary and sufficient for the third set of constraints in the problem above.[4] If a solution (i_2, a_2) does exist, then it satisfies $D'(a_2) = \pi'(a_2)(R - i_2) < \pi'(a_2)R$, which implies $a_2 < a_1$. That is, the effort by farmers will be less in the case of moral hazard than in the complete information equilibrium. This implies $i_2 > i_1$ (by the zero profit constraint), and $EU(a_2, i_1) < EU(a_1, i_1)$. The equilibrium is point 2 in Figure 7.1. Given interest rate i_2, the farmer maximizes her utility by choosing to commit effort a_2. The dashed line running from z to u_2 is the set of contracts that satisfy all three constraints; the borrower prefers (i_2, a_2) to any other point in that set.

The consequences of moral hazard in the credit market can be neutralized by the use of collateral when both borrowers and lenders are risk-neutral. Suppose that each borrower owns some asset (with value greater than R).[5] If the project fails, the borrower transfers the collateral pledged for the loan (C) to the lender. The equilibrium with moral hazard is now described by

$$\underset{a,i,C}{\text{Max}\ \pi} \quad (a)(R-i) - (1 - \pi(a))C - D(a)$$

subject to $\qquad\qquad \pi(a)i + (1 - \pi(a))C \geq \rho,$

$$\pi(a)(R-i) - (1 - \pi(a))C \geq W,$$

---

[4] At least when $0 < a < 1$. Our assumptions on $\pi(\ )$ and $D(\ )$ ensure that the choice of a will remain in the interior. The assumptions we have made imply that the first-order approach we have taken is valid. See Grossman and Hart (1983) for a discussion of the conditions under which the infinite number of inequalities in the third set of constraints can be replaced by a single first-order condition.

[5] We are assuming that borrowers and lenders place the same value on these assets, so we are not permitting transactions costs (Bell 1988) or systematic undervaluation of the collateral (Bhaduri 1983). We are also assuming that it would be costly to sell the asset in advance of the project, so borrowers still need to borrow in order to finance the project.

and
$$\pi(a)(R-i) - (1-\pi(a))C - D(a) \geq \pi(a')(R-i)$$
$$- (1-\pi(a'))C - D(a') \,\forall\, a' \in [0,1].$$

Once again, the first-order approach is valid. In equilibrium, $C^* = i^* = \rho$, and $a^* = a_1$. The borrower absorbs the entire risk of the transaction. The return to the lender no longer depends on the choice of a by the borrower, so moral hazard no longer exists. The loan is now riskless to the lender, so the interest rate is lowered (from equilibrium (1)) to the riskless rate. Borrowers are induced to put the optimal level of effort into the project. Lenders make zero profits, and borrowers achieve the same utility as they achieve in the complete-information equilibrium. (Calculate this to make it clear to yourself.) The result depends *crucially* on the assumed risk neutrality of both parties. If the borrower were risk-averse, the use of collateral could not entirely alleviate the difficulties induced by moral hazard, because the borrower would not be willing to absorb the entire risk of the transaction without some compensation from the lender.

Rural credit transactions are commonly associated with some form of collateral. Items for which there is a secondary market, and which are not themselves subject to moral hazard problems, are the most common forms of collateral (see Binswanger and Rosenzweig 1986). Therefore, jewellery or other household items commonly serve as collateral. In areas with well developed land markets, land is often pledged in exchange for a loan. Where other assets are not available, a wide variety of items including economic trees and standing crops, livestock, and farm equipment serve as collateral. These assets are less satisfactory as collateral because they are themselves subject to secondary problems of information asymmetries. For example, a farmer might treat a tractor or a bullock pledged as collateral with less care than otherwise; or, if there is unobserved (to the lender) variation in the quality of these assets, problems of adverse selection arise. In addition, collateral substitutes have been developed in some areas with poorly developed markets for the assets that conventionally serve as collateral. These include loan guarantees, provided most often by relatives, and *interlinked* transactions, in which the terms of an associated transaction in another market (e.g. a labour contract) serve to mitigate the moral hazard associated with the loan transaction (see Chapter 9).

There is a rapidly growing literature on another form of collateral substitute, which is joint liability. The extraordinary example of the Grameen Bank in Bangladesh motivates much of this work.[6] The idea is that by lending to a group, each member of which is liable for the repayments owed by each other member, lenders from outside a local community can take advantage of some of the information and enforcement mechanisms available within that community. If group members can impose penalties on each other which are otherwise

---

[6] Khandker *et al.* (1995) provides an accessible description of the Grameen Bank group lending scheme.

unavailable to the lender (for example various forms of social pressure), then it is possible that group loans will be defaulted less often than individual loans.[7] Alternatively, if lenders face a problem of adverse selection (similar to that discussed in Section II(b)), endogenously formed groups can serve as a screening device for lenders. Ghatak (1998) shows that there will be a tendency for endogenously formed groups to be homogeneous, as the various types of borrower self-select into groups composed of similar borrowers. This permits group lenders to write credit contracts which result in a separating equilibrium in a wider variety of circumstances than would be possible with individual lending.

(iii) Equilibrium with a fully informed monopolist

Suppose that a village has a single resident with enough wealth to act as a moneylender. (His wealth is larger than N, the number of residents in the village.) The moneylender lives in the village and has the opportunity costlessly to monitor the activities of anyone who borrows from him. He can deposit his wealth at the risk-free rate of ρ, so this is the opportunity cost of his funds. The moneylender will set the interest rate and level of effort to solve:

$$\underset{a,i}{\text{Max}} \quad i\pi(a)$$

subject to

$$\pi(a)(R - i) - D(a) \geq W$$

and

$$i\pi(a) \geq \rho.$$

This constraint set is identical to that of the case of perfect competition with complete information, so an equilibrium with lending will exist in the same set of circumstances as in that case. As in the case of a competitive credit market with complete information, this equilibrium is Pareto-efficient. Effort is set so that $\pi'(a_3)R = D'(a_3)$ (so $a_3 = a_1$), and the interest rate is set so that the borrower achieves his reservation utility: $\pi(a_3)(R - i_3) - D(a_3) = W$ (see Figure 7.1). The difference from case 1, of course, is that the farmers are pushed down to their reservation utility.

(iv) Competition between an informed local moneylender and uninformed outside lenders

This case may be the most informative. Suppose that there is an active, competitive market for credit from lenders not resident in the village. These lenders may be private urban lenders, moneylenders from other villages, or formal-sector (bank or government) lenders. These lenders all face the same opportu-

---

[7] Besley and Coate (1995) provide the first model in which 'social collateral' can be used to decrease the rate of default of group loans. Diagne (1997) provides a more careful treatment of the pathways through which 'social collateral' might be harnessed in group lending schemes.

nity cost of funds (ρ), and face prohibitive costs of monitoring the actions of borrowers in the village. There is also a resident moneylender (whose opportunity cost of funds is also ρ), who can monitor costlessly the actions of borrowers in the village. The local moneylender can use his informational advantage to collect rents even in the face of competitive (but uninformed) lenders from outside the village. The point is made most simply in the now-familiar Figure 7.1. Suppose that ρ and W are such that the equilibrium in subsection (ii) permits lending by uninformed outside lenders. The availability of these outside loans raises the reservation utility of local borrowers from W to W_2. The local moneylender now implements the contract outlined in subsection (iii), replacing W by W_2. The local moneylender is able to make positive profits ($= i_4\pi(a_4)$ $> i_1\pi(a_1) = i_2\pi(a_2) = 0$). The profits made by the moneylender in this instance reflect the power granted by his superior information concerning the actions of village residents.

(b) Adverse Selection

Another type of information asymmetry has received a great deal of attention in the literature on credit markets in developing countries. Contrary to the assumptions of Section II(a), there is a great deal of heterogeneity among farmers in any village. While lenders might have a good idea about the average characteristics of the pool of potential borrowers, they may not have complete information concerning the characteristics of any particular borrower. This may lead to problems of adverse selection. A few simple modifications to the models used in Section II(a) permit us to examine the consequences of adverse selection in credit markets.

Suppose that farming requires no effort, but that there are two types of potential borrowers indexed by $t \in \{1, 2\}$. Type 2 borrowers have access to land that is riskier but potentially more lucrative than that used by type 1 borrowers; that is, $\pi(1) > \pi(2)$, but $R(1) < R(2)$. In fact, we suppose that the expected return to farming each type of land is identical ($\pi(t)R(t) = \bar{R} \forall t$).[8] Also suppose that the reservation utility of the different types of borrower is constant ($W(t) = W \forall t$). The model is otherwise identical to that of Section II(a). The expected utility of a borrower is $U(i, t) = \pi(t)[R(t) - i]$ and the expected return from a loan at rate i to a type t borrower is $\Pi(i, t) = \pi(t)i$.

(i) Competitive equilibrium with complete information
As a benchmark, we first assume that perfectly informed lenders compete to make loans within the village. Lenders can distinguish between the types of

[8] That is, the distribution of returns for type 2 projects is a *mean-preserving spread* of the distribution of returns for type 1 projects.

borrower, so they can offer different interest rates to each type. An equilibrium with lending to borrower type t will be an interest rate $(i_1(t))$ such that (a) $U(i_1(t), t) \geq W$; (b) $\Pi(i_1(t), t) \geq \rho$; and (c) there is no interest rate $i(t)$ that yields a return greater than or equal to ρ to a lender and which a type t borrower would prefer to $i_1(t)$. If there is an equilibrium with lending, it is characterized by solving, *for each t,*

$$\underset{i(t)}{\text{Max}} \quad \pi(t)(R(t) - i(t))$$

subject to

$$i(t)\pi(t) \geq \rho$$

and

$$\pi(t)(R(t) - i(t)) \geq W.$$

There will be lending in equilibrium to both types if $\bar{R} - \rho > W$, otherwise neither type will receive loans. If there is lending, $i_1(t) = \rho/\pi(t) \, \forall \, t$, and the lender makes zero expected profits. Substitution of this equilibrium relation into the borrower's utility function shows that $U(i_1(t), t) = \bar{R} - \rho \, \forall \, t$. If there is lending, both types of farmers will borrow, and $i_1(1) < i_1(2)$.

(ii) Competitive equilibrium with adverse selection

Suppose that the lenders in the competitive credit market cannot differentiate between borrowers of different types, though they know the relative proportions of type 1 and type 2 farmers in the village. First, note that, at any given interest rate i,

$$U(i, 1) = \pi(1)[R(1) - i] < \pi(2)[R(2) - i] = U(i, 2),$$
$$\text{but } \Pi(i, 1) = \pi(1)i > \pi(2)i = \Pi(i, 2).$$

So safer borrowers achieve a lower expected utility from a given interest rate, but provide higher expected income to the lender. These results follow directly from the limited liability nature of the credit contract, which limits the loss faced by a borrower when her crop fails. Recall that the participation constraint is $\pi(t)(R(t) - i) \geq W$. Obviously, $\partial U(i, t)/\partial i < 0$. Define $i^*(1)$ as the highest interest rate at which type 1 borrowers are willing to borrow. So $i^*(1)$ is implicitly defined by the equation $\bar{R} - \pi(1)i^*(1) = W$. Define $i^*(2)$ analogously. $i^*(1) < i^*(2)$, so, as the interest rate increases, households with safer projects drop out of the pool of borrowers first. For interest rates less than $i^*(1)$, all potential borrowers demand credit. If the interest rate increases past $i^*(1)$, the relatively safe type 1 borrowers stop demanding credit, while type 2 borrowers continue to demand loans. As the safer borrowers drop out of the market, lender income falls discontinuously. Figure 7.2 illustrates the relationship between the interest rate charged by lenders and the expected income from lending. Lender income rises with increases in the interest rate until $i = i^*(1)$. Suppose $p(1)$ is the proportion of the population of potential borrowers who

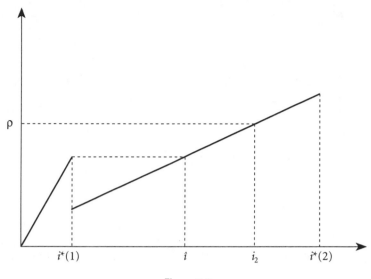

Figure 7.2

are type 1. Then the expected income from a loan at interest $i \leq i^*(1)$ is $E\Pi(i) = p(1)\pi(1)i + [1 - p(1)]\pi(2)i$. As i increases past $i^*(1)$, type 1 borrowers drop out of the market and lender income falls. As the interest rate continues to increase, lender income once again increases until $i^*(2)$, at which point type 2 borrowers stop demanding credit and no loans are made. For $i^*(1) < i \leq i^*(2)$, $E\Pi(i) = \pi(2)i$. For $i > i^*(2)$, $E\Pi(i) = 0$.

Lenders cannot distinguish between borrowers of different types. Therefore, the competitive equilibrium with adverse selection is defined as an interest rate i_2 such that (a) $E\Pi(i_2) \geq \rho$; and (b) there is no interest rate i for which $E\Pi(i) \geq \rho$ and both $U(i, t) \geq U(i_2, t)$ and $U(i, t) > W$ for any type t. In other words, an interest rate i is an equilibrium interest rate if lenders do not lose money on average at i, and if there is no other interest rate which any type of borrower would prefer at which lenders would avoid losing money. There are no explicit borrower participation constraints in this definition of equilibrium because these constraints are built into the function $E\Pi(i)$.

As long as $\bar{R} - \rho > W$, (the condition for lending to be possible in the case of complete information), there will be lending in the equilibrium with adverse selection. If $\rho > E\Pi(i^*(1)) \equiv p_1\pi(1)i^*(1)\rho + (1 - p_1)\pi(2)i^*(1)$ (as in Figure 7.2), then the equilibrium interest rate will be $i_2 = \rho/\pi(2) > i$ and only the risky type 2 borrowers will demand loans. If $\rho < E\Pi(i^*(1))$ (as in Figure 7.3), then the interest rate will be $i_2 = \rho/\{p(1)\pi(1) + [1 - p(1)]\pi(2)\}$, which is less than $i^*(1)$, and all potential borrowers will demand loans. It should be clear that $\tilde{i}$ is not an equilibrium. At that interest rate only risky borrowers would demand credit

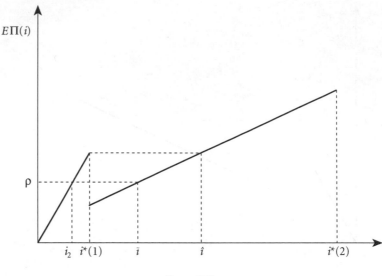

Figure 7.3

and lenders would make zero profits. But all borrowers prefer i_2 to $\tilde{i}$ and lenders also avoid losing money at i_2.

Many discussions of the implications of adverse selection for credit markets in less developed countries focus on the possibility of credit rationing. In this simple model, credit rationing does not occur. How does this model differ from the celebrated work of Stiglitz and Weiss (1981), which is the theoretical basis of the worry that credit rationing might be pervasive? The essential difference is that the current model presumes that lenders have access to an infinitely elastic supply of funds at a cost of ρ. Stiglitz and Weiss show that, when the relationship between the expected return to lenders and the interest charged is a non-monotonic function with an interior local maximum (as in our Figures 7.2 and 7.3), then there exists a supply of fund schedules that leads to a competitive equilibrium with rationing. Figure 7.4 (a modified version of their figure 4) illustrates the Stiglitz–Weiss result. The demand for loans is simply $N_1 + N_2$ for $i \le i^*(1)$, N_2 for $i^*(1) < i \le i^*(2)$, and 0 for larger i, where N_i is the number of the ith type of borrower. In the lower left quadrant we show the supply of funds to lenders as a function of the cost of those funds, ρ. We have drawn this schedule so that rationing will occur in equilibrium. (You should verify that other supply schedules will lead to equilibria without rationing.) The loan supply schedule in the upper right quadrant is derived by tracing the effect of the interest rate i on the expected return on loans, and hence on the supply of funds to lenders. The competitive equilibrium entails lenders charging $i^*(1)$ and earn-

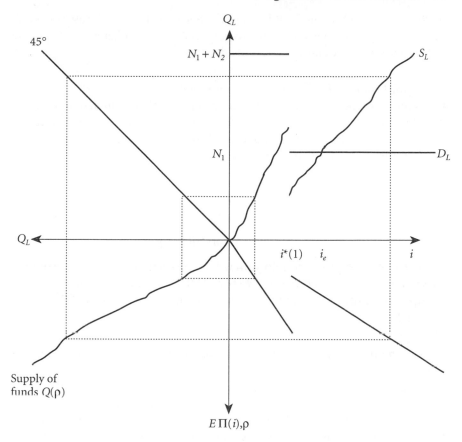

Figure 7.4

ing an expected return of $E\Pi(i^*(1))$. the demand for loans at $i^*(1)$ exceeds the supply of loanable funds, leading to a rationing of credit. An increase in the interest rate would cause type 1 borrowers to drop out of the market, leaving lenders with a riskier portfolio of loans and reducing expected returns to lending. At interest rate i_e loan supply equals loan demand (with only type 2 borrowers in the market), but lenders earn a lower expected return than at $i^*(1)$: a lender charging $i^*(1)$ could attract borrowers of all types, and would earn a higher expected return.

In a manner exactly analogous to that discussed in Section II(a), the existence of collateral can eliminate the problem of adverse selection. As in that case, a pledge of collateral equal in value to the repayment owed by the borrower places the entire risk of the transaction on the borrower. The return to the lender no longer depends on the unknown type of the borrower, hence adverse selection no longer exists. Once again, this result depends crucially on the assumed risk neutrality of the borrower. If the borrower is risk-averse, collateral can mitigate but not eliminate the consequences of adverse selection.

(iii) Equilibrium with a fully informed monopolist

Let us return to the case of a village with a monopolistic, omniscient moneylender. He knows which villagers have access to which type of land. As before, we assume that his opportunity cost of funds is ρ. His problem is to set an interest rate $i_3(t)$ for each type of borrower to solve:

$$\max_{i(t)} \quad \pi(t)i(t)$$

subject to $$\pi(t)(R(t) - i(t)) \geq W$$

and $$\pi(t)i(t) \geq \rho.$$

As long as $\bar{R} - \rho \geq W$, the equilibrium will involve lending to each type of borrower at interest rates $i_3(t)(\bar{R} - W)/\pi(t) = i^*(t)$. Each type of borrower achieves an expected utility of W, and the lender earns an expected return of $\bar{R} - \rho \geq W$ on each loan.

(iv) Competition between an informed local moneylender and uninformed outside lenders

Once again, suppose that there is an active, competitive market for credit from lenders not resident in the village. These lenders cannot distinguish between type 1 and type 2 farmers. They compete with a resident moneylender who knows the type of each farmer in the village. All lenders face an opportunity cost of funds equal to ρ. As in the case of moral hazard, the resident moneylender will be able to use his informational advantage to collect rents even in the face of this competitive pressure from uninformed lenders.

There are two cases to consider. First, suppose that $E\Pi(i^*(1)) < \rho \leq \bar{R} - W$ (as in Figure 7.2). The equilibrium with competitive, uninformed lenders would involve lending only to type 2 borrowers, with $i_2 = \rho/\pi(2)$. The local moneylender can charge different interest rates to different types of borrower; denote the interest charged by the local lender by $i_4(t)$. The availability of these outside loans to type 2 borrowers implies that the local moneylender cannot charge more than i_2 to type 2 farmers; so $i_4(2) = \rho/\pi(2)$. Type 1 farmers have no access to credit from outside lenders in this case; so the local lender can revert to his case 3 behaviour for this type of farmer and set $i_4(1) = (\bar{R} - W)/\pi(1) = \pi^*(1)$. The local lender earns rent on his loans to type 1 borrowers (his return on these loans is $\bar{R} - W > \rho$) because of his superior information.

Alternatively, suppose that $\rho \leq E\Pi(i^*(1))$ (Figure 7.3). In this case, the equilibrium with competitive uninformed lenders would involve outside lenders setting $i_2 \leq i^*(1)$ and lending to both types of farmer. The local moneylender can lend to type 1 farmers at any interest rate less than or equal to i_2. Suppose the local lender sets $i_4(1) = i_2$ (or just a bit below). Some (all) of the type 1 borrowers would not borrow from the outside lender, but instead would borrow from the local lender. The outside lenders would be faced with a riskier pool of borrowers at $i = i_2$ than they had in case 2 with no local lender. Their expected return from loans at i_2 would fall below ρ. Outside lenders, therefore, cannot offer loans at interest rate i_2. All type 1 borrowers will borrow from the local moneylender at $i_4(1) = i_2$, and the outside lenders will lend at $\tilde{i}$ to type 2 borrowers only. The local moneylender will set $i_2(2) = \tilde{i}$. The local lender again earns his rents on his loans to type 1 borrowers (His return on these loans is

$$\pi(1)i_4(1) = \frac{\pi(1)\rho}{p(1)\pi(1) + [1 - p(1)]\pi(2)} \geq \rho)$$

because of the power provided to him by his superior information concerning the characteristics of village residents.

III

The static consequences of these information symmetries are striking. They may lead to an inefficient allocation of credit, to excessive loan default as a consequence of moral hazard, to monopoly profits in the hands of lenders with relatively good information, or even to the collapse of the credit market. Yet more dramatic implications arise when the effects of credit market imperfections are considered in a dynamic context. In an important pair of papers, Banerjee and Newman (1993) and Galor and Zeira (1993) provide treatments of the dynamics of income distribution when credit markets are afflicted by problems of asymmetric information or imperfect contract enforcement.[9]

We saw in Section II that collateral can serve to mitigate some of the consequences of asymmetric information. In effect, individuals who can pledge collateral have improved access to credit markets. Consider the consequences of this in a general equilibrium. Suppose that with a certain investment individuals can start a business (or a farm). They hire a certain amount of labour at wage w, and at the end of the production period earn a profit (which is inversely related to the wage the entrepreneur pays). Now, suppose that, as a consequence of asymmetric information or imperfect contract enforcement, only households with wealth (that can be pledged as collateral) greater than a certain level, say C, can borrow enough money to finance the investment necessary to start a

---

[9] An excellent treatment of a simplified model is presented in Ray (1998).

firm. C will be a function of the wage, with $C'(w) > 0$, because firms earning a lower profit will have less incentive to repay the loan and thus more collateral will be required for a given loan size.

Imperfections of the credit market can have a dramatic impact on the labour market. Labour is supplied by those individuals with wealth below $C(w)$, while labour demand is determined by the entrepreneurs who are able to borrow and set up businesses. If the return from owning a business is higher than the return from working as a labourer, then this is a mechanism through which an unequal distribution of wealth can exist and become even more unequal over time. The few rich individuals have access to credit; they can borrow to finance businesses, earn a high return and remain rich. The large number of poor individuals cannot borrow and they all supply labour, driving down the wage. They remain poor, and the low wage further increases the returns (and thus the future wealth) of the rich entrepreneurs.

In this example, the dynamics of the distributions of income and wealth are driven by the properties of the credit market, and in particular by the fact that collateral can be used to mitigate the consequences of asymmetric information or imperfect enforcement of credit contracts.

REFERENCES

Adams, D., Graham, D., and Von Pischke, J. D. (1984), *Undermining Rural Development with Cheap Credit*. Boulder, Colo.: Westview Press.

Banerjee, A., and Newman, A. (1993), 'Occupational Choice and the Process of Development', *Journal of Political Economy*, 101.

Bell, C. (1988), 'Credit Markets, Contracts, and Interlinked Transactions', in H. Chenery and T. N. Srinivasan (eds.), *Handbook of Development Economics*. New York: North-Holland.

Besley, T., and Coate, S. (1995), 'Group Lending, Repayment Incentives and Social Collateral', *Journal of Development Economics*, 46.

Bhaduri, A. (1983), *The Economic Structure of Backward Agriculture*. New York: Academic Press.

Binswanger, H. P., and Rosenzweig, M. R. (1986), 'Behavioral and Material Determinants of Production Relations in Agriculture', *Journal of Development Studies*, 22.

Bulow, J., and Rogoff, K. (1989), 'A Constant Recontracting Model of Sovereign Debt', *Journal of Political Economy*, 97.

Chan, Y. S., and Thakor, A. (1987), 'Collateral and Competitive Equilibria with Moral Hazard and Private Information', *Journal of Finance*, 42.

Diagne, A. (1997), 'Default Incentives, peer Pressure, and Equilibrium Outcomes in Group-Based Lending Programs', unpublished paper, International Food Policy Research Institute.

Galor, O., and Zeria, J. (1993), 'Income Distribution and Macroeconomics', *Review of Economic Studies*, 60.

Ghatak, M. (1998), 'Joint Liability Contracts and the Peer Selection Effect', unpublished paper, University of Chicago Economics Department.

Grossman, S., and Hart, O. (1983), 'An Analysis of the Principal–Agent Problem', *Econometrica*, 51.

Kandori, M. (1992), 'Social Norms and Community Enforcement', *Review of Economic Studies*.

Khandker, S., Khalily, B., and Khan, Z. (1995), 'Grameen Bank: Performance and Sustainability', World Bank Discussion Paper no. 306, Washington.

Ray, D. (1998), *Development Economics*. Princeton: Princeton University Press.

Rogerson, W. (1985), 'The First-Order Approach to Principal–Agent Problems', *Econometrica*, 53.

Stiglitz, J., and Weiss, A. (1981), 'Credit Rationing in Markets with Incomplete Information', *American Economic Review*, 71.

8

Risk and Insurance in an Agricultural Economy

I

People who live in the rural areas of poor countries often must cope not only with severe poverty but with extremely variable incomes. This is most apparent for the majority who are directly dependant upon agricultural income. Weather variation, the incidence of disease, pests and fire, and a host of other less obvious factors cause farming yields to fluctuate unpredictably. Variations in the price of marketed output can also cause farm profits to vary. Fluctuations in income can present an acute threat to people's livelihoods even if, on average, incomes are high enough to maintain a minimal standard of living. Occasional famines provide the most egregious examples of the consequences of risk in poor societies, but risk also generates more commonplace worries such as the consequences of a bad harvest for a family's ability to afford school fees for children, or the implications of a wage-earner's illness for the ability to provide a healthy diet for the household.[1]

We have three main goals in this chapter. First, we will describe the Pareto-efficient allocation of risk within a community. Risk-pooling within a community could be achieved through formal insurance markets, or through a variety of informal transfer mechanisms. It will be seen that Pareto efficiency has very strong implications for consumption patterns in a risky environment. There are a number of reasons to expect that fully efficient risk-pooling rarely, if ever, is achieved. The second purpose of this chapter, therefore, is to examine the use of intertemporal consumption-smoothing through saving and credit markets as a substitute for full risk-pooling. Finally, if a risk-averse household is not able to achieve an entirely smooth consumption path through *ex post* mechanisms such as insurance, saving, and credit transactions, it has an incentive to devote

---

[1] See Walker and Ryan (1990), Bliss and Stern (1982), and Watts (1983) for rich descriptions of the risk faced by people living in different rural environments.

resources in an effort to secure a more stable income stream. In an agricultural economy, households might farm a diversified portfolio of land, adopt technologies (such as intercropping or drought-resistant crops) and contractual arrangements (such as sharecropping) that reduce the variance of income, or diversify their activities (through migration or local non-agricultural employment). Any of these *ex ante* actions might be costly, so that the households would be sacrificing income, on average, in order to assure a less risky stream of income.

II

There is a possibility that in some communities mechanisms exist to allocate risk efficiently.[2] Households within a village, kinship group, or other social network may share each other's risk through institutional arrangements which approximate the Pareto-efficient allocation of risk. The information flow within a cohesive community may be sufficiently rich that the incidence of random shocks to households' incomes is common knowledge, perhaps permitting community-level institutions to insure members against fluctuations in their incomes without the problems of moral hazard and adverse selection that would plague an outside insurer. Suppose that the community is a village. What are the implications of the existence of a smoothly operating set of institutions that achieves a Pareto-efficient allocation of risk?

To make the contrast with intertemporal smoothing most dramatic, we will first examine a village economy in which the Pareto-efficient allocation of risk is achieved, but in which there is no access to credit markets or even to storage. Let $i = 1, \ldots, N$ index the households that live in the village. There are T periods, indexed by t. s indexes the S states of nature, each with the objective and commonly known probability of occurrence π_s. In state s each household i receives an income of $y_{is} > 0$.[3] Let c_{ist} represent the consumption of household i if state s occurs in period t.[4] Suppose that each household has a separable utility function of the form:

---

[2] This possibility is explored informally in the large literature on the moral economy of peasant societies, most famously by Scott (1976). For reviews of the literature, see Platteau (1991) and Fafchamps (1992).

[3] For the moment we assume that income is exogenous. This is relaxed in Sections IV and V.

[4] We should denote consumption by $c_{ist}(h_{t-1})$ where h_{t-1} summarizes the history of states realized through period $t - 1$ to reflect the possibility that consumption might depend not only on the current state, but also on the entire history of states. However, we assume that the utility function is time-separable and that storage and borrowing across periods is not possible. The problem, therefore, separates by period, and current consumption depends only on the current state. To simplify notation, we delete h_{t-1}.

$$U_i = \sum_{t=1}^{T} \beta^t \sum_{s=1}^{S} \pi_s u_i(c_{ist}), \tag{1}$$

where $u(\ )$ is twice continuously differentiable with $u' > 0$, $u'' < 0$ and $\text{Lim}_{x \to 0} u'(x) = +\infty$.[5] A Pareto-efficient allocation of risk within the village can be found by maximizing the weighted sum of the utilities of each of the N households, where the weight of household i in the Pareto programme is λ_i, $0 < \lambda_i < 1$, $\sum \lambda_i = 1$:

$$\underset{c_{iht}}{\text{Max}} \sum_{i=1}^{N} \lambda_i U_i, \tag{2}$$

subject to the resources available in the village at each point in time in each state of nature:

$$\sum_{i=1}^{N} c_{ist} = \sum_{i=1}^{N} y_{ist} \, \forall \, s, t. \tag{3}$$

$$c_{ist} \geq 0 \, \forall \, i, s, t. \tag{4}$$

Equation (3) is the set of village resource constraints. Equation (4) contains the non-negativity constraints, which will not bind if the village has any resources in each period along each possible history.

The first-order conditions corresponding to c_{ist} and c_{jst} imply

$$\frac{u_i'(c_{ist})}{u_j'(c_{jst})} = \frac{\lambda_j}{\lambda_i} \, \forall \, i, j, s, t. \tag{5}$$

This equality extends across all N households in the village in any state at any point in time. The marginal utilities and therefore consumption levels of all households in the village move together. Therefore, the marginal utility of any household is a monotonically increasing function of the average marginal utility of households in the village in any state. This implies that the consumption of any household is a monotonically increasing function of average village consumption. In a Pareto-efficient allocation, then, transient changes in income are fully pooled at the community level. There is no incentive for risk diversification at the household level, because, after controlling for aggregate consumption, household consumption is not affected by shocks to a household's income. The only risk faced by the household is that faced by the community as a whole.

To see this result in its most stark form, suppose that everyone in the village has an identical constant absolute risk aversion utility function, so that

---

[5] The assumption that households maximize expected utility is for expositional convenience. The development that follows depends only on the assumption that the utility function is additively separable over time.

$u_i(x) = -(1/\sigma)e^{-\sigma x}$. Applying this utility function to the first-order condition (5) and taking logs, we find

$$c_{ist} = c_{jst} + (1/\sigma)(\ln(\lambda_i) - \ln(\lambda_j)). \tag{6}$$

As before, this equality holds across all N households in the village at any point in time. If we sum across these N equalities,

$$c_{ist} = \bar{c}_{st} + \frac{1}{\sigma}\left(\ln(\gamma_i) - \frac{1}{N}\sum_{j=1}^{N}\ln(\gamma_j)\right), \tag{7}$$

where

$$\bar{c}_{st} = (1/N)\sum_{j=1}^{N} c_{jst}.$$

So household consumption is equal to the average level of consumption in the village plus a time-invariant household fixed effect which depends upon the relative weight of the household in the Pareto programme. Equation (7) implies that the change in a household's consumption between any two periods is equal to the change in average community consumption between the two periods. This result depends on our choice of utility functions; in general, the change in a household's consumption is a monotonically increasing function of the change in average community consumption. In addition, notice that household income y_{is} does not appear in (7). After controlling for average consumption, a household's consumption is unaffected by its own income.

In a Pareto-efficient allocation of risk within a community, households face only aggregate risk. Idiosyncratic income shocks are completely insured within the community. The power of this conclusion obviously depends upon the relative importance of aggregate and idiosyncratic income risk within the relevant community. Within small regions, the incomes of households engaged in rainfed agriculture are likely to have a high covariance, reducing the effectiveness of local risk-sharing arrangements (Ruthenberg 1971; Binswanger and Rosenzweig 1986). Nevertheless, even in these regions there appears to be ample scope for risk-pooling. For example, Carter (1997) estimates that less than half the variance of rainfed farm yields in semi-arid Burkina Faso can be accounted for by common village-level variation: the majority of the yield variance is idiosyncratic to the household.

From the second welfare theorem, we know that the Pareto-efficient allocation of risk can be supported by a competitive equilibrium with complete contingent markets. However, the notion that such a rich set of competitive markets exists is incredible. Any risk-pooling mechanism must overcome the information and enforcement problems associated with insurance contracts. The insurer might be subject to either moral hazard or adverse selection (or both). In addition, it is likely to be impractical to write contracts in enough detail to specify each particular state that might occur, or to verify to third parties that particular states have occurred in order to enforce a contract. In the presence of these information and enforcement obstacles, a complete set of markets will not exist and the competitive equilibrium will not be Pareto-efficient. However, efficient (or nearly efficient) risk-pooling could be supported by a variety of other mechanisms. For example, in Chapter 9 we discuss the hypothesis that interlinked, repeated personalized transactions between households provide an essential framework for economic activity in small communities. It may be the case that such personalized transactions enable transfers between agents which serve to pool risk at the community level. Sahlins (1972) provides a discussion of systems of 'generalized reciprocity', in which those whose income temporarily is relatively large provide gifts to those whose income temporarily is relatively small. It is not necessarily true that gifts between specific individuals are reciprocated, but the giver can expect that, if she is ever in the position of having a temporary income shortfall, gifts will be forthcoming from someone in the community who simultaneously is enjoying a temporary windfall. Sahlins argues that systems of generalized reciprocity usually are found within kinship groups, but other communities can support similar risk-pooling arrangements. Here are two examples from the large literature on these risk-pooling systems.

Cashdan (1985) describes a system of gift exchange among Basarwa farmer–herders in northern Botswana. Most of the Basarwa studied by Cashdan subsist by providing livestock-herding services to richer non-Basarwa cattle-owners. In exchange for their labour, they receive milk from the cattle, perhaps some of the offspring, and the opportunity to use the draught power of the animals to cultivate their own fields. As the herd sizes (and therefore labour demands) of the wealthy cattle-owners fluctuate, the Basarwa workers find themselves forced to move to the cattle posts of new employers. Land is abundant and freely available for cultivation, but it takes time (two to three years) to clear and fence an optimally sized farm in the new location. These unpredictable employment changes, therefore, generate random variations in the income of these Basarwa households. Moreover, 'the probability of moving to a new location in a given year . . . is largely independent for the different households' (Cashdan 1985: 471). Therefore, a substantial portion of the income risk faced by these households is idiosyncratic and can be addressed by local risk-sharing mechanisms. Cashdan reports that, within a given locality, households that have been resident for longer (because they have not recently been forced to change employers) have relatively high incomes, and these households provide gifts of food to newer residents with smaller farms and incomes. The important idiosyncratic risk which is insured by this mechanism is certainly observable to all members of the community, and Cashdan implies that the probability of being forced to move is relatively exogenous to the behaviour of the households.

The problems of information asymmetries within the Basarwa community, therefore, seem relatively unimportant with respect to this source of risk. Whether the insurance extends to other sources of risk cannot be inferred from Cashdan's paper. Ethnic identity and the social costs of disengaging from the system of generalized reciprocity seem to play a crucial role in enforcing the obligation of temporarily wealthy households to transfer food to newer residents of a cattle post.

Platteau and Abraham (1987) discuss the importance of 'reciprocal credit' in a risk-pooling system of fishermen in a South Indian village. These fishermen live close to the margin of subsistence, and are engaged in a very risky activity. (The coefficient of variation of their daily catches exceeds unity.) There is little covariation in these incomes across households in the village, so there is ample scope for insurance within the village. Insurance is effected through frequent, very small, 'credit' transactions within the village. The acceptance of a loan by a fisherman

implicitly recognizes that he will be concerned with the future economic fortune of his creditor. Such a commitment implies that in the case that the creditor falls into distress, the borrower will not only have to return his debt immediately, but also that he must be ready to come to the help of his benefactor even if he has already succeeded in paying back his initial loan. Conversely, if the debtor again finds himself on the brink of a subsistence crisis, the creditor is expected to come to his rescue irrespective of whether or not he has cleared his first debt. (Platteau 1991: 151)

These credit transactions, therefore, serve to pool risk between borrowers and lenders within a small community. A similar arrangement is documented by Udry (1990), who finds that households in villages in northern Nigeria often simultaneously participate on both sides of an active credit market. The credit transactions pool risk between the borrowers and lenders through the use of contracts in which the repayment owed by the borrower depends upon the realization of random production shocks by both the borrower and the lender. A key feature of both the South Indian and northern Nigerian examples is that the risk-pooling arrangements occur within the confines of small communities within which information concerning the outcomes of, respectively, fishing and farming activities flows very freely. Moreover, in each instance the local community has access to enforcement mechanisms (primarily social pressure) with which to bring pressure on recalcitrant participants (Platteau 1991: 152; Udry 1990: 259).

The documented existence of *ex post* risk-pooling mechanisms within a variety of communities in less developed countries raises the possibility that some communities may have developed insurance systems which permit the allocation of risk to approach Pareto efficiency. This line of reasoning has motivated a number of quantitative studies of risk-sharing. For example, Townsend (1994) and Ravallion and Chaudhuri (1997) examine consumption outcomes rather than specific risk-pooling mechanisms in the ICRISAT Indian study villages. There is a high degree of co-movement in consumption across households within this set of villages, despite the fact that there is a substantial amount of idiosyncratic income variation. Nevertheless, a fully Pareto-efficient allocation of risk is not achieved in these villages. Deaton (1992*a*) and Grimard (1997) examine patterns of consumption to test the hypothesis of efficient risk-pooling within villages and ethnic groups, respectively, within Côte d'Ivoire. There is little evidence of any risk-pooling within villages, and somewhat stronger evidence of partial risk-pooling within ethnic groups. In neither case is full risk-pooling achieved. Udry (1994) rejects the hypothesis that Pareto-efficient risk-pooling is achieved in northern Nigerian villages using the specific mechanism of reciprocal credit transactions. In every case so far examined in the literature, therefore, the hypothesis of Pareto-efficient risk-pooling within rural communities in poor countries has been rejected.

III

A fully Pareto-efficient allocation of risk within local communities is rarely, if ever, achieved. Some idiosyncratic variation generally remains uninsured. Moreover, cross-sectional risk-pooling cannot contribute to households' efforts to cope with the effects of aggregate community-level shocks to income. The complementary *ex post* mechanism for insulating consumption from the effects of income fluctuation is consumption-smoothing over time using saving and credit transactions. Consider a household with no opportunity for cross-sectional risk-pooling, but with unlimited access to a credit market.[6] The household utility function is the same as that of equation (1), but it will be useful to rewrite (1) (dropping the i subscripts) as

$$U_t = E_t \sum_{\tau - t}^{T} \beta^{\tau - t} u(c_\tau) \tag{1'}$$

to emphasize the decision problem that the household faces over time. U_t is the expected utility of the household over the remainder of its lifetime. Suppose that in any period the household can borrow or lend on a credit market with a certain interest rate r_t. Let the household's asset stock at the start of period t be A_t (which is positive when the household is a lender, and negative when it is a borrower). The household receives a random income y_t and decides how to allocate its resources between consumption and net saving for the next period:

$$A_{t+1} = (1 + r_t)(A_t + y_t - c_t). \tag{8}$$

[6] This section relies on Deaton (1992*b*).

The household chooses consumption to maximize (1') subject to (8), non-negativity constraints on c, and the transversality condition $A_{T+1} \geq 0$. Note that the household can be a debtor in any but the final period.

The period t value function for the household's problem satisfies

$$V_t(A_t + y_t) = \underset{c_t}{\text{Max}} \{u(c_t) + \beta \; E_t \; V_{t+1}[(1 + r_t)(A_t + y_t - c_t) + y_{t+1}]\}. \quad (9)$$

The value of current resources (assets plus current income) is equal to the maximized value of current consumption plus the discounted expected value of resources next period. Optimization and the envelope condition imply

$$u'(c_t) = \beta(1 + r_t) \; E_t u'(c_{t+1}) \quad (10)$$

Saving or lending decisions are made so that the marginal utility of current consumption is set equal to the discounted expected marginal utility of next period's consumption. If the yield on assets just offsets the subjective discount rate $(\beta(1 + r_t) = 1) \; \forall \; t$, (10) simplifies to $u'(c_t) = E_t u'(c_{t+1})$.

If we make the assumption that u is quadratic, then (10) becomes

$$c_t = E_t c_{t+1}. \quad (11)$$

In this special case, therefore, households make consumption plans such that expected consumption is constant.[7] Since $A_{T+1} = 0$, the budget constraint (3') (with r_t constant at r) implies that the discounted value of consumption from any time t to T equals the value of the household's assets at t plus the discounted value of its income stream from t to T. If we combine this result with (11) and let T go to infinity, we arrive at the permanent income hypothesis:

$$c_t = \frac{r}{1+r}\left(A_t + E_t \sum_{\tau=t}^{\infty}(1+r)^{-(\tau-t)} y_\tau\right) \quad (12)$$

Current consumption, therefore, is the annuity value of current assets plus the present value of the expected stream of future income.

If the permanent income hypothesis is valid, how will household consumption respond to random variations in household income? The answer depends on the information associated with the income shock. The change in consumption will be equal to the annuity value of the present value of the change in the expected stream of future income. If the income shock is transitory, and there is little or no change in the household's expectations concerning its future income stream, then consumption will change little in response to the income shock. If the income shock causes a large change in the household's expectations concerning its future income stream, then the income shock will be seen as

---

[7] In the language of stochastic processes, consumption follows a martingale.

permanent and consumption will change dramatically in response to the income shock.

There is good evidence from a variety of studies that households engage in a substantial degree of consumption-smoothing. A particularly interesting study is Paxson (1992), which uses deviations of rainfall from its average level to identify transitory income shocks affecting Thai rice farmers. She uses these estimates to calculate the marginal propensity to save transitory income, and finds that these farmers save three-quarters to four-fifths of transitory income changes. This is less than the marginal propensity to save of one, which is predicted by the permanent income hypothesis, but it is strong evidence of significant intertemporal consumption-smoothing.[8] Despite evidence of consumption-smoothing using saving and credit transactions, the permanent income model can generally be rejected for households in all parts of the world. Microeconomic data from the United States and Japan indicate that even in these countries consumers are often liquidity-constrained (Hayashi 1987). As we have seen in Chapter 7, there are strong reasons to believe that rural households in developing countries do not have access to perfect credit markets. Morduch (1992) finds evidence of borrowing constraints strongly affecting the behaviour of relatively poor households in a set of villages in semi-arid India. Moreover, he finds that the households that seem to be liquidity-constrained engage in less risky production activities than unconstrained households. Using data from a broader set of Indian villages and different econometric techniques, Rosenzweig and Binswanger (1993) also find evidence of limitations on households' *ex post* smoothing capabilities. They show that wealthier households, less constrained in their ability to absorb income variability, invest in significantly more risky production activities and earn significantly higher mean returns from these activities than poorer households. The inability of poorer households completely to insulate their consumption from income risk, therefore, has adverse consequences for both the distribution of income and for productive efficiency.

Deaton (1991) shows that, even if households have no access to a credit market at all, they may still be able to achieve a high degree of intertemporal consumption-smoothing through the use of assets as buffer stocks. As long as the household has positive saving, temporary income shortfalls can be smoothed through dissaving and short-term windfalls can be saved. However, once the household's wealth falls to near zero, the possibility of further smoothing shrinks and consumption can become quite volatile. This pattern has been noted in the extensive literature on famines, in which it is observed that famines

---

[8] It should be noted that Paxson does not reject the null hypothesis that the marginal propensity to save equals one. However, she does reject the implication of the permanent income hypothesis that the marginal propensity to save out of changes in permanent income should be zero: she finds that this marginal propensity is positive.

often occur only after a succession of weather failures, or after people's savings are wiped out through other means (Watts 1983; Ravallion 1997). If the assets that are used to buffer consumption from income fluctuations are themselves used in the production process, then there can be important effects on future income from even temporary shocks to current income. This is one of the bases of Polly Hill's (1977) observation that farming households can be 'too poor to be efficient' and is explored more formally by Rosenzweig and Wolpin (1993). They observe from a sample of rural households in India that bullocks are often purchased and sold to smooth consumption when income fluctuates. However, bullocks play an important role in the production process of these farm households. In order to mitigate the effects on consumption of a transitory decline in income, a household might sell off a bullock. But the household's farm profit in the next year would be lower as a consequence of the loss of this productive asset.[9] Udry (1995) shows that, as long as a household has stocks of an asset that is *not* used in production, this asset will be used to smooth consumption; however, once this asset is drawn down near zero, as for instance after a succession of bad harvests, then assets used in production may be sold in order to smooth consumption. Rosenzweig and Wolpin (1985), for example, show that households subjected to two consecutive years of drought are 150% more likely to sell land.

IV

How does the consumption pattern of households that smooth consumption over time through credit markets compare with that discussed in Section II, when the household has access to complete risk-pooling? When there is complete risk-pooling, the household's consumption responds only to average community consumption. Holding community consumption constant, a shock to a household's own income, whether transitory or permanent, has no effect on household consumption. We made the additional assumption that the community had no access to credit markets, and also that no goods were stored. With this assumption, community income equals community consumption in each period. Therefore, even a transitory shock to community income causes the household to change its consumption. In contrast, where there is no risk-pooling but the household has access to a perfect credit market, community income is irrelevant to the household's consumption decision, but consumption will vary with changes in the household's permanent income.

[9] This may be a reason why households in Burkina Faso resisted selling their inventories of livestock to smooth the dramatic loss of income during the Sahelian drought of the 1980s: see Fafchamps *et al.* (1998).

It can be seen, therefore, that consumption-smoothing through insurance and consumption-smoothing through transferring resources over time are conceptually very distinct. However, it may be difficult to distinguish the two models by examining the relationship between household consumption and household and village income.[10] Both the permanent income model and the full insurance model imply that changes in household income may have only a small correlation with changes in household consumption. This result would occur if the household has access to full insurance and its income is not highly correlated with village income, and it would occur if the household is smoothing consumption intertemporally if the variations in its income are predominantly due to transitory shocks. Furthermore, both the permanent income model and the full insurance model would imply that household consumption might be highly correlated with village consumption and uncorrelated with transitory shocks to household income if these transitory shocks are largely uncorrelated across households in the village, while permanent shocks to households' incomes are largely common to the whole village.

Deaton and Paxson (1994) provide a simple method for distinguishing economies well characterized by intertemporal consumption-smoothing from those characterized by an approximately Pareto-efficient allocation of risk. The idea is to examine the distribution of consumption of a cohort of people over time. In a Pareto-efficient allocation characterized by equation (7), this distribution will remain stable over time: all idiosyncratic risk has been insured against. If the permanent income hypothesis is approximately true, the distribution of consumption will broaden (see equation (12)) as different individuals over time receive different news concerning their future income prospects.

We have presented the insurance and intertemporal smoothing mechanisms as though they are mutually exclusive. Of course, this is not true. If both borrowing and lending in a perfect capital market and insurance within the village are possible, then household consumption will still depend only on average consumption within the village, but village consumption can deviate from village income. The village-level analogue to the permanent income hypothesis will imply that village consumption as a whole (and therefore household consumption) will have little responsiveness to transitory shocks to village income. Household consumption will change only in response to variations in the permanent income of the village.

If consumption-smoothing is possible through either or both of these two *ex post* avenues, then risk-averse households will act in some other respects as if they were risk-neutral. In particular, variants of the neoclassical separation theorem will hold. For example, consider again the situation of a Pareto-efficient

---

[10] The following argument is drawn from Alderman and Paxson (1994).

allocation of risk within a community. Suppose that production is possible. Labour is inelastically supplied, but current output must be invested in order to produce next year. Consumption and income now depend on the history of past realized states, because investment creates a link across periods. The notation must be enriched to permit this dependence,[11] so household i's income in state s of period t after a history of states through period $t-1$ (h_{t-1}) is

$$y_{ist}(h_{t-1}) = g_i(s, k_{i,t-1}(h_{t-1})).$$ (13)

$g_i(\ )$ is a production function with $\partial g_i/\partial k_i > 0$ and $\partial^2 g_i/\partial k^2 < 0$. The capital invested on i's farm in period $t-1$ (in order to produce output in period t) depends on the history of states realized up to and including period $t-1$. Naturally, the resource constraints (3) must be modified to reflect the commitment of current resources for future production:

$$\sum_{i=1}^{N} k_{it}(h_{t-1}) = \sum_{i=1}^{N} [y_{ist}(h_{t-1}) - c_{ist}(h_{t-1})].$$ (3')

The first-order conditions for the Pareto programme now imply that the investments made in period $t-1$ for production in period t satisfy

$$\sum_{s} \lambda_s(h_{t-1}) \frac{\partial g_i(s,k)}{\partial k_{i,t-1}(h_{t-1})} = \sum_{s} \lambda_s(h_{t-1}) \frac{\partial g_j(s,k)}{\partial k_{j,t-1}(h_{t-1})},$$ (14)

where $\lambda_s(h_{t-1})$ is the Lagrange multiplier corresponding to the resource constraint (3') in state s of period t after history $t-1$. $\lambda_s(h_{t-1})$ is the increment in the value of the Pareto programme resulting from an increase in resources in state s of period t, so (14) implies that the marginal value of investment in period $t-1$ (weighted over the S states which might occur in period t) is equated across households. Investment, therefore, is determined entirely by considerations of productive efficiency, and the separation theorem holds. In particular, differences in risk aversion or wealth levels across households have no effect on the allocation of investment in a Pareto-efficient allocation. This result can be put into even more stark form if we assume that $y_{is}(h_{t-1}) = \theta_s g_i(k_{i,t-1}(h_{t-1}))$ so that production risk is characterized by a simple multiplicative factor. In this case, (14) becomes

$$\frac{\partial g_i(k)}{\partial k_{i,t-1}(h_{t-1})} = \frac{\partial g_j(k)}{\partial k_{j,t-1}(h_{t-1})},$$ (14')

and the marginal product of investment is equated across all households.

The same result is obtained if the permanent income hypothesis is true and all production risk is transitory. Therefore, if either cross-sectional or

---

[11] See fn. 4.

time-series *ex post* smoothing mechanisms exist and are effective, the neoclassical separation theorem holds and production decisions do not depend on the preferences of individual households. It is clear, therefore, that a successful *ex post* smoothing strategy has a dramatic effect on household behaviour. We have seen that there is evidence from a wide variety of studies that households in poor, risky agrarian environments engage in both cross-sectional risk-pooling and consumption-smoothing over time. However, there is equally good evidence that these strategies are not wholly successful. The information and enforcement difficulties associated with both insurance and credit transactions frustrate households' efforts to insulate their consumption from income shocks. Given the lack of access to complete and smoothly operating insurance and credit markets, households devote substantial resources to stabilizing the incoming stream of income in order to protect themselves from the dire consequences of substantial income fluctuations.

V

When the *ex post* mechanisms for mitigating the adverse consequences of income fluctuations fail, risk-averse households invest in *ex ante* means of reducing income fluctuations. Much of the rest of this book is concerned with some of the strategies used by households to ensure that their incomes do not fluctuate too severely. The effects of this imperative are felt throughout the economies of poor countries. For example, new technologies which have positive (but uncertain) expected profits might not be adopted, or might be adopted more slowly. (See, for example, the discussion of the adoption of the spread of new technologies for grain production in semi-arid Africa in Sanders *et al.* 1996.) Farmers might use conservative agronomic practices which lower risk and expected returns, such as planting low-yielding but rapidly maturing varieties of crops to minimize the probability that rainfall shortages will cause crop failure, or planting multiple crops on widely dispersed fields. Households might work in a diverse range of activities rather than specialize in a single profit-maximizing business in order to diversify some of the income risk. Households might spread their members across space through migration or marriage in order to reduce the variance of aggregate household income. Or they might agree to the use of contracts (such as sharecropping), which provide poor incentives for producing profit-maximizing levels of output but reduce the variance of income.[12] All of these measures reduce expected profits, but also reduce the variance of income.

---

[12] Dasgupta (1993: chs. 8 and 9) provides a review of much of the relevant literature on these and similar mechanisms.

The effect of imperfect *ex post* consumption-smoothing on production decisions can be seen with a simple modification of the model presented in Section III. Suppose that households face a liquidity constraint such that in any period $A_t + y_t - c_t \geq 0$. In addition, suppose that farmers face a portfolio choice (think of it as a choice about how much acreage to allocate to each of two different crops) between two activities, one of which is more risky than the other. In particular, let period t income be determined by the realization of a zero mean independent and identically distributed (i.i.d.) shock ϵ_t and the previous-period portfolio choice x_{t-1}, so that $y_t = y(x_{t-1}, \epsilon_t)$. $\partial y_t / \partial \epsilon_t > 0$, and the portfolio choice is such that $\partial y_t / \partial x_{t-1} > 0$ if $\epsilon_t > 0$ and $\partial y_t / \partial x_{t-1} < 0$ if $\epsilon_t < 0$. In good times choosing more of the risky activity increases output, while in bad times choosing more of the risky activity reduces output. x is costless, so if the household is maximizing expected income it will choose x_{t-1}, such that $E_{t-1} \delta y_t / \partial x_{t-1} = 0$.[13]

The period t value function for the household now satisfies (compare with (9))

$$V_t(A_t + y_t) = \text{Max} \{u(c_t) + \beta E_t V_{t+1}[(1 + r_t)(A_t + y_t - c_t) \\ + y(x_t, \epsilon_{t+1})] + \lambda_t(A_t + y_t - c_t)\} \qquad (15)$$

where λ_t is the Lagrange multiplier corresponding to the liquidity constraint in period t. Consumption in period t will be chosen to satisfy

$$u'(c_t) = E_t \beta(1 + r_t) V'_{t+1}[(1 + r_t)(A_t + y_t - c_t) + y(x_t, \epsilon_{t+1})] + \lambda_t, \qquad (16)$$

with complementary slackness between λ_t and $(A_t + y_t - c_t)$. By the envelope property, x_{t-1} will satisfy

$$E_{t-1} \frac{dV_t(\cdot)}{dx_{t-1}} = E_{t-1} U'(c_t) \frac{\partial y}{\partial x_{t-1}} = 0. \qquad (17)$$

Substituting (16) for $u'(c_t)$, we have

$$E_{t-1}[\beta(1+r)V'_{t+1}(\cdot) + \lambda_t] \frac{\partial y}{\partial x_{t-1}} = 0. \qquad (18)$$

So if $\lambda_t = 0$ in all states of period t, so that the individual knows that the liquidity constraint will not bind in period t, then x_{t-1} is chosen so that

$$E_{t-1} V'_{t+1}(\cdot) \frac{\partial y}{\partial x_{t-1}} = 0. \qquad (19)$$

On the other hand, if $\lambda_t > 0$ for some states of period t, then x_{t-1} is chosen so that

---

[13] This is the specification used by Morduch (1992).

$$\beta(1+r)E_{t-1}V'_{t+1}(\cdot)\frac{\partial y}{\partial x_{t-1}} = -E_{t-1}\lambda_t\frac{\partial y}{\partial x_{t-1}} > 0, \tag{20}$$

where the latter inequality holds because the liquidity constraints bind ($\lambda_t > 0$) in low-income states of period $t(\epsilon_t > 0)$, and in those states $\partial y/\partial x_{t-1} < 0$. Therefore, the expected marginal utility of undertaking the risky activity must be larger—and thus the level of risk-taking must be lower—when the liquidity constraint might bind than when it is known that it will not bind.

It is to be expected that poorer households are more likely to be subject to binding liquidity constraints. These households, therefore, will choose a more conservative portfolio of activities than richer households. Poorer households will choose activities that reduce the variance of their incomes, but that also have lower expected incomes than the activities chosen by wealthier households.

REFERENCES

Alderman, H., and Paxson, C. (1994), 'Do the Poor Insure? a Synthesis of the Literature on Risk Sharing Institutions in Developing Countries', in E. Bacha (ed.), *Economics in a Changing World*, iv, *Development Trade and the Environment*. London: Macmillan.

Binswanger, H. P., and Rosenzweig, M. (1986), 'Wealth, Weather Risk and the Composition and Profitability of Agricultural Investments', *Economic Journal*.

Bliss, C., and Stern, N. (1982), *Palanpur: Studies in the Economy of an Indian Village*. New York: Oxford University Press.

Carter, M. (1997), 'Environment, Technology and the Social Articulation of Risk in West African Culture', *Economic Development and Cultural Change*, 45.

Cashdan, E. (1985), 'Coping with Risk: Reciprocity among the Basarwa of Northern Botswana', *Man*, 20.

Dasgupta, P. (1993), *An Inquiry into Well-Being and Destitution*. Oxford: Clarendon Press.

Deaton, A. (1991), 'Saving and Liquidity Constraints', *Econometrica*, 59.

—— (1992a), 'Saving and Income Smoothing in the Côte d'Ivoire', *Journal of African Economies*, 1.

—— (1992b), *Understanding Consumption*. Oxford: Clarendon Press.

—— and Paxson, C. (1994), 'Intertemporal Choice and Inequality', *Journal of Political Economy*, 102.

De Waal, A. (1989), *Famine that Kills: Darfur, Sudan, 1984–1985*. Oxford: Clarendon Press.

Fafchamps, M. (1992), 'Solidarity Networks in Rural Africa: Rational Peasants with a Moral Economy', *Economic Development and Cultural Change*, 41.

—— Udry, C., and Czukas, K. (1998), 'Drought and Saving in Burkina Faso: Are Livestock a Buffer Stock?' *Journal of Development Economics*, 55.

Grimard, F. (1997), 'Household Consumption Smoothing through Ethnic Ties: Evidence from Côte d'Ivoire', *Journal of Development Economics*, 53.

Hayashi, F. (1987), 'Tests for Liquidity Constraints: A Critical Survey and Some New Observations', in T. Bewley (ed.), *Advances in Econometrics*. Cambridge: Cambridge University Press.

Hill, P. (1977), *Population, Prosperity and Poverty: Rural Kano, 1900 and 1972*. Cambridge: Cambridge University Press.

Morduch, J. (1992), 'Risk, Production and Saving: Theory and Evidence from Indian Households', unpublished paper, Harvard University.

Paxson, C. (1992), 'Using Weather Variability to Estimate the Response of Savings to Transitory Income in Thailand', *American Economic Review*, 82.

Platteau, J.-P. (1991), 'Traditional Systems of Social Security and Hunger Insurance: Past Achievements and Modern Challenges', in E. Ahmad, J. H. Drèze, P. J. Hills, and A. K. Sen (eds.), *Social Security in Developing Countries*. Oxford: Clarendon Press.

——and Abraham, A. (1987), 'An Inquiry into Quasi-Credit Contracts: the Role of Reciprocal Credit and Interlinked Deals in Small-scale Fishing Communities', *Journal of Development Studies*, 23.

Ravallion, M. (1987), *Markets and Famines*. Oxford: Oxford University Press.

——(1997), 'Famines and Economics', *Journal of Economic Literature*, 35.

——and Chaudhuri, S. (1997), 'Risk and Insurance in Village India: Comment', *Econometrica*, 65.

Rosenzweig, M., and Binswanger, H. P. (1986), 'Behavioral and Material Determinants of Production Relations in Agriculture', *Journal of Development Studies*, 22.

——and——(1993), 'Wealth, Weather Risk and the Composition and Profitability of Agricultural Investments, *Economic Journal*, 103.

——and Wolpin, K. I. (1993), 'Credit Market Constraints, Consumption Smoothing and the Accumulation of Durable Production Assets in Low-Income Countries', *Journal of Political Economy*, 101.

——and——(1985), 'Specific Experience, Household Structure, and Inter-generational Transfers: Farm Family Land and Labor Arrangements in Developing Countries', *Quarterly Journal of Economics*, 100.

Ruthenberg, H. (1971), *Farming Systems in the Tropics*. Oxford: Clarendon Press.

Sahlins, M. (1972), *Stone-Age Economics*. Chicago: Aldine-Atheton.

Sanders, J., Shapiro, B., and Ramaswamy, S. (1996), *The Economics of Agricultural Technology in Semiarid Sub-Saharan Africa*. Baltimore: Johns Hopkins University.

Scott, J. (1976), *The Moral Economy of the Peasant*. New Haven: Yale University Press.

Townsend, R. (1994), 'Risk and Insurance in Village India', *Econometrica*, 62.

Udry, C. (1990), 'Credit Markets in Northern Nigeria: Credit as Insurance in a Rural Economy', *World Bank Economic Review*, 4.

——(1994), 'Risk and Insurance in a Rural Credit Market: An Empirical Investigation in Northern Nigeria', *Review of Economic Studies*, 61.

——(1995), 'Risk and Saving in Northern Nigeria', *American Economic Review*, 85.

Walker, T., and Ryan, J. (1990), *Village and Household Economies in India's Semi-arid Tropics*. Baltimore: Johns Hopkins University.

Watts, M. (1983), *Silent Violence: Food, Famine and Peasantry in Northern Nigeria*. Berkeley: University of California Press.

9
Interlinkage of Transactions and Rural Development

I

Over the last couple of decades, the theoretical literature on rural development has sometimes emphasized the role of interlinked, often personalized, transactions between economic agents in providing a key element of the underlying institutional framework. In this, the economic literature has only recently caught up with the relevant literature in economic anthropology.[1] Anthropologists have often pointed to the multi-stranded nature of relationships in small face-to-face communities. Gluckman, in his studies of tribal Africa, has called such societies 'multiplex', with each individual playing not one but a variety of roles in interacting with the fellow members of his community. Generalizing from his experience with the hill peasants of Orissa, Bailey (1971) notes: 'the watershed between traditional and modern society is exactly this distinction between single-interest and multiplex relationships'. He goes on to comment that, in the cognitive map of the peasant, single-interest, functionally specialized relationships are to be made—with due caution—only with outsiders, those who are outside his moral community.

These interlinked transactions differ qualitatively from the anonymous and systemic interdependence of economic action in competitive general equilibrium theory, and are more in the form of package deals, with the terms of one transaction contingent upon the terms in another. The usual examples in the rural development literature take the form of landlord–tenant relations intertwined with creditor–borrower relations between the same parties, or of employers hiring workers on terms that are interlocked with those on which the former provide credit (or land) to the latter, or of simultaneous deals in the commodity and credit markets between a trader and a farmer where the latter

---

[1] For a review of the economic issues in the literature to date in this perspective, see Bardhan (1984: ch. 12).

gets credit on the pre-commitment of future crop delivery to the former. An understanding of the nature of these relations is clearly important in any policy agenda of institutional reforms.

Much too often in the past, particularly in the radical institutionalist literature, these relations have been described as remnants of feudalism. But feudalism as a historical category is highly inappropriate to cover such relations, even in most pre-capitalist cases.[2] Besides, there are some qualitative aspects of these relations that are common in both capitalist and pre-capitalist economies. For example, *personalized* transactions often characterize enduring relationships in 'customer' markets—as opposed to what Okun (1981) called 'auction' markets—even in industrially advanced countries; and interlinked transactions are not unknown in the package deals and tie-in sales in sophisticated markets.

However, more important than the problem of careless labelling of the relations is the policy question. If, in our reformist zeal, we do not pay enough attention to the underlying economic rationale of pre-existing institutions and their interconnections, and try to hack away parts of them, we may not always improve (and may even worsen) the lot of the poor tenant–labourer–borrower, the intended beneficiary of the reform programme. A well-intentioned land redistribution programme may, for example, be rendered counter productive by the absence of a simultaneous programme of credit reform; even in credit reform, public banks spreading to reach out to the peasants may meet with limited success in the face of the potential borrower interlocked in her credit-cum-land or -labour relationship with the local lender–landlord–employer. Piecemeal laws trying to put a ceiling on rents or interest rates or a floor to minimum wages may be rendered ineffective by suitable readjustments of prices or selective rationing in interlinked transactions.

On the other hand, in trying to understand the micro foundations of pre-existing institutions, we should not be blind to their adverse consequences. For example, the very nature of rationale for personalized interlinking may at the same time act as a formidable barrier to entry for other parties and may give the dominant partner in a transaction some additional leverage. The thin line between *understanding* an institution and *justifying* it is often blurred, particularly by careless interpreters of the theory.

In this chapter we keep both kinds of considerations in mind in discussing certain common types of interlinked transaction that characterize agrarian environments in some poor countries. In Section II we analyse a simple model of credit–labour interlinkage, and in Section III an equally simple model of credit–trade interlinkage. Section IV concludes with some general observations.

[2] There are many historians—e.g. Anderson (1974)—who regard feudalism as a non-universal socioeconomic organization specific to the experience of Europe and, at most, Japan.

II

In a survey of a random sample of 110 villages in East India, Bardhan and Rudra (1981) observed that about four-fifths of the villages have a system of loans by the landlord–employer in the slack season against a commitment by the peasant labourer to supply labour services in the peak season, a system usually known as *dadan* in this region. In many of these cases, the number of labour days in which the loan is repaid by the labourer is calculated at a wage rate that is below the market wage rate prevailing at the time of repayment.

Such voluntary credit–labour linkage (terminable and renewable every crop season) may be interpreted simply as an intertemporal barter transaction, ensuring a double coincidence of wants arising from the irregularities of the agricultural crop cycle. In order to survive the slack season, labourers look for a credit transaction in which they can repay the loan in the form of future labour services, but this will not be acceptable to creditors apart from the employer–creditor, who is in great need of labour in the peak season. Many such village economies are characterized by a dominant landlord who, because of the size of his assets and urban connections, is able to obtain credit more cheaply than other local agents. Thus, the landlord is able to act as a financial intermediary between an outside loan market and his labourers. However, the landlord is also positioned as a monopolist in establishing the terms of trade between current consumption and future labour services. If the landlord can obtain unlimited funds at a fixed interest rate, r, then monopoly profits are earned by a two-part tariff on consumption credit. Labourers pay a marginal interest rate per unit of consumption credit equal to the landlord's opportunity cost plus a fixed 'entry fee' for the privilege of borrowing at this rate. The provision of labour services in future periods constitutes repayment of principal and interest, including the entry fee, on a consumption loan. The entry fee represents the monopoly profits on the transaction.

Consider a stylized agrarian economy with two periods.[3] In the first, there is no work. In the second, there is a spot labour market where labour services are traded at a given wage rate, W. The revenues of the single dominant landlord are a monotonically increasing and strictly concave function, $F(L)$, of the quantity of labour employed, L. There is a pool of n peasants who borrow from and work for this landlord. Each peasant has an identical utility function, $U(C_1, C_2)$, defined over consumptions, C_1 and C_2, in each of the two periods, with the usual properties of strict concavity and consumption in each period being a 'normal' good.

The landlord and the peasants can trade labour in the spot market or undertake an interlinked transaction which entirely bypasses the spot market. Linked

---

[3] The following model is based on Bardhan (1984: cha. 6).

credit–labour transactions may be seen as an implicit contract specifying three items: (1) an amount of consumption credit, c, which the landlord extends to peasants during period 1; (2) a commitment of labour services, l, to be provided by each peasant in period 2; and (3) a wage, w, at which the committed labour services are compensated. Implicit contracts are, by assumption, costlessly enforceable.

Consider an implicit contract (c, l, w). Each peasant has committed l units of labour to the landlord at a wage of w, and, if the peasant's second-period labour endowment is one unit, trades $1 - l$ units of labour at the spot wage. Hence under the contract, first-period consumption is equal to c, and second-period consumption is equal to $wl + W(1 - l)$. Substituting these into the utility function gives the utility of the contract to peasants as

$$U = U[c, wl + W(1 - l)]. \tag{1}$$

Profits to the landlord are given by

$$\pi = F(L) - W(L - nl) - nlw - (1 + r)cn. \tag{2}$$

The implicit contract may now be viewed in the following way. The landlord extends to the peasants a loan of c which is to be repaid by their providing labour services, which are compensated at a discount $(W - w)$ below the market wage. The market value of these labour services is Wl, whereas the peasant is compensated only by an amount lw. The difference, constituting the loan repayment, we call

$$R = l(W - w) \tag{3}$$

Using (3), (1) and (2) may be rewritten as

$$U = U(c, W - R) \tag{4}$$

and

$$\pi = F(L) + nR - WL - (1 + r)cn. \tag{5}$$

From (4) and (5), one may note that these do not directly involve the contract values of l and w, except to the extent they jointly affect R. This means that in equilibrium the contract wage, w, is indeterminate, depending on the number of hours worked for the landlord. From (3), a loan repayment of a given size can be made equivalently by working more hours at a smaller discount or fewer hours at a larger discount.

Peasants can borrow from a source other than the landlord (say, the professional moneylender in the village or in the nearby small town) at an exogenous interest rate of $r^0 > r$; similarly, they can work at the spot market at the wage rate W. These define a reservation utility of $V(W, r^0)$ for the peasant. The implicit contract must ensure for the peasant a utility level at least equal to this reservation utility, and profit maximization by the landlord implies that this voluntary compliance constraint must hold with strict equality, so that

$$U(c, W - R) = V(W, r^0) \tag{6}$$

From (6) we can write the loan repayment as an implicit function,

$$R = R(c, W, r^0). \tag{7}$$

Given exogenous values of W and r^0, the implicit function defines the maximum repayment a peasant is willing to make for a consumption credit of c. R_c, the partial derivative of the function with respect to c, i.e. the peasant's willingness to pay for a marginal increase in consumption credit, should be equal to the peasant's intertemporal marginal rate of substitution in consumption, given by the ratio of the marginal utilities in the U function.

Substituting the R function from (7) into (5), the landlord's profit function, and maximizing it with respect to L and c, we get

$$F'(L) = W \tag{8}$$

and

$$R_c(c, W, r^0) = 1 + r. \tag{9}$$

These equations determine the equilibrium values of labour input, L^*, and consumption credit, c^*, and thus the loan repayment, R^*.

Some of the comparative-static results are as follows. A higher spot wage, W, lowers labour input, increases consumption credit, and raises the loan repayment. A higher interest rate faced by the landlord leaves labour input unchanged, lowers consumption credit, and lowers the loan repayment. A higher interest rate faced by peasants also leaves labour input unchanged, lowers consumption credit, and raises the loan repayment.

Using R_c from (9), the opportunity cost of credit to the landlord can be equalized to the peasants' intertemporal marginal rate of substitution, so that

$$\frac{U_1(c, W - R)}{U_2(c, W - R)} = 1 + r. \tag{10}$$

This suggests a further interpretation of the equilibrium implicit contract. Suppose that the landlord charges peasants an interest rate on consumption loans of r plus an 'entry fee' of f for the privilege of borrowing at this rate. A peasant will optimally choose a consumption credit, c, that satisfies the optimal intertemporal consumption condition,

$$\frac{U_1(c, W - (1+r)c - f)}{U_2(c, W - (1+r)c - f)} = 1 + r. \tag{11}$$

If $f = R^* - (1 + r) c^*$, then the peasant will optimally choose a credit of $c = c^*$. Thus, the equilibrium implicit contract effects an outcome equivalent to a two-part tariff on consumption loans by which the landlord establishes a fixed entry fee and a marginal interest rate equal to his own cost of credit. The peasant chooses the size of the loan and then repays principal and interest, including the entry fee, in labour services valued at the spot wage.

Thus, the credit–labour interlinkage serves as a form of effective nonlinear pricing on the part of the landlord (even when outright nonlinear contracts, such as the case of different people charged different interest rates depending on the size of the loan, are socially disapproved or legally disallowed). It enables the landlord to extract the entire consumer's surplus from those who borrow from him, even though at the margin the price charged is equal to his opportunity cost of raising credit.

III

One of the most pervasive interlinked contracts in poor countries all over the world is that between a trader–lender and a farmer–borrower. The former often lends to the capital-strapped farmer in exchange for a promise to deliver the crop at a pre-agreed price discount.[4] (Sometimes this is called contract-farming, which has been an increasingly important form of organization in export agriculture in Africa over the past few decades.) We analyse the problem in a model[5] qualitatively similar to that in the preceding section, but now we move from the world of consumption credit for a labourer to that of production loans for a farmer.

Suppose now we have, for simplification, a (concave) production function, $F(K)$, where output depends only on the working capital, K, that the farmer has to borrow. As before, the opportunity cost of credit to the linked lender (the trader, in this case) is r, which is lower than r^0, the rate that the (small) farmer faces were he to raise credit outside. Let i be the interest rate charged by the trader–lender, such that $(1 + i)$ is $\alpha(1 + r)$. The market price of output is p, but the price offered by the trader is q, which is βp. For the moment, α and β could be less than, equal to, or greater than unity. An interlinked contract between the farmer and the trader may thus be represented by (α, β).

Given these terms, the farmer maximizes his income, Y, with respect to K:

$$Y = \beta p F(K) - \alpha(1 + r)K. \tag{12}$$

---

[4] Although in this section we emphasize the credit market imperfection, one should note that the interlinked contract also saves the trader and the farmer the transaction cost of finding each other in the product market, just as in the preceding section the interlinked contract also saves transaction costs in the labour market.

[5] This model is based on Gangopadhyay and Sengupta (1987). It does not consider uncertainty. For a model with linked product and credit contracts with uncertainty, see Bell and Srinivasan (1989).

The first-order condition of maximization yields

$$\beta p F'(K) = \alpha(1 + r). \tag{13}$$

The minimum income the farmer can get even without entering the contract with the trader is

$$\underline{Y} = \max_K [pF(K) - K(1 + r^0)]. \tag{14}$$

The trader maximizes his income.

$$\pi(\alpha, \beta) = (1 - \beta)pF(K) - (1 - \alpha)(1 + r)K, \tag{15}$$

subject to (13) and the constraint that the farmer gets at least his reservation income, $\underline{Y}$. It is in the interest of the trader to drive the farmer's income level to this minimum. The first term on the right-hand side of (15) is the trader–lender's gain from trading and the second term is his interest income.

It is now easy to show that the trader's optimal contract (α^*, β^*) is given by

$$\alpha^* = \beta^* = \gamma = \frac{\underline{Y}}{\max_K [pF(K) - K(1+r)]} < 1, \tag{16}$$

where γ is less than unity since $r^0 > r$. π from (15) can be rewritten as $[pF(K) - (1 + r)K] - Y$. If Y is pressed down to $\underline{Y}$, then π will be maximized for the trader when he maximizes $[pF(K) - (1 + r)K]$. The first-order condition for this maximum, combined with (13) yields $\alpha^* = \beta^*$. In that situation Y, from (12), is $\alpha^*[pF(K) - (1 + r)K]$, which, when equalized to $\underline{Y}$ from (14), yields $\alpha^* < 1$.

Thus, the farmer is given an interest discount (i.e. $i < r$), which is compensated by the underpayment in the output market $(q < p)$.[6] Even though the farmer faces a credit market imperfection $(r^0 > r)$, interlinkage allows the trader to counteract the possible effect of this imperfection on the farmer's production efficiency and to squeeze the maximum surplus over the farmer's reservation income.[7] An obvious policy conclusion is that, if our objective is to prevent underpayment to farmers in the output market, an intervention in the credit market may be called for; an intervention directly in the output market will lead to inefficiency.

---

[6] We are, of course, ignoring the additional underpayment that is often involved in the real world in the form of the farmer having to sell immediately after the harvest and not being able to wait for a better price in the post-harvest season.

[7] See Gangopadhyay and Sengupta (1987) for additional results in the case where farmers differ in their reservation income levels.

IV

In the preceding two sections, interlinkage provides the lender a way of ensuring that the borrower chooses an efficient level of the loan, so that he can then remove from the latter the entire surplus by a suitable 'tax'. There are other examples in the literature where interlinkage serves similar surplus-enhancing functions for the landlord–creditor. For example, in situations of moral hazard with respect to unobserved work effort (or risk-taking), interlinked transactions can internalize some externalities. Braverman and Stiglitz (1982) analyse a tenancy-cum-credit contract from this point of view. The landlord, by altering the terms and amount of the loan that he makes available to the tenant, can induce her to work harder or to undertake projects that are more to the landlord's liking (for example projects with yields of higher mean as well as greater variance). Thus, if there is a positive externality of credit, there will be an incentive for the landlord to encourage the tenant to become indebted to him. In the context of moral hazard it is also important to note that interlinked transactions can save on contract enforcement costs by making the possible discovery of dishonesty or default or shirking by an agent in one transaction too costly for her in terms of the threat to other transactions of its spillover effects (and the general loss of goodwill in the small closed world of a peasant community).

The preceding two sections model ways of counteracting the effects of imperfections in the credit market;[8] in similar ways interlinkage may provide a way of partially circumventing incomplete or non-existent markets (like that of insurance). Kotwal (1985) shows how, in the absence of an insurance market, credit as a weather-dependent side payment in tenancy (whereby in a bad year the landlord gives credit to the tenant who pays him back in a better year) may solve the trade-off problem between risk-sharing and incentives that, as we have discussed in Chapter 6, is central to the tenancy literature.

As we have seen, while interlinkage may serve the cause of efficiency, it may at the same time allow a monopolist to extract the total surplus, i.e. to be an extortionate monopolist. Even in a situation of potential oligopolistic competition, the very nature of personalized interlinking may act as a formidable barrier to entry for other parties. As Ray and Sengupta (1989) show, in a two-stage model of Bertrand competition, the ability to interlock yields differential advantages to the lenders (one, say, a landlord, and the other a trader), depending on the

---

[8] It is an open question why credit transactions are so frequently interlinked with other transactions. Rogerson (1985) argues that, in repeated principal–agent games (with a risk-neutral principal and risk-averse agents), the principal needs to control the intertemporal allocation of consumption of the agent (and hence needs to control the agent's access to credit), in order to gain more leverage on the use of the non-contractible input by the agent. On the agent's side, credit is often such an overwhelming constraint that the agent is often prepared to forgo some freedom of operation in another market to obtain credit.

varying characteristics of the borrowers. For a group of heterogeneous borrowers, there emerges a predictable division of these borrowers among the lenders.[9]

In a model of fragmented duopoly, where the duopolists each have a 'captive' segment (where each is a monopolist) and a common 'contested' segment (where each competes in the usual way with the other duopolist), Basu and Bell (1991) have shown how interlinkage may be a part of the duopolist lender's strategic interest in expanding his captive segment: a landlord may employ more labourers than otherwise, as he keeps in mind the leverage this gives him in the credit market. Mishra (1994) has extended this line of inquiry to show that a duopolist (say, a landlord–creditor), through precommitment to a suitable choice of his captive segment (e.g. a pool of labourer–borrowers), can prevent the entry of competitors (say, pure creditors) in the contested segment.

Most models of interlinkage attribute the decision to interlink entirely to the principal (say, the landlord), as the agent (e.g. the peasant) is by assumption pressed down to a given reservation utility, and so neither gains nor loses from interlinkage. If one goes beyond models with 'utility-equivalent contracts' for the peasants, it is possible to capture some of the adverse effects for them of the additional monopoly power that interlinkage may, as suggested above, bestow on the landlord–creditor. In addition, it is important to point out that personalized interlocking of labour commitments and credit transactions (involving selective exclusion of others) often divide the workers and weaken their collective bargaining strength *vis-à-vis* employers.[10]

Bell (1988) notes how in a Nash bargaining framework the peasant may be worse off with an interlinked set of transactions than with a set of separate bilateral bargains[11] (even when the utility possibility frontier itself shifts outward with interlinking). Figure 9.1 illustrates this simple idea. The lower curve represents the landlord–peasant utility possibility frontier *without* credit interlinkage, and the upper curve represents the frontier *with* interlinkage. D is the disagreement payoff point (where the peasant gets her minimum reservation utility), and P is the standard equilibrium in a principal–agent situation, which shifts to P' with interlinkage (with the peasant still down to her reservation utility). At P', compared with P, the peasant is no worse off, and the landlord is better off. But in a bargaining framework, let us suppose that N represents the

---

[9] Ray and Sengupta (1989) spell out the conditions necessary for the 'interlocker's edge' in surplus extraction over say, the pure moneylender. These conditions include an inability to have direct nonlinear pricing in the credit market, special advantages the interlocker may enjoy either in terms of the market domain or observability of contract variables, etc.

[10] In their survey in rural West Bengal, Bardhan and Rudra (1981) found that, in villages where some form of group bargaining or labour agitation for agricultural wage increase took place, most of the labour respondents who had interlinked credit contracts with their landlords reported non-participation in the movements, and the majority of them cited their ties with the landlord as the primary reason for their non-participation.

[11] For a more complex analysis of the effects of interlinking on welfare, in both partial and general equilibrium, in a bargaining context, see Bell (1988).

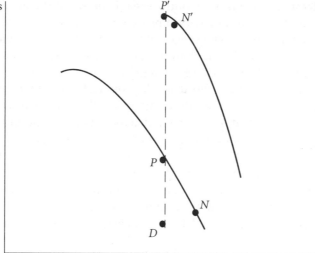

Figure 9.1

Nash bargaining solution without interlinkage. Now with interlinkage it is possible to end up at N', where the peasant is worse off,[12] even though interlinkage has shifted the utility possibility frontier outward (as implied by the usual efficiency rationale for interlinking discussed earlier).

So far we have generally considered only cases of two-party interlinking. There are, however, many cases of more complicated three-cornered interlinked exchange. For example, Bhalla (1976) cites a case from her study of Haryana villages in North India: the worker gets supplies of essential consumer goods on credit from the village shopkeeper or grain dealer, which are repaid with her labour services to the landlord–employer (in the form of underpaid wages), who in turn repays the original creditor by adjusting his account with the latter for grain deliveries or purchases. In three-way relations it may be possible for the strong party (say, the landlord) to extract more surplus from the worker than if he were involved in only a dyadic relation. Basu (1986) has constructed a model where the landlord can even press the worker *below* the latter's reservation utility in the dyadic case, by credibly threatening that, if the worker does not accept his terms, not merely will he refuse to employ her, but he will persuade the shopkeeper not to trade with her; the threat is credible because the shopkeeper, if he has to choose between a larger and a smaller customer, will opt for the former.

[12] This result is, of course, sensitive to the solution concept used. For example, if we replace Nash's solution with that of Kalai and Smorodinsky (1975)—who use an axiom of monotonicity instead of the Nash axiom of independence of irrelevant alternatives—the result will be quite different.

Finally, let us comment on a controversial issue about the impact of inter-linking on adoption of productivity improvements. This issue was first formally raised by Bhaduri (1973), who suggested that a landlord–lender may discourage such improvements by the sharecropper–borrower, since the former may lose more in interest income, even though his rental income goes up, as the latter becomes better off and less dependent on the landlord for consumption credit. Several people have made the counterpoint that, especially in the kind of institutional setting Bhaduri had in mind, a monopolistic landlord can always manipulate the interest or the rental rate to gain from a productivity increase. In addition, Srinivasan (1979) shows in a model of tenancy-cum-credit, that a productivity improvement need not lead to a fall in consumption credit to the the tenant. Since this latter model may be of some independent interest from the point of view of interlinkage in the context of production uncertainty (ignored in the models of Sections II and III), we shall briefly sketch a simplified version of it.

There are two periods. In the first, the slack season, the sharecropper borrows an amount B from the landlord for her consumption in that period as she has no other source of income and no other source of credit. The mean output x, harvested in the second period, is assumed to be given (i.e. not subject to choice), whereas the actual output is θx, where θ is a random variable (the probability distribution of which is known), with an expected value of unity. The sharecropper gets to keep a fraction α of the harvest, and i is the rate of interest on her borrowing B.

If the harvest turns out to be sufficiently good, the sharecropper pays her rent and repays her loan in the second period and consumes the rest. But if the harvest net of loan repayment is too small to cover her minimum subsistence consumption in the second period, denoted by $\underline{c}$, she repays the balance at a stipulated price of working γ days of labour per unit of the loan amount owed to the landlord–employer. In other words, any default in loan repayment has to be paid to the landlord with obligatory and 'underpaid' labour service (i.e. rendered at less than the labourer's opportunity cost). Such labour service, denoted by l, causes disutility to the sharecropper, denoted by $v(l)$. We shall take her utility function in each period to be additively separable, composed of $u(c) - v(l)$, where $u(c)$ is utility from consumption. We shall assume u to be concave and v to be convex, in the usual way. Also, $u(\underline{c}) = v(0) = 0$, by normalization. We shall call V the expected value of the sharecropper's discounted sum of utilities over the two periods and β the discount factor. The sharecropper chooses her level of borrowing B in the first period to maximize V.

Since there is no obligatory labour in the first period, the sharecropper's utility is just given by $u(B)$. In the second period her consumption is $[\alpha\theta x - (1 + i)B]$ and no obligatory labour if $\theta\alpha x > \underline{c} + (1 + i)B$. Otherwise, her consumption is $\underline{c}$, and her obligatory labour is given by $\gamma\{[\underline{c} + (1 + i)B] - \alpha\theta x\}$.

Denoting $\{\underline{c} + (1 + i)B\}/\alpha x$ as z, the sharecropper's maximand is

$$V(B) = u(B) + \beta\{\int_{\underline{\theta}}^{z}\{-v(\gamma\alpha x(z-\theta))]f(\theta)\,d\theta + \int_{z}^{\bar{\theta}} u(\alpha\theta x - \alpha xz + \underline{c})f(\theta)\,d\theta\},$$
$$(17)$$

where $f(\theta)$ is the probability density of θ, with $\underline{\theta}$ and $\bar{\theta}$ as the minimum and maximum values respectively of θ.

From the first- and second-order conditions of maximization in (17), we can work out the comparative statics of how B will change with changes in mean output x. In particular,

$$\frac{dB}{dx} > 0 \quad \text{if} \quad v'(0)/u'(c) > 1/\gamma.$$

In this last inequality the left-hand side is the sharecropper's opportunity cost of leisure (evaluated at the point of maximum leisure and minimum consumption) or the marginal rate of substitution between labour and consumption; the right-hand side is the implicit wage paid by the landlord for obligatory labour. (The left-hand side will be even higher at higher consumption.) This inequality condition is the essence of the unpleasantness of obligatory labour, i.e. of having to provide labour services at below opportunity cost. So under this condition consumption borrowing is an increasing function of mean output. Thus the sharecropper will not reduce her borrowing when productivity increases.

Going back to the general question of interlinking and innovation, some complications arise[13] in situations of moral hazard or of bilateral bargaining (both ignored in the preceding model). For example, in the tenancy-cum-credit model with uncertainty and moral hazard, with respect to the tenant's effort, any binding restriction on the landlord's control over the two instruments of crop share, α, and the interest rate, i, may make it difficult for the landlord to balance the need to share risks and the need to provide incentives for effort, and thus may render some productivity increases unprofitable for him. In bilateral bargaining settings, when neither the landlord nor the tenant has unilateral power, the decision to adopt yield-increasing improvements may be the outcome of a cooperative game. The improvements may be rejected if there is a non-neutral shift in the bargaining frontier (say, with an improvement that also increases risk), or even when there is a neutral shift, if there is a large enough change in the tenant's disagreement payoff as a result of the improvements.

---

[13] For a fuller discussion see Bell (1988).

REFERENCES

Anderson, P. (1974), *Lineages of the Absolutist State*. London: New Left Books.

Bailey, F. G. (1971), 'The Peasant View of the Bad Life', in T. Shanin (ed.), *Peasants and Peasant Societies*. Harmondsworth: Penguin Books.

Bardhan, P. (1984), *Land, Labor, and Rural Poverty*. New York: Columbia University Press.

—— and Rudra, A. (1981), 'Terms and Conditions of Labor Contracts in Agriculture: Results of a Survey in West Bengal, 1979', *Oxford Bulletin of Economics and Statistics*, 43.

Basu, K. (1986), 'One Kind of Power', *Oxford Economic Papers*, 38.

—— and Bell, C. (1991), 'Fragmented Duopoly: Theory and Application to Backward Agriculture', *Journal of Development Economics*, 36.

Bell, C. (1988), 'Credit Markets and Interlinked Transactions', in H. B.Chenery and T. N.Srinivasan (eds.), *Handbook of Development Economics*, i. Amsterdam: North-Holland.

—— and Srinivasan, T. N. (1989), 'Some Aspects of Linked Product and Credit Market Contracts among Risk-neutral Agents', in P. Bardhan (ed.), *The Economic Theory of Agrarian Institutions*. Oxford: Clarendon Press.

Bhaduri, A. (1973), 'A Study in Agricultural Backwardness under Semi-feudalism', *Economic Journal*, 83.

Bhalla, S. (1976), 'New Relations of Production in Haryana Agriculture', *Economic and Political Weekly*, 27 March.

Braverman, A., and Stiglitz, J. F. (1982) 'Sharecropping and the Interlinking of Agrarian Markets', *American Economic Review*, 72.

Gangopadhyay, S., and Sengupta, K. (1987), 'Small Farmers, Moneylenders, and Trading Activity', *Oxford Economic Papers*, 39.

Kalai, E., and Smorodinsky, M. (1975), 'Other Solutions to Nash's Bargaining Problem', *Econometrica*, 43.

Kotwal, A. (1985), 'The Role of Consumption Credit in Agricultural Tenancy', *Journal of Development Economics*, 18.

Mishra, A. (1994), 'Clientelization and Fragmentation in Backward Agriculture: Forward Induction and Entry Deterrence', *Journal of Development Economics*, 45.

Okun, A. M. (1981), *Prices and Quantities: A Macroeconomic Analysis*. Washington: Brookings Institution.

Ray, D., and Sengupta, K. (1989), 'Interlinkages and the Pattern of Competition', in P. Bardhan (ed.), *The Economic Theory of Agrarian Institutions*. Oxford: Clarendon Press.

Rogerson, W. P. (1985), 'Repeated Moral Hazard', *Econometrica*, 53.

Srinivasan, T. N. (1979), 'Bonded Labor Contracts and Incentives to Adopt Yield-Raising Innovations in Semi-feudal Agriculture', *Economic Journal*, 89.

10

Human Capital
and Income Distribution

I

Improvements in the health and education of people are central to the development process. Clearly, people place a high value on the health and education of themselves and their family members, and thus improvements in these fields must be a goal of development. At the same time, the health and education of an individual have an important effect on that individual's capability to produce. A healthier, better educated person is capable of producing more, and this improved productivity is rewarded in the labour market. The commitment of current resources to improving an individual's health or education, therefore, increases that person's future productivity and income.

The use of the term 'human capital' as shorthand for the cluster of such factors as nutrition, health, formal education, and on-the-job training, which are embodied in an individual and which provide future advantages, focuses attention on the role of expenditures on these factors as investments. This focus is a powerful analytical device, and will prove particularly useful in exploring the links between the distribution of expenditures on human capital and the distributions of income and wealth. At the same time, however, this focus should not detract from the recognition of the value that people place on good health and education in themselves, apart from their instrumental role in generating future income.

The population of a poor country, of course, is not uniformly poor. There is persistent poverty in every poor country, and in many cases there is a high degree of income inequality. One of the most visible manifestations of this inequality is the wide dispersion in the health and education attained by people living in any poor country. In this chapter we will explore the idea that there is joint causation between income and human capital, and that this, combined with increasing returns to investments in human capital and (imperfect) credit markets, generates a *poverty trap*. Relatively wealthy individuals are able to invest in human capital, and this enables them to earn enough income to remain wealthy. Conversely, the poor are unable to invest in human capital, and thus earn low incomes and remain poor. The joint causation of human capital investment and income, therefore, can provide a theory of the distribution of income. An example of such a theory is provided in Section III of this chapter.

Economists hypothesize that the educational attainment, health, and nutrition of an individual affect that person's labour power. An improvement in health, nutrition, or education increases a person's productivity and thus her income. There is in fact a very strong association between household income (or wealth) and these aspects of well-being. Any empirical investigation of the influence of human capital on income, however, is made difficult by the fact that people value the health and education of themselves and their family members. Richer people can afford to acquire more of these valued goods. The positive association between income, health, and education might reflect the positive elasticity of demand for the components of human capital rather than a direct link between human capital and productivity. Some of the challenges of investigating the empirical relationships between human capital and income are briefly discussed in Section II of this chapter.

The level and distribution of human capital within an economy also have important effects on the rate of technological innovation in that society. These links are explored in some detail in Chapter 12.

II

That there is two-way causality between income and human capital can hardly be disputed. There is clearly a demand-side effect of income on each of the components of human capital. The very phrase 'human capital' reminds us of the reverse causation, from an individual's health and education to her productivity, wage, and income. The strength of each of these relationships, however, is an empirical matter and is subject to ongoing debate.

To illustrate the difficulty of measuring the strength of these relationships, consider what might be the simplest of the relationships: the income elasticity of demand for calories. Conventional estimates of this elasticity in poor countries range from around 0.5 to about 1. Behrman and Deolalikar (1987), Bouis and Haddad (1992), and Bouis (1994), however, all argue that the actual elasticity is near zero. It can be argued that the standard estimates are biased upwards for four important reasons. First, there is the likelihood that income is not exogenous, owing to the feedback from nutrition to productivity. Second, many estimates of the calorie demand are calculated from reports of expenditure on broad groups of food, converted to calories via standard nutrition tables; as incomes rise, people may be consuming more expensive foods within these groups, biasing upwards the calculated income elasticity of demand for calories. Third, much of the food consumed in poor countries is produced on people's own farms and thus is also a component of income; thus, any measurement error in the production of food on one's own farm is common to both income and calories, biasing upwards the calculated elasticity. Finally, unrecorded gifts of food probably flow mostly from richer to poorer households, so calorie consumption is understated for the poor and overstated for the rich, again biasing the estimated elasticity upwards.

These comments nicely illustrate some of the difficulties of measuring the relationship between income and human capital outcomes, but the conclusion of the above authors is probably overstated. Instrumental variable procedures have been used both to address the endogeneity of income and to correct the bias induced by measurement error, and attention has been drawn to the strong nonlinearities that appear to exist in the relationship between income and calorie consumption (see Thomas and Strauss 1997). The weight of the evidence is that the elasticity of demand for calories is relatively high (but less than 1) for poor households, declining to around zero as household income rises.

Despite the cavils regarding the specifics, the general point, i.e. that the demand for the components of human capital increases with income, is well established. There is also strong evidence regarding the strength of the reverse relationship, from aspects of human capital to productivity and income. Consider first the effect of education on productivity. There is clear-cut evidence of a strong positive relationship between the schooling of a child and that child's future earnings. There is however a variety of conceptual and statistical difficulties which complicate the interpretation of this regularity.[1] However, it is most convincingly explained with reference to the role of education as an investment in human capital which increases the future productivity of the individual. Moreover, it appears to be the case that the increase in earnings associated with additional education is much higher in poor countries than in rich countries—on the order of twice as high (see Psacharopoulos 1985 and Schultz 1988).

The possibility that a worker's health and nutritional status affect her productivity underlies the notion of the efficiency wage discussed in Chapter 4. Although the initial theoretical work on the implications of a direct link from

---

[1] Most importantly, it is possible to construct any number of arguments that rationalize the fact that the wealthy are relatively well educated without a causal relationship between education and productivity, Spence's (1973) screening model being the most familiar. Schultz (1988) provides a good review of the statistical problems associated with estimating the effect of education on productivity. The most important of these is the fact that an individual's level of education is not randomly allocated across any population, but rather is chosen. Therefore, statistical evidence regarding the relationship between education and earnings can be misleading owing to correlations between education and omitted factors (like ability, or class background), which themselves affect earnings.

health and nutrition to productivity rested on quite weak empirical grounds, evidence regarding the importance of this relationship has grown rapidly in the past decade. The work reviewed by Strauss and Thomas (1995) now clearly establishes that health and nutritional status are important determinants of productivity and earnings in poor countries.

III

This section examines the implications of the interdependence between income and human capital using a model due to Ljungqvist (1993). This model serves to illustrate three important theoretical points. First, the feedback between income and human capital investments can serve as the basis of a theory of the distribution of income. Richer families are able to invest more in human capital, and thereby to earn more in the future. This reasoning applies to the distribution of income within a nation, and also can serve as part of the explanation for international differences in average income. Second, this reasoning depends on a form of increasing returns in human capital investment. If the returns to investing in human capital are smoothly diminishing, then (at least in the long run) everyone will wind up with a similar level of human capital. Finally, the persistence of inequalities in incomes and human capital depends on imperfections in the capital market. If everyone has access to the same investment opportunities, then (again, at least in the long run) incomes and levels of human capital will converge. To illustrate these points, the model makes dramatic simplifications. Perhaps most importantly, it makes the now-standard assumption in the literature on human capital that education serves only to increase future income: it is not valued itself.

We begin by assuming that all agents have the same preferences and basic abilities. The agents live forever and maximize a standard, additively separable, utility function,

$$\int_0^\infty e^{-\rho t} U(c_t) dt, \tag{1}$$

where c_t is the consumption at time t of the single good that is produced. The good is internationally traded, and each country's output is determined by constant returns to scale production function using physical capital (K_t), unskilled labour (U_t), and skilled labour (S_t), i.e. $F(K_t, U_t, S_t)$. An unskilled labourer can be (instantaneously) transformed into a skilled labourer using $\gamma (<1)$ skilled labourers (educators). This education enables the worker to remain skilled for one period, after which she must be retrained. The natural interpretation is that each period represents a generation, and that the agents represent a type of family dynasty.

We will consider only steady-state equilibria; therefore we drop the time subscript t from all notation. There are three types of employment: working as a skilled labourer (S), working as an educator (E), and working as an unskilled labourer (U). Normalizing the population to 1, we have $S + E + U = 1$. Let H be the number of educated workers. Thus, $S + E = H$. Recalling that educated workers have to be retrained after one period, it can be seen that in a steady state the number of teachers required to maintain the stock H of educated workers is $E = \gamma H$. Thus, the number of skilled workers engaged in production is $S = (1 - \gamma)H$, and the number of unskilled workers is $U = 1 - H$. We assume that workers cannot borrow to finance their education. Therefore, the cost of education (the wages of the teacher) must be accumulated as savings before a worker can be educated.

It can now be seen that the state of the country's economy (in steady state) is determined fully by the number of educated workers, H. Physical capital is internationally traded at a discount rate equal to ρ. Thus, for any number of educated workers, the equilibrium stock of capital in the country is determined implicitly by

$$\rho = F_3((1 - \gamma)H, 1 - H, K(H)), \tag{2}$$

where the subscript i indicates the partial derivative with respect to the ith argument. In turn, the wages of educated workers (skilled labourers and educators) and uneducated workers are determined by

$$w_s(H) = F_1((1 - \gamma)H, 1 - H, K(H)), \tag{3}$$
$$w_U(H) = F_2((1 - \gamma)H, 1 - H, K(H)).$$

The rate of return on human capital investments $r(H)$ is determined implicitly by

$$\gamma w_s(H) = \int_0^1 e^{-r(H)\tau}(w_s(H) - w_U(H))\mathrm{d}\tau. \tag{4}$$

The left-hand side is the cost of education, while the right-hand side is the discounted value of the increase in wages consequent upon being educated.

A number of educated workers H will characterize a stead-state equilibrium if, at the factor prices determined by that number, educated workers choose to maintain their training (by paying for renewed education in each period) and uneducated workers choose not to invest in education. Educated workers will choose to maintain their education if the rate of return on human capital as defined in (4) is at least as high as ρ, the return on investing in physical capital. This will be the case as long as the wage differential between trained and untrained workers is large enough. If we assume that the technology is such that the marginal rate of substitution between skilled and unskilled workers is diminishing for any positive K, then the wage differential is decreasing in H. Therefore, if there is an H^* such that $r(H^*) = \rho$, then $r(H) > \rho$ for all $H < H^*$.

that is, if there is some number of trained workers such that the wage differential in a steady state is large enough that the return to being trained is as high as the return on physical capital, then the return to training will be greater than the return to physical capital for any steady state with a smaller number of trained workers.

The existence of some $H^* > 0$ is guaranteed if the education technology is sufficiently productive relative to the return on physical capital,[2] and if

$$\text{Lim}_{H \to 0} w_U = 0 \text{ and } \text{Lim}_{H \to 0} w_s > 0. \tag{5}$$

The assumptions in (5) guarantee that, as the number of skilled workers declines, the ratio of the skilled to the unskilled wage gets arbitrarily large. Thus, there is a number of educated workers $H^* > 0$ at which the return to investment in education is at least as high as the return to holding physical capital. In steady states with this or any lower number of educated workers, dynasties of educated workers will choose to invest in the education of each successive generation of workers.[3]

It now remains to be seen whether there exists a number of educated workers $H \in (0, H^*)$ such that uneducated workers do not invest in education, and thus remain employed as unskilled labour. If so, then this number of educated workers characterizes an equilibrium for this economy.

Since, for any number of educated workers $H \in (0, H^*)$, the return to investing in education is at least as high as that to investing in physical capital, uneducated workers would choose to invest in education if they had sufficient capital, or if they could borrow to finance the training. Our assumption of an imperfect capital market, such that future labour earnings cannot serve as collateral for a loan for education, is therefore essential. Were there to be a perfect capital market, there could be no steady state with $H < H^*$, and people would be indifferent between investing in education and investing in physical capital.

Consider an uneducated individual with no assets. The rate of time preference is equal to the interest rate, so she prefers a constant stream of consumption. If she chooses to remain uneducated, her constant flow of consumption is

$$c_u = w_u. \tag{6}$$

Once she has been trained, she can consume at the constant rate of

$$c_s = w_s. \tag{7}$$

She can become an educated worker by paying the cost of γw_s. In order to accumulate the savings required to pay for training, she will have to reduce her

---

[2] Specifically, $1 - \rho\gamma > e^{-\rho}$ guarantees that education is sufficiently productive to be profitable as H approaches zero.

[3] We have simplified a bit here. It is possible that $r(1) > \rho$, in which case there is no H^*. In this case, in any steady state all educated workers choose to reinvest in education each period.

consumption below c_u for some period. During this accumulation phase, it will be optimal to choose a constant consumption stream, say $c_a < c_u$. Given c_a, the length of time $T(c_a)$ it will take to accumulate γw_s is determined by

$$\int_0^{T(c_a)} e^{\rho t}(w_u - c_a)dt = \gamma w_s. \tag{8}$$

This uneducated worker can choose low current consumption with rapid accumulation, and thus early training, or higher current consumption with slower accumulation, and a longer delay until she achieves the higher consumption level of c_s. She thus chooses c_a to

$$\underset{c_a}{\text{Max}} \int_0^{T(c_a)} e^{-\rho t}U(c_a)dt + \int_{T(c_a)}^{\infty} e^{-\rho t}U(c_s)dt, \tag{9}$$

subject to $c_a < w_u$. Suppose c^* solves (9). The worker will decide *not* to invest in education if

$$\int_0^{T(c^*)} e^{-\rho t}U(c^*)dt + \int_{T(c^*)}^{\infty} e^{-\rho t}U(c_s)dt \leq \int_0^{\infty} e^{-\rho t}U(c_u)dt. \tag{10}$$

Consider the inequality (10) as $H \to 0$. Given the assumptions in (5), as the number of educated workers gets smaller, the unskilled wage approaches zero, while the skilled wage remains bounded away from zero. c^*, which is strictly less than the unskilled wage, approaches zero faster than the unskilled wage. At the same time, the cost of education (γw_s) gets larger relative to the unskilled wage. The time it takes to accumulate the savings required for training increases. If we make the usual Inada assumption that the marginal utility of consumption approaches infinity as consumption approaches zero, then the loss of utility for giving up consumption to accumulate savings for education outweighs the delayed gain from higher consumption in the future. For any small enough H, inequality (10) holds and an uneducated worker with no assets has to remain uneducated. Any $H \leq H^*$ for which (10) holds therefore, can be an equilibrium. Educated workers choose to remain skilled. (H is less than or equal to H^*, so the return to investment in education is at least as great as the return to physical capital.) Uneducated workers with no assets remain unskilled and assetless, because the cost of forgoing enough consumption for long enough to accumulate the savings needed to finance training is too high.

This model provides a simple theory of persistent income inequality generated by inequalities in human capital. The rich can afford to invest in human capital, and as a consequence earn high incomes and remain rich. The poor cannot afford training, and thus earn low incomes and remain poor. There are two features of the model that are essential for generating this persistent inequality. First, there is a crucial imperfection in credit markets. Workers cannot borrow to finance their educations, presumably because the future increased earnings from training cannot be pledged as collateral for a loan. If education loans *were* to be available, then, as long as education was a valuable investment (that is, as long as the return to education was at least as large as the return to physical capital), uneducated workers would simply borrow enough to fund training, repaying the loan from the consequent increased earnings. Income inequality would not persist without a failure of the credit market.

Second, there is a strong form of increasing returns to human capital investment. In this model, a worker is either educated or uneducated—education is not divisible. A small expenditure on training (less than that required to train a worker fully) therefore earns no return at all. It is the difficulty of reducing consumption by enough, and for long enough, to save up the lump sum required to finance education that prevents uneducated workers from becoming trained. If investment in human capital instead displayed 'normal' diminishing returns, currently uneducated workers would gradually accumulate education until all workers were equally well trained. It will be recalled from Chapter 4 that a similar assumption regarding increasing returns to nutrition generated an efficiency wage in the labour market.

Finally, it should be noted that the twin assumptions of an imperfect capital market and increasing returns to human capital investment (along with the variety of more specific technical assumptions that we have made) generate not only a theory of the distribution of income, but also a continuum of equilibria. We have seen that it is possible to have steady-state equilibria with an entire range of trained workers. Steady-state equilibria exist with large numbers of trained workers, a relatively low differential between skilled and unskilled wages, and a rate of return to education that just equals the return to investment in physical capital. Equilibria also exist with small numbers of trained workers, very large differences in the wages earned by skilled and unskilled workers, a very high return to education, and a pool of untrained workers who cannot afford to reduce their consumption by enough to save up the funds required for training.

In this chapter, we have discussed only one of several possible mechanisms through which the interaction between human capital and income can generate poverty traps and persistent income inequality. It is important to recall other possible mechanisms, three of which have been discussed in less detail earlier. Nutrition is one such potential mechanism; this has been discussed briefly in Chapter 4. Dasgupta (1993) provides a full model in which the interconnections between nutrition and income result in a particularly virulent poverty trap. Second, in our discussion of migration in Chapter 5, we mentioned a model in which the externalities associated with neighbourhoods, particularly through the local externalities associated with education, can cause persistent poverty. Finally, in Chapter 7 we discussed a model in which credit market imperfections interacted with occupational choice to yield a poverty trap.

REFERENCES

Behrman, J., and Deolalikar, A. (1987), 'Will Developing Country Nutrition Improve with Income? A Case Study for Rural South Asia', *Journal of Political Economy*, 95.

Bouis, H. E. (1994), 'The Effect of Income on Demand for Food in Poor Countries: Are Our Databases Giving Us Reliable Estimates?' *Journal of Development Economics*, 44.

—— and Haddad, L. (1992), 'Are Estimates of Calorie-Income Elasticities too High? A Recalibration of the Plausible Range', *Journal of Development Economics*, 39.

Dasgupta, P. (1993), *An Inquiry into Well-Being and Destitution*. Oxford: Clarendon Press.

Ljungqvist, L. (1993), 'Economic Underdevelopment: The Case of a Missing Market for Human Capital', *Journal of Development Economics*, 40.

Psacharopoulos, G. (1985), 'Returns to Education: A Further International Update and Implications', *Journal of Human Resources*, 20.

Schultz, T. P. (1988), 'Education Investments and Returns', in H. Chenery and T. N. Srinivasan (eds.), *Handbook of Development Economics*, i. Amsterdam: North-Holland.

Spence, A. M. (1973), 'Job Market Signalling', *Quarterly Journal of Economics*, 87.

Strauss, J., and Thomas, D. (1995), 'Human Resources: Empirical Modeling of Household and Family Decisions', in J. Behrman and T. N. Srinivasan (eds.), *Handbook of Development Economics*, iiiA. Amsterdam: Elsevier Science.

Thomas, D., and Strauss, J. (1997), 'Health, Wealth and Wages of Men and Women in Urban Brazil', *Journal of Econometrics*, 77.

11

Poverty Alleviation: Efficiency and Equity Issues

I

In the poor countries of sub-Saharan Africa and South Asia (the areas where mass poverty in the world is geographically concentrated), poverty by any reasonable measure is so pervasive that policies of poverty alleviation encompass practically the whole range of development policies. Most policies that affect the national economy significantly have substantial implications for the poor. The efficiency–equity trade-off that is at the heart of much of mainstream policy economics is thus central to the policy debates on poverty. A society may very well consider the objective of redistribution in favour of the poor a sufficiently worthwhile goal to warrant some sacrifice in terms of efficiency. But if such a redistribution comes at a substantial cost in terms of misallocated resources and aggregate income losses, it may not be politically or economically sustainable; in fact, it can be a much more serious issue in economic policy in poor countries (both because the poor form a much larger proportion of the population and because one can afford such losses less at low levels of income) than the controversies that rage around the efficiency impact of the 'welfare' budget in rich countries.

This issue is reflected in a running policy debate over the last twenty-five years on the relative importance of market-driven growth trickling down to the poor versus a programme of massive and direct intervention to help the poor. In this chapter, after noting some aspects concerning the measurement of poverty, we briefly consider some of the issues in this debate, and proceed to situations where the efficiency–equity trade-off may be false or exaggerated (particularly when agency costs and coordination problems are taken into account), which in turn may have interesting policy implications in terms of possible efficiency-enhancing redistributive projects. In this context we shall also discuss the relative efficiency effects of asset distribution policies (like land reform) as opposed to tax-transfer policies that take the form of subsidies. Within transfer policies in general we shall discuss the merits and costs of efficient targeting, including issues of self-selection by the poor and of targeting underprivileged groups and backward areas. Finally, we consider governance structures and focus on the role of local self-governing institutions in improving efficiency and equity in poverty alleviation.

II

For a long time, the common practice in measuring poverty has been to count the numbers of people who fall below some poverty line (defined with varying degrees of arbitrariness) for income or consumer spending. Some adjustments are usually made to the poverty line in terms of changes in cost-of-living or household demographics. A large literature has developed on the various problems with this common poverty measurement practice,[1] including the limits of the usual income-centred or commodity-centred concept of well-being. One equity issue that has been emphasized is that the head-count measure is not sensitive to differences in the depth of poverty or to inequality *among* the poor. The literature, though not the common political parlance, has therefore moved towards more sophisticated measures, such as that in Foster *et al.* (1984): for a non-negative living standard indicator (say, consumption) y distributed with density $f(y)$, and with a poverty line z, the poverty measure P is given by

$$P = \int_0^z \left(\frac{z-y}{z} \right)^\alpha f(y) \mathrm{d}y, \quad \alpha \geq 0. \tag{1}$$

When α is 0, P is the same as the head-count measure; and when α is 1, P is what is known as the poverty gap index (therefore depending on the distances of the poor below the poverty line as well as on the number of the poor). As α increases, P becomes increasingly sensitive to the living standard indicator of the poorest people.

Given the various sources of arbitrariness in poverty measurement, one can still draw upon stochastic dominance criteria to make unambiguous comparative rankings of poverty. For example, if we do not know the precise poverty line z (but are sure that it does not exceed $\bar{z}$) or the precise poverty measure P, even then, as Atkinson (1987) shows, we can make unambiguous comparative rankings of poverty if the cumulative density function of y in one case lies completely outside that in another, up to $\bar{z}$. (If the cumulative density functions cross each other, then the ranking is ambiguous.)

---

[1] For an overview of the issues in poverty measurement practice, see Ravallion (1994).

In the recent empirical literature, decline in the poverty measure has often been found to be closely associated with high economic growth (most notably in East and South-east Asia). Lipton and Ravallion (1995) report estimates for eight developing countries (Bangladesh, Brazil, Côte d'Ivoire, India, Indonesia, Morocco, Nepal, and Tunisia) that a 2 per cent annual rate of growth in consumption per person will typically result in a decline in the poverty gap index of 3 to 8 per cent, using local poverty lines and assuming growth to be distributionally neutral. Whether growth will be distributionally neutral depends, of course, on the initial distribution of (physical and human) assets, the nature of imperfections in markets (particularly the capital market), the pattern of growth, factor bias in technology, and government policies (on, say, taxes and social welfare).

In general, the most important way for economic growth to help the poor is by expanding their opportunities for productive and remunerative employment (including self-employment on farms and in artisan shops). There is now some measure of agreement that policies that contribute to growth by improving the allocative efficiency of resource use (say, by reducing distortions in relative prices, exchange rates, and trade policies) may help the poor. This is particularly so if the traded goods sector is more labour-intensive than the non-traded goods sector, and if exports are more labour-intensive than import substitutes (assuming, of course, that the workers have some basic education and skills). Underpricing of scarce inputs—such as capital, energy, and environmental resources—often leads to the adoption of capital-intensive and environment-damaging projects that have adverse distributional consequences. Movements of domestic terms of trade in favour of agricultural commodities and a removal of restrictions on their trade may help the poor if the sector consists of a large number of small farmers who market a significant part of their output, and if the wages of landless labourers do not lag far behind the price rises.

Thus, the access of the poor to the avenues of growth is critical for poverty reduction. For many reasons, some of the poor may be excluded from the growth process. One of the most important cases arises in situations of severe capital market imperfections, when the escape routes from poverty for the unskilled and the assetless may remain blocked. The nature of the growth process itself can cause problems. For example, the centripetal forces of growth with increasing returns (agglomeration economies of scale[2]) may drain resources away from backward regions, reinforcing regional polarization, as economic geographers have repeatedly shown. Large projects of industrialization and commercialization may uproot and disenfranchize sections of the

[2] In the 'new economic geography' literature, which began with Krugman (1991), the agglomeration economies are endogenously determined by the interaction among economies of scale at the plant level, transportation costs, and factor mobility.

poor from their traditional habitats and their access to common property resources. In most of these cases the gainers can afford to compensate the losers, but in the actual political process they seldom do. Furthermore, in countries with high and persistent inequality, the trickle-down effects of even fairly high rates of growth have been so slow that without remedial pro-poor policy actions it will take an unconscionably long time before a sizeable dent is made in the backlog of poverty. Even where growth has been associated with substantial reductions in poverty, the association is often mediated by pro-poor social expenditure policies that are facilitated by growth, as Drèze and Sen (1989) have pointed out.

Just as growth can facilitate redistribution, there are many redistributive projects which, by relieving the severe constraints faced by the poor and improving their conditions, can help economic growth in the process. This runs somewhat contrary to the preoccupation of mainstream economics with the equity–efficiency trade-off, with its emphasis on the various costs of redistribution in terms of reduced economic incentives and performance. (In a widely cited passage, Okun (1975), for example, described redistribution as carrying money from the rich to the poor in a 'leaky bucket'.) There are, however, many situations, particularly in poor countries, when this famous trade-off may be false or at least exaggerated. One such situation, which non-economists are quick to point out, is when rampant poverty breeds crime (and other 'extra-legal appropriative activities', to use Grossman's (1992) term) and political instability, which can have damaging consequences for investment and macroeconomic efficiency in general. A second case relates to an old idea in development economics about the link between nutritional intake and work efficiency in situations of extreme poverty, which asserts that a better fed work-force is more productive. A potentially important corollary of this original brand of efficiency wage theory is, as we noted in Chapter 4, that a more egalitarian distribution of land, for example by reducing the malnourishment (and thus improving the employability) of the currently unemployed, may lead to a rise in the aggregate output in the economy, as shown by Dasgupta and Ray (1986).

A third type of situation, actually quite pervasive, arises when redistributive policies help economic growth by correcting market failures that particularly affect the poor. The imperfections of the credit and insurance markets are especially important here. These originate from problems of moral hazard, adverse selection, and enforcement, and the poor with low collateral or risk-bearing capacity find it particularly difficult to overcome these problems. These imperfections and the usually costly private adjustments to them (such as entering interlinked contracts with lenders, which squeeze the surplus out of the borrower, as we have seen in Chapter 9, or informal risk-sharing arrangements with kin members, which act like an implicit tax system with its deadweight losses), can cause poverty traps in which the poor get caught.[3] Expanding the opportunities for credit, for example, can help the poor to invest in education as a way of climbing out of poverty. It can also make small farmers and artisans more economically viable by allowing them to enlarge their scale of production, to take up more high-return, high-risk projects or occupational choices, and in general to avoid constrained myopic policies. In this way, redistributive policies can increase a society's aggregate potential for productive investment, innovation, and human resource development.

Some of these activities (like better education and health of the poor) also have important positive externalities for the rich. In addition, positive externalities arise in the context of gender-specific poverty alleviation policies. Better education for women is often associated with the better education, nutrition, and health of children (particularly daughters); better opportunities for outside work for young women can lead to socially more beneficial fertility behaviour (through, say, raising the age at marriage). Such externalities make gender equity and efficiency go together. Then there are important dynamic externalities that can arise from community or neighbourhood-specific characteristics; these may refer to physical infrastructure (e.g. roads, communications, irrigation and power systems) improving the productivity of private investment, or to adult human capital endowments (influencing the educational investment decisions of the young) in the neighbourhood, or, somewhat more intangibly, to what is often described as 'social capital' in the form of social networks, peer group effects, role models, connections in the job market, etc.

The lack of this social capital (over and above the usual lack of physical and human capital) has been emphasized in the studies by sociologists of poverty traps in the inner-city ghettos in the United States (see e.g. Wilson 1987), but similar effects may be observed in poor countries for backward areas or socially disadvantaged groups, or even for the rural sector in general, from which there is a continuous 'brain drain' to the cities. If these externalities are important, anti-poverty programmes have to go beyond policies addressed to individuals and households *per se*; policies aimed at poor areas and groups as a whole may be fruitful in terms of both equity and efficiency. We shall come back in Section IV to discuss the issue of preferential job and education policies for some disadvantaged groups in this context.

---

[3] For theoretical growth models that analyse the dynamic processes emanating from credit market imperfections and generating poverty traps even in the long run, see Banerjee and Newman (1993), Galor and Zeira (1993), and Aghion and Bolton (1997). In understanding why some families never get rich across generations, Galor and Zeira emphasize the impact of non-convex technology, where the credit-constrained poor family cannot overcome the minimum threshold size in investment in human capital; Banerjee and Newman show that poor people unable to afford the collateral required to be self-employed entrepreneurs or employers crowd the labour market and depress the wage rate (as we briefly noted in Chapter 7), and therefore the bequest they leave to their children; Aghion and Bolton focus on the capital market and the relationship between wealth inequality and the cost of borrowing and hence access to investment opportunities for the poor.

Going back to the case of credit and insurance market failures, such failures point to a general principle now recognized in the literature on imperfect information and agency costs: when information is incomplete and competing claims are seldom resolved in costlessly enforceable contracts, the usual separability of equity and efficiency of mainstream economics breaks down. Under the circumstances, the terms and conditions of contracts in various transactions that directly affect the efficiency of resource allocation crucially depend on who owns what and who is empowered to make which decisions. In general, redistributions of property rights, if they align control of non-contractible actions more closely with residual claims over the outcomes of these actions (for example a tenancy reform in agriculture which assigns residual claimancy rights to the tenant whose productive efforts are difficult to monitor for the landlord), will improve efficiency.

This general idea also has implications for economic governance structures.[4] Government failures in policy design and implementation (including in poverty alleviation) are caused partly by information and transaction costs. A realignment of the governance structure in favour of decentralization or devolution of power to a local level can create important incentives by placing decision-making in the hands of those who have localized information that outsiders (e.g. the central bureaucrats) lack. In situations where the state bureaucracy is thus informationally hamstrung while similar information problems render individual market contracts incomplete or unenforceable (as in the case of credit and insurance, mentioned above), a local community organization, if it has stable membership and well developed mechanisms for transmitting private information and norms among its members, has the potential to provide more efficient coordination than either the state or the market. We shall discuss this in the context of poverty alleviation in Section V.

III

Since credit market failure is widely regarded as one of the crucial factors behind the persistence of poverty, intervention in this market has been one of the major planks of anti-poverty policy. Over the last three decades there have been many cases in poor countries of the government trying to provide subsidized credit to the poor. The results have been mixed (as, for example, in the case of one of the largest credit programmes for asset-building by the rural poor in the world, the Integrated Rural Development Programme in India). Wealthier borrowers have often appropriated the credit subsidies meant for the

---

[4] For a comparative evaluation of markets, states, and communities in the context of coordination failures caused by agency problems, see Bowles and Gintis (1995).

poor. In general, underpricing of credit has led to inefficient use of capital. Credit administered through government or semi-government agencies weakens incentives to invest wisely or repay promptly: building the political connections to get debt relief and rent-seeking sometimes become more important than responsible investment behaviour. Political patronage in the matter of loan disbursement or moratorium has rendered the whole financial system quite shaky in some countries. Even ignoring the problem of political clientelism, the fundamental dilemma of the credit market is that outside agencies (including government banks) do not have enough local information about the borrower and monitoring is costly, and so they insist on collaterals that ration out many of the poor; on the other hand, the local lenders who have more personalized information about the borrower often use this informational entry barrier to the credit market to charge high interest rates.

In localized pockets in different parts of the world today, there are some success stories in resolving this dilemma through the use of borrower groups as mechanisms of overcoming information and enforcement problems—as in the widely cited Grameen Bank experiment in Bangladesh, where credit for groups of poor women is (supposedly) organized along lines of joint liability. Such group lending schemes seem to work best in small, relatively closed communities, where peer monitoring and social sanctions against local deviants are easier to organize and sustain over repeated transactions, and where the group members have largely uncorrelated but similar levels of income. In addition, when loan contracts are linked with explicit or implicit insurance against adverse shocks to income, borrowers default much less.

In a world of private and asymmetric information, a credit subsidy to a poor family may not be the best way to overcome the barriers faced by borrowers; in terms of efficiency, a lump-sum grant or asset transfer to the same family may be superior. Hoff and Lyon (1995) have a theoretical model to illustrate this in the context of financing investment in education or starting a new business (the probability of successfully completing the project being private information to the investor).[5] Suppose individuals (assumed risk-neutral) each have one such risky project that they are able to undertake with outside finance. Assume that all projects have the same rate of return R if they succeed and the same return of 0 if they fail, but the projects differ in their probability of success, p. If i and j are two individuals, and if $p_i > p_j$, then i is said to have a better project than j. If a project fails, the borrower has no income and cannot repay his or her debt.

Individual borrowers know the probability of success of their project, but lenders do not. (Lenders know only the distribution of project types.) A lending contract therefore can do no more than specify a collateral requirement and an interest rate. In a competitive market the interest rate will reflect the *average*

---

[5] We follow here the summary version of the argument given in Hoff (1996).

probability of success of the borrowers who provide that collateral. The best projects therefore cross-subsidize the worst, which induces entry by individuals with *negative* value projects. Let p^* be the success probability of the lowest-quality project that enters the credit market at any given collateral requirement and interest rate. Normalizing the opportunity cost of capital used in a project to be 1, the surplus, i.e. the combined revenues of lender and borrower, from a project of type p is $(pR - 1)$.

The lender knows only the distribution of project types in the economy. From his point of view, the expected surplus from a project undertaken by an individual who would be willing to undertake a project with success probability $p \geq p^*$ can be depicted as the area $S - L$ in Figure 11.1, where $h(p)$ denotes the

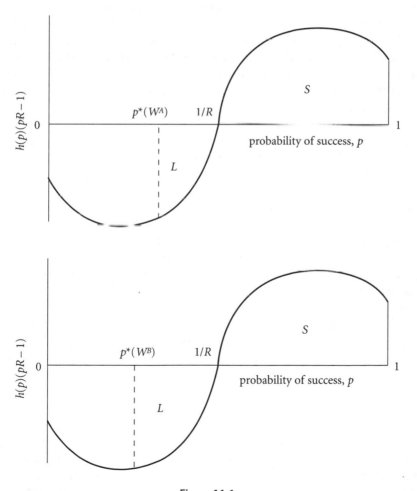

Figure 11.1

probability density function of project types. As illustrated in the figure, there is a set of possible projects that have a negative return and that generate an expected loss of L; and there is a set of possible projects that have a positive return, generating expected revenues of S. As depicted, $S - L > 0$; this condition must be satisfied if the individual is to be able to borrow at all.

The lower is an individual's stake (in the form of collateral pledged to the lender) in her project, the more risk she is willing to take with the lender's money, and the lower is the success probability p^* at which a project will be, for her, just worth undertaking. Now consider two prospective borrowers, A and B, with A's initial wealth exceeding that of B (i.e., $w^A > w^B$). By observing the stake that each has in her project, a lender can infer their reservation success probability, p^*. Thus, conditional on the information available to the lender, A has a higher probability of repaying her loan than B and, accordingly, will be charged a lower interest rate in the market. Consider varying B's wealth level. As it falls, so does the probability of success at which B finds it worthwhile to undertake a project; as in the comparison provided by the two panels of Figure 11.1, the area L becomes larger and larger. If B's wealth is sufficiently low, then $p^*(w^B)$ may be so low that the lender expects no surplus from a project that B would be willing to undertake, and so B will not be able to borrow.

In this context, consider the policy options of awarding a grant that adds to the size of collateral offered by B as opposed to the standard policy of subsidizing her cost of borrowing. Hoff and Lyon (1995) prove that the former option dominates. The intuition is that the grant, by adding to the borrower's collateralizable wealth, makes her bear more of the consequences of her 'hidden' action (i.e. unobserved by the lender) and thus improves the link between performance and rewards. But a subsidy to borrowing aggravates the inefficiency caused by the fact (a source of negative externality) that individual borrowers do not take into account the cost borne by others (in the form of a higher interest rate charged) when they default, as the interest rate has to reflect the average risk of individual borrowers, who to the lender are observationally equivalent. In the context of asymmetric information, which creates a potential for negative externalities that may result in shutting low-wealth individuals out of a market, asset redistributive policy thus is not merely more equitable, but also may enhance efficiency by internalizing those externalities through an increase in the collateral of the poor borrower.

Among asset-redistributive poverty alleviation measures, one of the most popular (though resisted tenaciously and sometimes violently by the vested interests) is land reform. As noted in Chapter 6, in traditional agriculture (outside the plantation economy), where the use of lumpy inputs such as farm machinery is limited, the economies of scale in production are not substantial, and the small farm with a differential advantage in labour cost is often more productive than the large farm, as empirical evidence from many poor countries suggests. Of course, the larger farmer is likely to have better access to production credit (particularly significant as purchased inputs become more important in modern agriculture) and to information and marketing networks, and a greater capacity to diffuse and insure against risks. If these services can be made available to the small farmer (with proper attention paid to possible adverse incentive effects like those following from problems of moral hazard in insurance against risks), land redistribution may boost productivity and reduce poverty. But to be realistic, one should recognize that in some densely populated poor countries (e.g. Bangladesh) the 'surplus' land for redistribution (with any reasonable ceiling on large farms) is likely to be far short of what is needed to make a big dent in poverty. The redistribution of land from large to small farmers may also reduce the demand for hired labour (while correcting the underutilization of family labour on small farms), and may depress the wage rates for landless labourers, particularly if they get no land in the land reform.

Tenancy reform, by rearranging property rights in favour of the actual cultivator of the land, can improve production incentives. Security of tenure, if properly implemented, can provide incentives for long-term improvements on the land.[6] It should, however, be noted that, without adequate enforcement of tenurial security, and without effective ceilings on farm size, restrictions on tenancy have led in many areas to the eviction of tenants or the conversion of erstwhile tenants into wage labourers. Besides, as Hayami and Otsuka (1993) point out with examples from the irrigated rice sector in the Philippines, such restrictions may close the possibility for agricultural labourers at the bottom to climb the tenancy ladder.

One beneficial byproduct of land reform, underemphasized in the usual economic analysis, is to change the local political structure in the village. Redistributive land reform gives more 'voice' to the poor and induces them to get involved in local self-governing institutions and in the common management of local public goods. Furthermore, local markets (say, for farm products or credit or water) function more efficiently when the levelling effects of land reform improve competition and make it more difficult for the rural oligarchy to corner markets.

Given the strength of opposition of vested interests, many regard the political prospects for land reform in most developing countries as bleak, and therefore drop it altogether from the agenda of poverty alleviation. This is not always wise. Some aspects of land reform (e.g. extension of tenurial security) may be less difficult to implement than others (e.g. land ceilings). Besides, in the dynamics of political processes and shifting coalitions, the range of feasibility often changes; and options kept open can contribute to the political debate and

---

[6] For a discussion of the complexity of the issues involved, see Chapter 6.

influence the political process. Some policy advisers (from international lending agencies) who rule out land reform as politically infeasible are at the same time enthusiastic supporters of other poverty alleviation policies, which may be not a great deal less politically difficult; an example is the strict targeting of food subsidies, leading to a cut in the substantial present subsidies to the vocal urban middle classes. In the game of political coalition formation, a radical policy sometimes becomes implementable if it helps cement strategic alliances, say between sections of the urban upper classes (including white-collar workers) and the rural poor.

IV

One of the most widely discussed efficiency issues in connection with various transfer programmes and the maintenance of a safety net for poor families relates to targeting and cost-effectiveness.[7] With structural adjustment programmes necessitating large cuts in budgetary subsidies in many countries, targeting transfers to vulnerable sections of the population has become even more important, since the leakages from transfer programmes to non-target groups are often considerable while failure to reach all in the target group is much too common. But the administrative costs of targeting can be high, particularly as reliable and cheaply administered means tests are infeasible in many contexts in less developed countries. Behavioural responses (especially in the form of reduced labour supply and displaced private transfers) may create extra costs to targeted interventions, as some of the case studies in van de Walle and Nead (1995) testify. In this section we shall focus on the incentive problems of different kinds of targeting (particularly self-targeting and group or area-specific targeting in poverty alleviation programmes).

To give an illustration of the behavioural response and the associated issue of self-targeting, we shall consider a model of incentive arguments for work requirements in poverty alleviation programmes, due to Besley and Coate (1992). They follow John Stuart Mill's (1848) characterization of the problem as one of 'how to give the greatest amount of needful help, with the smallest encouragement to undue reliance on it'.

Suppose the government wishes to assist only those who would earn less than z (the poverty line) without intervention, while preserving incentives for individuals to make choices that will put them in a position to earn more than z. Let the population consisting of n individuals be of two types according to their income-generating ability $a \in \{a_L, a_H\}$, where $a_L < a_H$ and H stands for high and L for low. A fraction γ of the population has ability a_L. We shall take a_L and a_H

---

[7] For a review of the policy options and evidence on these issues see Lipton and Ravallion (1995).

also to be the individuals' wage rates. Each individual has the utility function given by $y - d(e)$, where y is income and e is labour effort, and $d(\cdot)$ is increasing and strictly convex.

A poverty-alleviating transfer programme is a pair of benefit packages $\{b_i, c_i\}$, with $i = L, H$, where b_i denotes the transfer amount for individuals of ability type i and c_i denotes a cost in terms of a public-sector work requirement to receive the transfer. (We shall ignore here the productivity effects of this public sector work.) The government's objective is to minimize the cost of the programme, $n[\gamma b_L + (1 - \gamma)b_H]$, subject to the constraint that each individual obtains an income of at least z.

Individuals of ability a_i must choose whether or not to claim the benefit package $\{b_i, c_i\}$ that is intended for them. Even if they do so, they may continue to supply some labour to the private labour market. Let $e(b, c, a_i)$ denote the private-sector labour effort supply of an individual with wage rate a_i who accepts a package $\{b, c\}$. It is easy to show that

$$e(b, c, a_i) = \hat{e}(a_i) - c \text{ if } c \leq \hat{e}(a_i),$$
$$= 0 \qquad \text{otherwise,} \tag{2}$$

where $\hat{e}(a_i)$ is the amount of labour that would be supplied to the private sector in the absence of the transfer programme.[8]

Given this labour supply, the individual's private-sector earnings will be

$$y(c, a_i) = a_i(\hat{e}(a_i) - c) \text{ if } c \leq \hat{e}(a_i)$$
$$= 0 \qquad \text{otherwise.} \tag{3}$$

The individual's utility level is given by

$$v(b, c, a_i) = b + y(c, a_i) - d(e(c, a_i) + c). \tag{4}$$

We shall assume that only one group in the target population (type L) is poor without government intervention, i.e.

$$y(0, a_H) > z > y(0, a_L). \tag{5}$$

Now let us suppose that the government knows the distribution of abilities in the population, but cannot observe each individual's ability or private-sector earnings. High-ability individuals may find it worthwhile to claim that they are of low ability in order to get the transfer. For the poverty-alleviating transfer programme to be implementable, it must therefore satisfy the incentive compatibility condition that high-ability (low-ability) individuals prefer their own benefit package to masquerading as low-ability (high-ability) individuals and receiving the other's benefit package. Under unobservable private-sector earnings, this condition implies

---

[8] We shall ignore, for simplification, the income effect of b on the labour supply.

$$v(b_L, c_L, a_L) \geq v(b_H, c_H, a_L)$$

and

$$v(b_H, c_H, a_H) \geq v(b_L, c_L, a_H).$$

The problem for the government is to minimize costs subject to this incentive compatibility constraint and a voluntary participation constraint (i.e. that the individual will voluntarily take up the package $\{b_i, c_i\}$ intended for her only if she is better off by so doing).

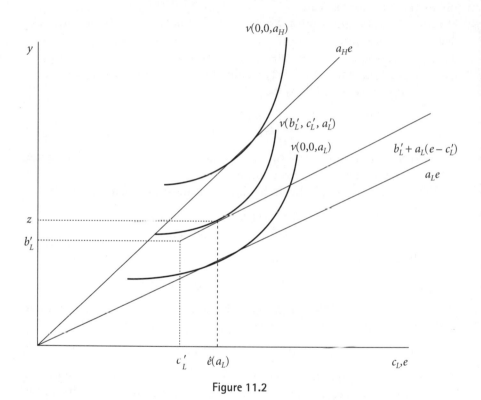

Figure 11.2

By imposing a work requirement on those who claim to be of low ability, the government can achieve self-selection. This is because high-ability individuals have a higher opportunity cost of supplying labour effort than the low-ability individuals. In Figure 11.2, low-ability individuals, in the absence of transfers, face a budget line $a_L e$ and choose to put in $\hat{e}(a_L)$ amount of effort. High-ability individuals face a higher price effort represented by the budget line $a_H e$. Suppose now that individuals who claim to be of low ability are offered the package (b_L', c_L'). If a low-ability individual took up this package, she would face a budget line with slope a_L emanating from point (b_L', c_L'). As illustrated in Figure 11.2, this individual would work $\hat{e}(a_L) - c_L'$ in the private sector and enjoy a post-transfer income of z. In contrast, if a high-ability individual were to take up this package, she would face a budget line with slope a_H emanating from (b_L', c_L'). This is everywhere below her *status quo* budget line, and therefore she has no incentive to masquerade. Thus, the transfer programme described by $\{(b_L', c_L'), (0,0)\}$ is incentive-compatible, despite offering different transfers to the two ability types.

There is, of course, a cost to using work requirements to achieve self-selection, since the poor will be working less in the private sector as a consequence of the work requirement and therefore will require a higher transfer to lift them to the poverty line. Thus, the key trade-off is between the cost savings arising from lower transfers to the non-poor and the cost increases resulting from higher transfers to the poor. Besley and Coate (1992) resolve this trade-off by calculating the work requirement that offers a benefit sufficient to get the self-categorized low-income individuals to the poverty line and at the same time makes the self-categorized high-ability individuals indifferent between claiming to be of low ability and receiving no transfers at all. This optimal work requirement c_l^* is defined by

$$v(0, 0, a_H) = v(z - y(c_L^*, a_L), c_L^*, a_H). \tag{6}$$

Self-targeting can also be important in other kinds of transfer programmes: for example, the public distribution of subsidized food could cover only coarse grains or other 'inferior' goods that the non-poor usually do not consume. (Of course, here, as well as in public works programmes involving the requirement of heavy manual work unattractive to the non-poor, bogus master rolls still divert some funds to non-poor middlemen.) Subsidizing coarse grains through food stamps is generally preferable (assuming that the administrative costs of food stamps are not high) to public procurement and distribution (as in India), since the government does not have to be involved in the purchase, transport, and storage of the commodities (a significant part of the large budgetary food subsidy in India). To counter the effect of a rise in food prices, as happened with the food stamp programme in Sri Lanka, governments should consider indexing the value of the stamps to the price of coarse grains or other such goods bought only by the poor. In the case of public works programmes, while some costs in terms of foregone alternative earnings have to be taken into account, their major role in very poor rural areas is to provide a fall-back option for agricultural labourers in lean seasons and bad crop years, thus increasing their usually low bargaining power in the labour market, and, by providing a minimum economic security, helping them to make more productive but risky investment decisions. Of course, such works programmes cannot help those in the needy population who are unemployable because of physical and other disabilities;

they will need disability-specific in-kind transfers (such as medical treatment or old-age pensions or nutrition for pregnant and nursing women).

Similar to the examples of coarse grains and works programmes, distribution of rudimentary social services such as primary education or basic health care is usually somewhat pro-poor, as some of the existing studies of the incidence of the benefits of public spending on social services suggest. This is presumably because the rich often turn to the private market for primary education and basic health care, and because the poor generally have larger families or more dependants. The distribution of the benefits of public spending for higher education and expensive medical care in urban hospitals is likely to be much more regressive. So the existing practice in many countries of charging low prices across the board for different social services regardless of cost, accompanied by quantity rationing or quality reductions when budgets are tight, has not served the poor in either the quantity or quality of services. High-cost services consumed by the rich are often subsidized more than low-cost services, so selective increases in user fees (with exemptions for the very poor or for some basic services) can serve both efficiency and equity considerations (provided that the requisite administrative infrastructure is in place).[9]

A major political problem for targeted anti-poverty programmes is that the process of transition from a universal to a narrowly targeted programme may seriously erode its political support base. As Gelbach and Pritchett (1995) show, a classical social choice theory model, in which agents vote simultaneously over the level of taxation and the degree of targeting, will have no equilibrium with positive levels of targeted transfers, and a voting equilibrium often will exist with no targeting (but non-zero taxation and redistribution). Then they show that, in a game in which the policy-maker chooses the degree of targeting while voters choose the level of taxation, the redistributive efficiency gains from targeting may well fail to outweigh the resulting reduction in funds available for redistribution. They cite empirical examples from food subsidy programmes in Sri Lanka and Colombia to indicate that episodes of increased targeting have been followed by reductions in overall benefits.

Let us now turn to the issue of group- or area-specific targeting in poverty alleviation. There are some groups and areas that are historically handicapped and their initial conditions may lock them into poverty unless special remedial attempts are made to change the situation.[10] Take the case of women. Women in

---

[9] There is a separate debate, in the literature on the effects of schooling, about whether expanding access to schools should be given priority over improving their quality, when funds are scarce. See e.g. the debate on this matter between Eric Hanushek and Michael Kremer in the *World Bank Research Observer*, 10, 1995; however, both authors agree that improving school quality will increase attendance, that investments in textbooks and radio education are more important than in reducing class size, and that new organizational forms and performance incentives may provide better and less expensive education.

[10] The equity argument here should actually be more refined. As Roemer (1995) has pointed out,

many parts of the world face special social and economic constraints in acquiring and using human capital. One of the usually overlooked constraints is the lack of childcare facilities, which often forces young daughters of poor working women to skip school to take care of their younger siblings, perpetuating the cycle of low education and low-paid jobs for women from one generation to the next. The legal and cultural barriers to entering the labour market are often formidable for women, and if they do break in they are often segregated in casual or dead-end low-paying jobs. Their domestic commitments (and culturally induced low self-esteem) seriously restrict their mobility and ability to seize better work opportunities. Women are often excluded from credit programmes because they cannot provide collateral—in South Asia they lack secure property rights to land, and in Africa formal land titling programmes have sometimes deprived women of their traditional rights to land. Health risks associated with childbearing and with taking care of other family members, and the consequent interruptions in employment, can make women risky clients for banks, as the experience of self-employed women's organizations like SEWA in India has shown. Women's access to extension services is also limited, which is of particular consequence in Africa, where women are heavily involved in production decisions for some crops. And women lack protection from violence in many societies, further limiting their activity and autonomy. All this suggests that the usual public interventions at the household level may be woefully inadequate, calling for more effective gender targeting of policy in expanding women's economic and social opportunities.

We noted in Section II that, in the case of some disadvantaged groups or backward neighbourhoods or regions, there may be important externalities, which again suggests that anti-poverty policies need to go beyond individuals and households. There is clearly a trade-off here between the increased cost of group-targeting (which will inevitably involve some of the non-poor within a group) and the efficiency gain from internalizing the positive externalities. In this connection it is important to analyse the efficiency implications of preferential treatment to disadvantaged minorities in jobs, education, business contracts and permits, etc. Variants of such a policy have been tried in Malaysia, India, the southern Philippines, and elsewhere. They have often generated a great deal of political controversy, but systematic economic analysis, either theoretical or empirical, of their efficiency effects is scarce, at least compared with the corresponding work on the effects of affirmative action in the United States. Even though some of these policies (for example quotas in India in civil service jobs and concerning admission to higher education for some low-caste or tribal

equality of opportunity (as opposed to outcome) may imply that people should be indemnified against the handicaps of being in a particular group which are beyond their control (e.g. ethnicity, gender, home or neighborhood environment in early age), but not against the consequences of their autonomous actions (e.g. effort or decisions taken), causing intra-group variations in performance.

groups) are not directly relevant to the very poor, they can have indirect effects on their chances for upward mobility.

The standard efficiency argument against job quotas for minorities is that it splinters the labour market, distorts the allocation of labour between covered and other sectors, and may adversely affect the incentives for skill acquisition among members of the quota-protected group. But if group-specific dynamic externalities and social capital are important determinants of economic success as in the models of Benabou (1996) and Durlauf (1996), preferential policies can increase efficiency by changing the way workers are sorted across occupations and firms. In addition, if employers hold negative-stereotype views about minority worker productivity, and if in such cases the return to acquiring signals of ability is low or signals are uninformative, maintaining preferential job policies for a time can help eliminate stereotypes and thus improve incentives on the part of minority workers for skill acquisition. But there are circumstances, as Coate and Loury (1993) have pointed out in a job assignment model of self-confirming negative stereotypes in equilibrium, where the employer, by patronizing the disadvantaged group under the preferential system, may undercut the incentive for skill acquisition and thus fail to eliminate stereotypes. (These disincentive effects are mitigated if promotions within a firm, as opposed to entry-level jobs, are heavily performance-based.)

To the extent that preferential policies are supposed to cope with an historical handicap, their economic rationale is akin to that behind the age-old argument for infant-industry protection in early stages of development. Some disadvantaged groups need temporary protection against competition so that they can participate in learning by doing and on-the-job skill formation until they catch up with the others. Some of the standard arguments against infant-industry protection are then equally applicable against preferential policies. For example, the 'infant', once protected, sometimes refuses to grow up; preferential policies, once adopted, are extremely difficult to reverse. The Indian Constitution stipulated a specified duration for job reservation for the lowest castes and tribes; not only has this been continued indefinitely, but the principle of 'reservation' has now been extended to a large number of other castes. Another argument against infant-industry protection is that, even when the goal is justifiable, it may be achieved more efficiently through other policies. For example, a disadvantaged group may be helped by a preferential investment policy or development programmes in a particular area where the group is concentrated, or with preferential loans, scholarships, job training programmes, and extension services for its members, instead of job quotas that bar qualified candidates from advanced groups. Such indirect policies of helping out backward groups are also less likely to generate political resentment (particularly because in this case the burden may be shared more evenly, whereas in the case of job quotas the redistributive burden falls on a small subset of the majority community).

V

Finally, we discuss the issue of governance structure in poverty alleviation programmes. There is an increasing awareness that the cause of both efficiency and equity in these programmes will be served better if we move away from state paternalism as well as harsh market processes, and instead rely more on local self-governing institutions and community involvement to improve the material conditions and the autonomy of the poor. Even when the state is obligated to spend a significant part of the budget on anti-poverty programmes (as for example in India), too often very little aid reaches the real poor, in the absence of organized pressure from the intended beneficiaries, owing to the fact that the programmes are administered by a distant, uncoordinated, and corrupt bureaucracy that is unaccountable and insensitive to the needs of the local poor. Even when it does reach the poorest people, it often perpetuates a cycle of dependency and an attitude of malfeasance and opportunism among them, milking the state cow for its uncertain bounties. The disproportionate benefits, of course, go to those who have the resources, connections, and dexterity to manipulate the milking process and to the large army of middlemen, contractors, officials, and politicians.

Devolution of power to the local community usually brings some responsibility in decision-making and in implementation and can provide incentives for improving the quality and cost-effectiveness of such programmes. Local information can often identify cheaper and more appropriate ways of providing public services. There is also scattered evidence that the serious problem of absenteeism of salaried teachers in village public schools and of doctors in rural public health clinics is significantly reduced when they are made accountable to the local community. Peer monitoring and enforcement of local social sanctions and a common set of norms can provide the basis of social insurance schemes and group borrowing, as we noted in Section III. In remote regions of poor countries, decentralization also provides a more effective channel of transmitting (and acting upon) early warnings about problems that might develop into disasters (droughts, epidemics, etc.). In Chapter 13 we suggest that decentralization with local accountability may also help in the management of common property resources on which the daily livelihood of the rural poor depends, such as forestry, grazing, irrigation, fisheries, and so on, and that there are several documented examples in different parts of the world of successful and autonomous local community-level cooperation in the management of these resources. In some cases—for example in forest protection and in the regeneration and development of wasteland in India—there are now some successful instances of joint management by the state and the local community, with the latter taking major responsibilities.

One should, however, resist the temptation to romanticize the value of the local community as a social and economic organization, as is common among many environmentalists, NGO activists, and other assorted anti-state anti-market social thinkers. On the efficiency question, the major trade-off is between the need for policy coordination at some central level when there are economies of scale and of scope and interjurisdictional externalities on the one hand, and for local information and accountabilty on the other. The importance of the two sides in this trade-off varies from case to case, and it is difficult to pass general judgement on the appropriate extent of decentralization in the governance structure without looking into the empirical details of each case. Besides, proximity and small numbers at the local level make collusion easy and arm's length transactions (and an impartial auditing of accounts) difficult to ensure. There is considerable scope for corruption and cost-padding here; of course, these can be kept in check if accountability mechanisms (e.g. external auditing, public hearings on major items of expenditure, and other local institutions of transparency) are in place.

On the equity side, it is important to keep in mind that, in situations of severe social and economic inequality at the local level, decentralization can be highly inadequate in helping the poor. It may be easy for the local overlords to capture the local community institutions, and the poor may be left grievously exposed to their mercies and their malfeasance. Such capture is more difficult at the national level because the local élite of different regions may partially neutralize one another. Since there are certain fixed costs of organizing resistance groups or lobbies, the poor may sometimes be more unorganized at the local level than at the national level, where they can pool their organizing capacities.

REFERENCES

Aghion, P., and Bolton, P. (1997), 'A Theory of Trickle-Down Growth and Development', *Review of Economic Studies*, 64.

Atkinson, A. B. (1987), 'On the Measurement of Poverty', *Econometrica*, 55.

Banerjee, A., and Newman, A. (1993), 'Occupational Choice and the Process of Development', *Journal of Political Economy*, 101.

Benabou, R. (1996), 'Equity and Efficiency in Human Capital Investment: The Local Connection', *Review of Economic Studies*, 62.

Besley, T., and Coate, S. (1992), 'Workfare versus Welfare: Incentive Arguments for Work Requirements in Poverty-Alleviation Programs', *American Economic Review*, 82.

Bowles, S., and Gintis, H. (1995), 'Efficient Redistribution: New Rules for Markets, States, and Communities', unpublished paper, University of Massachusetts.

Coate, S., and Loury, G. (1993), 'Will Affirmative Action Policies Eliminate Negative Stereotypes ?' *American Economic Review*, 83.

Dasgupta, P., and Ray , D.(1986), 'Inequality as a Determinant of Malnutrition and Unemployment: Theory', *Economic Journal*, 96.

Drèze, J., and Sen, A. (1989), *Hunger and Public Action*. Oxford: Oxford University Press.

Durlauf, S. (1996), 'A Theory of Persistent Income Inequality', *Journal of Economic Growth*, 1.

Foster, J., Greer, J., and Thorbecke, E. (1984), 'A Class of Decomposable Poverty Measures', *Econometrica*, 52.

Galor, O., and Zeira, J. (1993), 'Income Distribution and Macroeconomics'. *Review of Economic Studies*, 60.

Gelbach, J., and Pritchett, L. (1995), 'Does More for the Poor Mean Less for the Poor? The Politics of Tagging', unpublished paper, World Bank.

Grossman, H. (1992), 'Robin Hood and the Distribution of Property Income', IRIS Center Working Paper no. 43, College Park, Maryland.

Hanushek, E. (1995), 'Interpreting Recent Research on Schooling in Developing Countries', *World Bank Research Observer*, 10.

Hayami, Y., and Otsuka K. (1993), *The Economics of Contract Choice*. Oxford: Clarendon Press.

Hoff, K, (1996), 'Market Failures and the Distribution of Wealth: A Perspective from the Economics of Information', *Politics and Society*, 24.

—— and Lyon, A. (1995), 'Non-leaky Buckets: Optimal Redistributive Taxation and Agency Costs', *Journal of Public Economics*, 58.

Kremer, M. (1995), 'Research on Schooling: What We Know and What We Don't: A Comment on Hanushek', *World Bank Research Observer*, 10.

Krugman, P. (1991), *Geography and Trade*. Cambridge, Mass.: MIT Press.

Lipton, M., and Ravallion, M. (1995), 'Poverty and Policy', in J. Behnman and T. N. Srinivasan (eds.), *Handbook of Development Economics*, iiiA. Amsterdam: Elsevier.

Mill, J. S. (1848), *Principles of Political Economy*, Books IV and V, Harmondsworth: Penguin.

Okun, A. M. (1975), *Equality and Efficiency: The Big Tradeoff.* Washington: Brookings Institution.

Ravallion, M. (1994), *Poverty Comparisons*, Fundamentals of Pure and Applied Economics, 56, Chur, Switzerland: Harwood Academic Press.

Roemer, J. (1995), 'Equality of Opportunity and Affirmative Action', Working Paper, University of California at Davis Department of Economics.

van de Walle, D., and Nead, K. (eds.) (1995), *Public Spending and the Poor: Theory and Evidence*. Baltimore: Johns Hopkins University Press.

Wilson, W. J. (1987), *The Truly Disadvantaged*. Chicago: University of Chicago Press.

12

Technological Progress and Learning

I

The process of economic development is characterized by a transformation of the technologies used in production. Technological change in the poor countries has often been seen as a process through which techniques of production invented and first used in the rich countries are imported and adapted for local use. Experimentation and learning have only a minor role to play in this process of technology transfer; production technologies are chosen 'off the shelf' and are often embodied in capital goods imported from rich countries. The crucial determinants of this type of technological change are current and expected factor and product prices—poor countries need devote few resources to the process of invention itself.

If the changes in technology that occur as the currently poor countries develop are well described by this notion of technology transfer, then it provides one of the 'benefits of backwardness' described by Gerschenkron (1962). Poor countries can free-ride on the investments in technology made in rich countries, and this might be one mechanism through which the convergence of productivity levels between poor and rich countries could occur.

It can be argued, however, that technological change in poor countries is more complex than a simple transfer of blueprints (or machines) from rich countries. Evenson and Westphal (1995) provide the useful vocabulary of 'tacitness' and 'circumstantial sensitivity' when characterizing technology. Techniques of production are tacit if they are not fully embodied in a set of artefacts—a collection of machines, seeds, manuals, or blueprints, for example. The tacit elements of a technology might be employed quite differently across producers using ostensibly identical techniques of production. Moreover, the performance characteristics of a particular technique of production might be sensitive to the circumstances under which it is used. Non-tradable inputs (most obviously, land) vary in characteristics in ways that affect the performance of different technologies. The institutional context in which a technology is used (in particular, the relationship between workers and managers) can also influence the performance of techniques of production.

If a technology is characterized by tacitness or circumstantial sensitivity, then learning and innovation are involved wherever it is newly applied—even if the explicit elements of the technology are imported from a rich country. Thus, tacitness and circumstantial sensitivity limit the value of international spillovers, and require local investments in technology. This point could be over-emphasized—fundamental scientific advances remain a vital source of new potential for the entire world. But the translation from abstract principles into new designs and then the implementation of the new designs into production is not immediate or costless. It is locally produced and adapted knowledge that provides a source of growth.

To overcome the tacitness or circumstantial sensitivity of a newly developed or imported technology, there must be local investment in learning. Producers might engage in *learning-by-doing*, experimenting with the new technology to reveal the tacit elements of the technology or determine the sensitivity of the technology to local conditions. Alternatively, producers might *learn from others*—either from other producers engaged in learning-by-doing, or from locally based researchers and extension agents.

The two types of learning have dramatically different implications for policy and for the character of growth. When producers learn from their own experimentation, they undertake an investment that yields uncertain returns. When producers learn from each other, not only is there a risky investment, but that investment generates an information spillover. This learning externality underlies some modern models of growth, and provides a role for government or other social institutions which might supply a mechanism for rewarding experimenters for the positive externality generated by their activities.

Taken together, these two types of learning form the process of 'social learning', in which knowledge generated by experimentation by an individual or firm increases that producer's future profits and generates an information externality that benefits other individuals and firms. In the following section we present a simple model (after Foster and Rosenzweig 1995) as a basis for thinking about the process of social learning, and which can serve as the foundation for a model of economic growth with endogenous technological change. In Section III we link the process of technological innovation to investment in human capital, and show (using a simple variant of Acemoglu 1997) that, when labour markets are imperfect, underinvestment in human capital and a lack of technological innovation can be mutually reinforcing.

II

We consider a very simple form of learning about a technology, which might correspond to a situation in which the parameters of a new technology (perhaps a seed) depend upon local conditions (perhaps soil characteristics) which vary across the world. This 'target input' model (Prescott 1972; Wilson 1975; Jovanovic and Nyarko 1994) has the characteristic that the basic form of the technology is known with certainty. Only a random parameter (known as the 'target') remains unknown. The profit of a producer declines with (the square of) the distance between the input used and the unknown target level of input use. After the input has been applied and the output realized, the producer can deduce what the target level of the input must have been. Each application of the technology, therefore, is an experiment which yields information about the distribution of the unknown random parameter. Producers learn by doing, gaining information about the production function through their own experimentation. They may also learn from others, observing the experiments of their neighbours and drawing lessons about the distribution of the target input level.

This model has been employed profitably by Foster and Rosenzweig (1995) in their study of farmers' experimentation with Green Revolution seeds in India. This section presents a simplified version of their model, and retains the terminology of innovation in agriculture. The core ideas of social learning, however, are applicable to innovation more generally.

Suppose output is determined by the production function

$$q_{it} = 1 - (k_{it} - \kappa_{it})^2, \qquad (1)$$

where k_{it} is the level of input use chosen by person i in period t, and κ_{it} is the target level of input use. κ_{it} is not known as the time inputs are chosen. It is determined by

$$\kappa_{it} = \kappa^* + \mu_{it}, \qquad (2)$$

where μ_{it} is a normally distributed independent and identically distributed (i.i.d.) shock with mean zero and variance σ_u^2. At time t, person i does not know κ^*, but she has beliefs about κ^* which are distributed $N(\kappa_t^*, \sigma_{\kappa it}^2)$. 'Learning', in this model, is a process of gathering information which permits the individual to make a better and better estimate of the true value of κ^*.[1] We assume that the input is costless, so that output equals profits. This assumption doesn't affect our discussion of the process of learning itself, but it does greatly simplify the analysis of the adoption decision.

---

[1] For the sake of simplicity, we assume (rather unrealistically) that the farmer knows that the variance of $\mu_{it} = \sigma_u^2$.

Maximization of expected profit implies that $k_{it} = E_t(\kappa_{it}) = \kappa_t^*$. Therefore,

$$E_t(q_{it}) = 1 - \sigma_{\kappa it}^2 - \sigma_u^2. \tag{3}$$

Expected profit rises as $\sigma_{\kappa it}^2$ declines, that is, as the individual learns more about the true value of κ^*.

(a) Learning-by-doing

Consider farmer i in isolation. Each season she chooses an input level (k_{it}) and observes output (q_{it}). Thus, she can infer κ_{it}, and she uses this information to update her beliefs about κ^*. Suppose that the variance of her beliefs about κ^* in period $t-1$ is $\sigma_{\kappa i, t-1}^2$. Then after observing κ_{it} and applying Bayes's rule to update her beliefs about κ^*,

$$\sigma_{\kappa it}^2 = \frac{1}{\dfrac{1}{\sigma_{\kappa i, t-1}^2} + \dfrac{1}{\sigma_u^2}}. \tag{4}$$

Defining $1/\sigma_u^2 \equiv \rho_o$ as the precision of the information generated by observations from her own farm and $1/\sigma_{\kappa i0}^2 \equiv \rho_{i0}$ as the precision of i's initial beliefs about the value of κ^*, (4) becomes

$$\sigma_{\kappa it}^2 = \frac{1}{\rho_{i0} + I_{t-1}\rho_o}, \tag{4'}$$

where I_{t-1} is the number of trials of the new technology that i has observed on her own farm from period 0 to period $t-1$. So we can write expected profits as a function of the number of trials:

$$Eq_{it}(I_{t-1}) = 1 - \frac{1}{\rho_{i0} + I_{t-1}\rho_o} - \sigma_u^2. \tag{3'}$$

Additional experiments with the new technology increase future expected profits:

$$\frac{\partial Eq_t(I_{t-1})}{\partial I_{t-1}} = \frac{\rho_o}{(\rho_{i0} + I_{t-1}\rho_o)^2}. \tag{5}$$

Eventually, as the farmer collects more and more information, she becomes certain about the value of κ^*. Taking the limit of (4') as I increases, we have

$$\lim_{I\to\infty} \sigma_{\kappa it}^2 = 0 \text{ and } \lim_{I\to\infty} E(q_{it}) = 1 - \sigma_u^2.$$

(b) Learning from Others

Learning-by-doing can be a quite slow mechanism for achieving technological progress, particularly in agriculture, where it is usually necessary to wait at least a season, and often longer, to observe the outcome of an experiment. The process of learning would be much faster if information from neighbouring farmers could also be used. If neighbouring farmers share the same technology, in the sense that the distribution of the unknown target input level is the same, then they might be able to learn from each other. In agriculture in particular, the distance over which farmers can usefully learn from each other might be quite limited. (That is, some types of agricultural technology might be quite highly sensitive to local circumstances such as soil characteristics and weather patterns.) In the context of this model, it might be the case that the distribution of κ_{it} is different in different localities, so that observations from one location about realizations of κ_{it} in one place provide little information about its distribution in another.[2] For now, though, consider neighbouring farmers for whom the new technology has identical characteristics.

Suppose that farmer i can observe, with some error, the input choice and yield of each farmer j living in the same village. Thus, i observes $\kappa_{jt} + \epsilon_{jt}$, where $\epsilon_{jt} \sim N(0, \sigma_\epsilon^2)$.[3] In a richer model, one might permit the distribution of the noise in the information flow between farmers i and j to depend on their relationship. But we maintain the simpler model, which ignores the subtler issues of social networks within the village. Defining

$$\rho_v = \frac{1}{\sigma_u^2 + \sigma_\varepsilon^2} < \rho_o,$$

we have
$$\sigma_{\kappa it}^2 = \frac{1}{\rho_{i0} + I_{t-1}\rho_o + N_{t-1}\rho_v}, \tag{6}$$

where N_{t-1} is the number of trials of the new technology that i has observed on all the farms of her neighbours from period 0 to period $t-1$.

The externality generated by social learning is now apparent. If one farmer experiments with a new technology, this generates information for all her neighbours and increases their expected profits. Thus,

$$\frac{\partial E q_t (I_{t-1}, N_{t-1})}{\partial N_{t-1}} = \frac{\rho_v}{(\rho_{i0} + I_{t-1}\rho_o + N_{t-1}\rho_v)^2} > 0. \tag{7}$$

---

[2] See Munshi (1996) for a discussion of social learning in this situation.
[3] Again, suppose that σ_ϵ^2 is known.

A farmer's decision to use and thus experiment with a new technology has implications for all of her neighbours, and thus the adoption of technology is a social process. Decisions about technology use, we will see in the next section, depend not only on a farmer's evaluation of its profitability, but also on the nature of a farmer's interactions with the other farmers in her neighbourhood.

(c) Adoption of Technology

Suppose that the farmers have available a 'traditional' technology, the parameters of which are known with certainty. To simplify notation, we presume that the return from this technology is riskless and equal to q_a, but nothing in what we say depends on this assumption. For the moment, abstract from social learning and presume that each farmer learns about the parameters of the new technology independently. Let $\iota_t = 1$ if the farmer uses the new technology in period t and 0 if she uses the traditional technology. The value of the future stream of profits of farmer i from period t to period T is:

$$V_t(I_{t-1}) = \underset{\iota_s \in \{0,1\}}{\text{Max}} \ E_t \sum_{s=t}^{T} \delta^{s-t} [(1 - \iota_s) \, q_a + \iota_s \, q_s(I_{s-1})], \tag{8}$$

where $I_s = \sum_{t=0}^{s} \iota_t$. Focusing on period t,

$$V_t(I_{t-1}) = \underset{\iota_t}{\text{Max}} \ (1 - \iota_t) \, q_a + \iota_t \, E_t q_t(I_{t-1}) + \delta V_{t+1}(I_t). \tag{9}$$

Two comments are in order. First, note that, since expected profits are increasing in the number of trials of the new technology, once the farmer switches to the new technology she will continue to use the new technology for ever. That is, since $E_{qt}(I_{t-1})$ is strictly increasing in I_{t-1} (recall equation (5)) then if $\iota_t = 1$, $\iota_s = 1$ for all $s > t$. This observation underscores an important weakness of the target input model as the basis of a model of technological change. The history of technology is replete with examples of innovations that are attempted and then abandoned once proven less profitable than alternative technologies. The target input model begins with the assumption that the new technology is superior; the problem of learning is concerned with discovering the precise shape of the new technology. An alternative approach (adopted, for example, by Besley and Case 1997 and Ellison and Fudenberg 1993) would be to focus on discovering whether or not a new technology is profitable in a particular environment.

Second, the switch from the old technology to the new may take place when the old technology is still more profitable. Consider a farmer in period 0 and her decision to adopt the new technology. She will adopt the new technology in period 0 if

$$q_a - E\,q(0) \le \delta(V_1(1) - V_1(0)).\qquad(10)$$

So, if the loss in current expected profits is less than the (discounted) gain in future profitability from the additional trial of the new technology, the new technology will be adopted. The right-hand side of (10) is positive:

$$V_1(1) - V_1(0) = E_0 \sum_{s=1}^{T} \delta^s (q(s) - q(s-1)) = \sum_{s=1}^{T} \delta_s \left(\frac{1}{\rho_{i0} + (s-1)\rho_o} - \frac{1}{\rho_{i0} + s\rho_o} \right) > 0.\quad(11)$$

so the new technology may be used even if the current expected profit from the new technology is less than that which would be received from the old.

If farmers can learn from each others' experience with the new technology, the determination of which farmer will adopt the new technology will depend crucially on the farmer's interactions with everyone else in the village. The value of future profits to a farmer depends not only on her own experience with the new technology (I_t), but also on the experience of everyone else in the village (or other appropriately defined reference group (N_t)):

$$V_t(I_{t-1}, N_{t-1}) = \underset{\iota_t}{\mathrm{Max}}\,(1 - \iota_t)\,q_a + \iota_t\,E_t q_t(I_{t-1}, N_{t-1})$$
$$+ \delta V_{t+1}(I_t, N_t).\qquad(12)$$

Hence a farmer's expectations about her neighbour's use of the new technology have a direct effect on the value of the flow of profits expected by that farmer. The more experimentation she expects her neighbours to conduct, the higher the profit she expects. At the same time, a farmer who expects that many of her neighbours will adopt the new technology may delay her own adoption of that technology because the value of the information that she will receive from experimenting with the crop is lower the more other farmers experiment. To see this, note that our farmer will choose to use the new technology if

$$q_a - E_0\,q(0, N_0) \le \delta[V_1(1, N_0) - V_1(0, N_0)].\qquad(13)$$

The right-hand side is again positive, reflecting the increase in the flow of expected profits as a consequence of the information gained by the farmer experimenting with the new technology in period 0. However, the right-hand side is declining in N_0: if more other farmers use the new technology, less additional information is gained by the farmer experimenting herself. Thus, if many of your neighbours have characteristics that would lead them to adopt new technology early, it might be in your interest to refrain from experimenting yourself, until you see how they have got on with it.

The spread of technology, therefore, depends on social interactions in a number of ways. First, there is the direct effect of information flow within the community. People might be learning from each other's experiments. It is likely that the extent of learning from others depends on the technology itself and on a host of characteristics of the community itself. An important programme of empirical research, therefore, is to document the extent of 'information spillovers' generated by experimentation. Second, there is the issue of the impact of the externality. Is there any social mechanism which serves to reward experimenters for the value of their experiments to other farmers? This, of course, is the primary justification for intellectual property rights protection, but it may be the case (particularly in the context of agricultural innovation) that there is a number of less formal mechanisms that reward experimentation and innovation. Finally, the pattern of adoption of innovations depends on the nature of the game that is being played in the community. In the context of our model, each farmer is simultaneously faced with a problem akin to equation (12). How is the equilibrium N_0 determined? Is it the simple Markov-perfect equilibrium assumed by Foster and Rosenzweig? In this case, the externality generated by experimentation is not internalized by the farmer. Or are there enforcement mechanisms, multi-period punishments, or other institutional arrangements that make other equilibria possible?

The model presented in this section focuses on the adoption of a single innovation. Jovanovic and Nyarko (1994) address the issue of continuous technological progress. They model the problem of learning about an entire sequence of technologies indexed by $z = 1, 2, \ldots$ where $q_{it} = \gamma^z [1 - (k_{it} - \kappa_{zit})^2]$ and $\gamma > 1$. Learning about the distribution of κ_z provides some information about the distribution of κ_{z+1}. Thus, experimentation with technology z not only generates information which makes the use of that technology more profitable (for both the experimenter and her neighbours), but also makes further innovation more profitable.

The model of social learning presented here involves quite sophisticated behaviour on the part of innovators. Data from experimentation throughout a community are pooled (perhaps with some noise added as information flows from person to person), and the parameters of the technology are gradually learned. This accords well with some of the descriptions of innovative activity in poor countries; for example with Amanor's (1994) description of on-farm experimentation in Ghana. Other models of social learning, however, might be appropriate in some contexts. One interesting strand of recent research is exemplified by Ellison and Fudenberg (1993), who analyse how innovation would occur if producers used simple, exogenously specified rules of thumb to guide their adoption decisions. They focus on rules of thumb in which adoption decisions are a simple function of the lagged profitability of different techniques, modified by the relative popularity of the different techniques. They show that the success with which such naive rules lead to the adoption of more efficient technologies depends crucially on the precise rule of thumb that it is in use, and on the nature of the technology itself (particularly the degree to which its profitability depends on local conditions).

The simple model presented in this section illustrates two important characteristics of innovation in the context of social learning. First, innovation is a form of investment. Producers engage in costly experimentation, sacrificing current profits in exchange for knowledge which will increase profits in the future. Second, innovation generates spillovers. This is the case because new technology, in the sense of designs or methods for doing a task, is *non-rival*. Use of a new technique by one person does not prevent another person from also using the same technique. Thus, if one person learns about a new technology, others can benefit from that knowledge. It may be the case (depending on the technology and the social context) that this new knowledge is only partially (or not at all) *excludable*—it may not be possible to prevent others from observing your use of the new technology and thus benefiting from your experimentation. In this case, there is an externality generated by your investment.

III

Thus far, we have focused on the problem of learning—the locally produced and adapted knowledge that permits producers to change their techniques of production. However, even when all the characteristics of the new technology are known with certainty, adoption might not be a simple matter. Use of a new technology often requires a different economic environment from use of the old. Changes in the institutional context of production (new contracts, or new ways of organizing labour), or in infrastructure, or in the skills of the labour force might be required.

It is on the last of these that we focus in this section. Potentially profitable new technology might not be used if the available work-force does not have the requisite skills. This notion is at the centre of Rosenstein-Rodan's (1943) argument that 'the first task of industrialization is to provide for training and "skilling" of labour' (p. 204). Simultaneously, the return to human capital and hence workers' and firms' incentives to invest in training appears to be very sensitive to the rate of technological change in an economy. In a dynamic environment characterized by rapidly changing technology, the returns to education and training are exceptionally high.[4]

This interdependence between training and the adoption of technology need not be problematic. If the training is firm-specific, so that it is valuable only inside the firm providing the training, then the training will be provided and the technology adopted if the productivity gains outweigh the costs of the training and new technology. This is the efficient outcome. In the case where the skills

---

[4] Schultz (1975) forcefully states this argument, and Foster and Rosenzweig (1996) provide supporting evidence from the Indian green revolution.

imparted by training are generally useful, Becker (1964) shows that, in a competitive labour market, firms providing the skills charge the employees the present discounted value of the increased wages these employees will be able to earn in the future as a consequence of their improved skills. A significant component of training in poor countries, as in rich countries, takes place in apprenticeship programmes. Master mechanics, tailors, machine shop operators, and the like provide the training to apprentices required to keep the informal sectors of many economies vibrant.[5] Again, the skills will be provided and the technology adopted if and only if the productivity gains outweigh the costs of training and the new technology.

When markets are imperfect, however, a lack of coordination can inhibit both training and innovation. For example, liquidity constraints could limit the ability of workers to pay for the general training they receive (see Velenchik 1995), and this in turn could limit the profitability of adopting a new technology. Rosenstein-Rodan (1943) focused on labour market imperfections—if workers are not paid their marginal products, then future employers might not have to pay trained workers for the full value of their training. In his words, 'there are no mortgages on workers—an entrepreneur who invests in training workers may lose capital if these workers contract with another firm' (p. 204). When labour markets are imperfect, training can generate a positive externality to firms that employ labour in the future. When this externality is not internalized, workers and firms will invest in sub-optimal levels of training, and the profitability (and rate) of innovation may be too low. To formalize this argument, we present a simplified version of the model developed by Acemoglu (1997).

Suppose that there is an economy with a continuum of risk-neutral workers and risk-neutral firms, each with mass 1. The discount rate is r. (Perhaps this is a small open economy with access to international capital.) The economy lasts for two periods. Each firm requires one worker to produce y units of output in each period. In period 1, it is possible to make two sorts of investment to increase productivity in period 2. First, a new technology might be adopted at cost δ to be used for production in period 2. Second, a worker can be provided with general training which will increase her productivity in any firm in the second period. τ units of training can be obtained at a cost of $c(\tau)$, where $c(\cdot)$ is differentiable, strictly increasing and convex, and $c(0) = 0$.

The crucial assumption about the technology is that training and the new technology are complementary. To sharpen the point, we will assume that this complementarity is very strong: the new technology will not improve output unless used with a trained worker, and the training will not be useful unless used with the new technology. Define $\gamma_j = 1$ if firm j has invested in the new

---

[5] See e.g. Berry's (1985: ch. 6) rich description of motor mechanics in Ile-Ife, Nigeria.

technology and $\gamma_j = 0$ otherwise. If worker i with training τ_i is paired with firm j in the second period, then output is $y + \gamma_j \alpha \tau_i$, where $\alpha > 0$. Output increases in the second period only if a firm with the new technology is matched with a worker who has been trained. Finally, there is an exogenous profitability $s \in (0, 1)$ that a worker–firm pair in period 1 is forced to separate and match with a different partner in period 2. In a frictionless labour market, this separation does not create any problem, because there is a continuum of firms which will be able to employ any worker forced to leave her period 1 firm.

In an efficient allocation, the surplus generated by training and technology adoption is maximized

$$\max_{\gamma \in \{1,0\}, \tau} \gamma \alpha \tau - (1 + r)(c(\tau) + \delta \gamma). \tag{14}$$

The first term is the additional output generated by training and adoption of technology, and the second term is their cost (which is incurred in the first period), if $\gamma = 0$, the optimal level of training is obviously $\tau^l = 0$. If $\gamma = 1$, then the optimal level of training is τ^h such that

$$\alpha = (1 + r)c'(\tau^h). \tag{15}$$

If $\delta > 0$, it is clearly not profitable to innovate unless workers are trained. Suppose in addition that

$$\alpha \tau^h - (1 + r)(c(\tau^h) + \delta) > 0, \tag{16}$$

so that it is optimal to choose to adopt the technology and train the workers. Acemoglu (1997) shows that it is possible to support this efficient allocation in a competitive equilibrium. The intuition is simple. The wage for workers in the second period (w), working for firms that adopt the technology, is a function of their level of training, such that $w(\tau) - w(0) = \alpha \tau, \forall \tau$. In the first period, workers are paid a wage $v(\tau)$ which depends on the training they receive. In the competitive equilibrium workers pay for their training, so $v(\tau) = v(0) - c(\tau), \forall \tau$. If (16) holds, all workers choose $\tau = \tau^h$ and all firms choose $\gamma = 1$.

Suppose, however, that there is an imperfect labour market. We will not model the imperfection explicitly, but will suppose that firms are randomly matched with workers at the start of period 1. Given this match, they cannot switch before period 2, and hence they bargain over the division of the surplus in the relationship. At the end of period 1, a fraction s of the matches are dissolved and randomly matched with new partners for period 2. Again, given this match, no more switches are possible, and the firm and workers again bargain over the division of the remaining surplus. Suppose that the bargaining process is such that the worker gets a fraction β of the surplus, while the firm gets $(1 - \beta)$. This generates the following externality. Suppose that a trained worker is separated from her firm and matched with a new firm for period 2. The new firm now captures a proportion of the value of the investment that has been made in training that worker. Hence, in the first period firms and workers recognize that a third party might take some of the second-period benefits of the training, and they underinvest in training.

First, consider the simple case where we abstract from the adoption of technology. This will permit us to show the underinvestment in training result most clearly. Let $\delta = 0$, so that all firms adopt the new technology. At the start of period 2, with probability s, worker i is separated from her initial employer. She negotiates a contract with her new employer and receives a wage of $\beta(y + \alpha\tau_i)$. The firm and worker take account of the possibility of a separation in the first-period training decision. The surplus generated for the firm and worker by training level τ is:

$$TS = \frac{1}{(1+r)}\{(1-s)(y+\alpha\tau)+s[\beta(y+\alpha\tau)+(1-\beta)(y+\alpha\int \tilde{\tau}dF(\tilde{\tau}))]\}-c(\tau). \quad (17)$$

The final term is the cost of training, which is realized in the first period. The first term is discounted, for it is the benefit of training, realized in the second period. The first component is simple, for it is the probability that the match continues into the second period, times the output given the continued match. The second component is the probability that the match is dissolved times the returns to the worker in that case, plus the returns to the firm in that case. The worker gets $\beta(y + \alpha\tau)$ from her new firm. The firm gets $(1 - \beta)$ of the output given its new worker. $F(\tilde{\tau})$ is the distribution function of training among workers, so $y + \alpha \int \tilde{\tau}dF(\tilde{\tau})$ is the firm's expected output in period 2, given the dissolution of the first-period match. Choosing τ to maximize (17), we see that firms and workers will choose $\hat{\tau}$ such that

$$(1 + r)c'(\hat{\tau}) = (1 - s)\alpha + s\beta\alpha < \alpha, \quad (18)$$

so that $\hat{\tau} < \tau^h$. Despite the fact that all firms are assumed to have adopted the new technology, there is underinvestment in training. This is a consequence of the fact that in period 2, with probability s, only $\beta\alpha$ will be gained from the training, rather than α. The other portion of the gain, $(1 - \beta)$, was captured by the firm lucky enough to have been matched with the trained worker in period 2. Only if $s = 0$, so that matches do not dissolve, or if $\beta = 1$, so that workers capture all the benefit of their training, is this allocation efficient. The labour market imperfection, therefore, leads to underinvestment in training.

We now consider the way in which this market imperfection can interact with the choice to adopt new technology. Assume once more that $\delta > 0$, so that the technology is costly. However, maintain assumption (16), so that the technology (combined with optimal training) is socially valuable. Suppose that a proportion Φ of firms adopts the technology in the first period. A worker with training τ who with probability s is forcibly separated from her firm has a second-period expected wage of $y + \Phi\alpha\tau$. The firm and the worker at the start of period 1 choose τ and γ (recall that $\gamma \in \{0, 1\}$ indicates adoption of the technology) to maximize their joint surplus, which is analogous to (17):

$$\underset{\gamma \in \{0,1\}, \tau}{\text{Max}} \frac{(1-s)(y+\gamma\alpha\tau)}{(1+r)} + \frac{s[\beta(y+\Phi\alpha\tau)+(1-\beta)(y+\gamma\alpha\int\tilde{\tau}dF(\tilde{\tau}))]}{(1+r)} - (c(\tau)+\gamma\delta). \quad (19)$$

We will now show that it is possible that this economy has two equilibria: one in which all firms adopt the new technology and all workers receive (sub-optimal, but positive) training $\hat{\tau}$, and the other in which no firms adopt the technology and no workers are trained. In the latter equilibrium, there is no incentive to train workers because no firms adopt the new technology, and no firms adopt the new technology because of the dearth of trained workers.

To see that the first equilibrium is possible, suppose that $\Phi = 1$, and that all workers have training $\hat{\tau}$ (so $F(\tilde{\tau})$ has all of its mass at $\hat{\tau}$). Now consider a firm and worker choosing γ and τ to solve (19) with $\Phi = 1$ and $\int\tilde{\tau}dF(\tilde{\tau}) = \hat{t}$. If they choose $\gamma = 1$, then they will also choose $\tau = \hat{\tau}$, because (18) describes the relevant first-order condition. In the case of a separation, the second-period wage of the worker is $\beta(y + \alpha\hat{\tau})$ (because $\Phi = 1$) and the second-period earnings of the firm are $(1 - \beta)(y + \alpha\hat{\tau})$ (because all workers get $\hat{\tau}$ training). So the gain from adopting the innovation and choosing training level $\hat{\tau}$ is $\alpha\hat{\tau} - (1 + r)(\delta + c(\hat{\tau}))$.

Does anyone have an incentive to deviate from this possible equilibrium? Suppose a firm/employee pair decides not to innovate in the first period. What level of training would this pair choose? Training has no benefit if the pair remain together, but with probability s the worker will be separated and matched with a firm with the new technology (recall that $\Phi = 1$), and in that event her wage will be $\beta(y + \alpha\tau)$. The cost of training remains $(1 + r)c(\tau)$, so the deviating pair would choose $\tau = \bar{\tau}'$ such that

$$(1 + r)c'(\bar{\tau}') = s\beta\alpha < (1 - s)\alpha + s\beta\alpha. \quad (20)$$

So $\bar{\tau}' < \hat{\tau}$. The gain to a firm–worker pair of choosing $\gamma = 0$ and $\tau = \bar{\tau}'$ over choosing $\gamma = 0$ and $\tau = 0$ is $s\beta\alpha\bar{\tau}' - (1 + r)c(\bar{\tau}')$. (The first term is the expected extra income earned as a consequence of the training, and the second term is the cost of training.) Hence, if

$$\alpha\hat{t} - (1 + r)(\delta + c(\hat{\tau})) > s\beta\alpha\bar{t}' - (1 + r)c(\bar{t}') > 0, \quad (21)$$

no firm–worker pair will have an incentive to deviate from the equilibrium in which every firm adopts the technology and every worker receives training $\hat{\tau}$. Note that (21) is more restrictive than assumption (16), but is based on the same idea that the innovation–training combination is sufficiently profitable that it generates a surplus.

The allocation in which no firm adopts the technology and no worker is trained is also an equilibrium. Suppose $\Phi = 0$ and no worker is trained (all the mass of $F(\tilde{\tau})$ is at 0). If a firm–worker pair chooses not to adopt the technology, it will also choose zero training. There is no return from training if the pair stays together in the second period, nor (given $\Phi = 0$) is there any return to training if the pair is separated. Is there any incentive for this pair to deviate from this equilibrium? If they adopt the technology ($\gamma = 1$), they choose a level of training $\tau = \bar{\tau}^h$ where

$$(1 + r)c'(\bar{\tau}^h) = (1 - s)\alpha < (1 - s)\alpha + s\beta\alpha. \tag{22}$$

The left-hand side of (22) is the marginal cost of training. The right-hand side is the marginal gain from training, which is realized only if the pair remain together. So $\bar{\tau}^h < \hat{\tau}$. The gain to the pair from choosing to adopt the technology and train the worker is

$$(1 - s)\alpha\bar{\tau}^h - (1 + r)(\delta + c(\bar{\tau}^h)), \tag{23}$$

where the first term is the additional output from training and adopting the technology, which is realized only if the match is not dissolved, and the second term is the cost of adoption plus training. If (23) is negative, then no firm–worker pair has an incentive to deviate from the equilibrium in which no firm adopts the technology and no worker is trained. Note that it is possible for (23) to be positive, in particular if s is small enough. If the firm–worker pair is confident that they will not be separated, then any profitable technology will be adopted.

In this model, therefore, there can be two possible equilibria. These equilibria are Pareto ranked. In the high equilibrium, all firms adopt the technology and all workers are trained (to the level $\hat{\tau}$). Each pair generates a surplus equal to $\alpha\hat{\tau} - (1 + r)(\delta + c(\hat{\tau}))$, which by (21) is positive, and this surplus is split between the worker and the firm. The externality generated by the labour market imperfection leads to underinvestment in training ($\hat{\tau}$ is less than the optimal τ^h), but there is a sufficiently high level of training in the general work-force that firms are not inhibited from adopting the new technology. In the second equilibrium, there is no innovation, nor is any worker trained. No surplus is generated, so both workers and firms are strictly worse off than in the first equilibrium. No single worker–firm pair has an incentive to deviate from this bad equilibrium. It is not worth paying for the technology and the training of the worker because of the probability that the pair will be dissolved. The separated worker would be paired with a firm that has not adopted the technology, so her skills would be useless. The separated firm would wind up with a worker unable to utilize the new technology.

This model has formalized the argument of Rosenstein-Rodan (1943) that investment in human capital, in the specific form of training workers, generates an externality when labour markets are imperfect. Combining this insight with the notion that training and the adoption of new technology are complementary leads to the possibility of multiple Pareto-ranked equilibria. The model illustrates the possibility of an economy trapped in a poor equilibrium in which potentially profitable new technology is not adopted because of insufficient investment in the human capital of workers, and simultaneously there are low returns to investment in human capital because of the low rate of technological innovation. Moreover, it is impossible for an individual firm and its workers profitably to break out of this equilibrium owing to the externalities generated by training in the context of imperfect labour markets.

In this chapter, we have examined two aspects of technological change in poor countries. The first is learning and experimentation. We have argued that technological transformation of production in poor countries generally involves more than a simple transfer of ideas and/or machines from rich countries. Most often, innovation is required in order to adapt the technology to the conditions in which it is to be used. This innovation involves experimentation and learning, both from producers' own experience and from the experience of similarly situated producers in the same economy. The spread of technology, therefore, commonly involves *social learning*.

Second, we have argued that, even when the technology is well understood, adoption of a new technology might require a different economic environment than continued use of an existing technology. In this chapter, we focused on the possibility that new technologies require a more highly skilled labour force. This requirement, coupled with the existence of labour market imperfections, raised the possibility of an economy trapped, unable to adopt a new technology because of an inappropriately trained labour force, and unable to provide appropriate training because of the existing technology of production.

REFERENCES

Acemoglu, D. (1997), 'Training and Innovation in an Imperfect Labor Market', *Review of Economic Studies*, 64.
Amanor, K. S. (1994), *The New Frontier: Farmers' Response to Land Degradation, A West African Study*. London: Zed Books.
Becker, G. (1964), *Human Capital*. Chicago: University of Chicago Press.
Berry, S. (1985), *Fathers Work for their Sons: Accumulation, Mobility and Class Formation in an Extended Yoruba Community*. Berkeley: University of California Press.

Besley, T., and Case, A. (1997), 'Diffusion as a Learning Process: Evidence from HYV Cotton', unpublished paper, Woodrow Wilson School, Princeton University.

Ellison, G., and Fudenberg, D. (1993), 'Rules of Thumb in Social Learning', *Journal of Political Economy*, 101.

Evenson, R., and Westphal, L. (1995), 'Technological Change and Technology Strategy', in J. Behrman and T. N. Srinivasan (eds.), *Handbook of Development Economics*, iiiA. Amsterdam: North-Holland.

Foster, A., and Rosenzweig, M. (1995), 'Learning by Doing and Learning from Others: Human Capital and Technical Change in Agriculture', *Journal of Political Economy*, 103.

—— and —— (1996), 'Technological Change and Human-Capital Returns and Investments: Evidence from the Green Revolution', *American Economic Review*, 86.

Gerschenkron, A. (1962), *Economic Backwardness in Historical Perspective: A Book of Essays*. Cambridge, Mass.: Harvard University Press.

Jovanovic, B., and Nyarko, Y. (1994), 'The Bayesian Foundations of Learning by Doing', unpublished paper, New York University Department of Economics.

Munshi, K. (1996), 'Farmers as Econometricians: Social Learning and Technology Diffusion in the Indian Green Revolution', unpublished paper, Boston University.

Prescott, E. (1972), 'The Multi-Period Control Problem under Uncertainty', *Econometrica*, 40.

Romer, P. (1990), 'Endogenous Technological Change', *Journal of Political Economy*, 98.

Rosenstein-Rodan, P. (1943), 'Problems of Industrialization of Eastern and South-Eastern Europe', *Economic Journal*, 53.

Schultz, T. W. (1975), 'The Value of the Ability to Deal with Disequilibria', *Journal of Economic Literature*, 13.

Velenchik, A. (1995), 'Apprenticeship Contracts, Small Enterprises and Credit Markets in Ghana', *World Bank Economic Review*, 9.

Wilson, R. (1975), 'Informational Economics of Scale', *Bell Journal of Economics*, Spring.

13

Environment and Development

I

There is a two-way relationship between poverty and environmental degradation. The poor, particularly in rural areas, depend for their daily livelihood on local environmental resources—forests, fisheries, grazing lands, irrigation water, and so on. The local commons also provide some insurance for the poor as a fallback source of food and fodder in bad crop years. With the erosion of the local commons—the decimation of forests and grazing lands, the silting and increasing toxicity of rivers and ponds, the depletion of aquifers, and soil erosion and desertification—the life of the rural poor has become more insecure and impoverished in many parts of Africa and South Asia. The usual poverty estimates based on private consumption expenditure data do not capture this effect (except indirectly and partially through a rise in the prices of such items as firewood that enter the cost of living deflator). There is slow but increasing awareness that the data for national income growth rates need to be seriously corrected for the depreciation of the stock of 'natural' capital.[1] In many countries such depreciation of the environmental resource base has been disproportionately costly for the poor. The other side of the relationship between poverty and environmental degradation is that poverty in turn drives people to desperate short-run 'mining' of land and water and to other intensive resource extraction, straining the already fragile and limited environmental base, sometimes beyond the possibility for repair and renewal.

While this two-way relationship suggests yet another way in which it is difficult to escape from the vicious circle of poverty, the recent literature has pointed out,[2] on the basis of cross-section data, another kind of nonlinearity for

[1] For Costa Rica, for example, Solorzano *et al.* (1991) have estimated that, in 1989 the depreciation of three resources—forests, soil, and fisheries—amounted to about 10% of GDP and over a third of gross capital formation.

[2] See e.g. World Bank (1992), and Grossman and Krueger (1995). For a critical discussion of the U-shaped curve, see Arrow *et al.* (1996) and the comments on it in the Policy Forum of the *Environment and Development Economics*, Feb. 1996.

countries that do succeed in escaping: a U-shaped curve relating economic growth and environmental quality; i.e., as income per capita rises, environmental quality first gets worse and then improves. This may be partly because the income elasticity of demand for a better environment is positive (as awareness increases after a point and as the consumption basket shifts from basic necessities to luxuries), partly because the pollution intensity of production changes as a country's output composition shifts from agriculture to manufacturing and then to services, and partly because the technological and organizational capacity for the abatement of pollution improves as a country gets richer to offset the increasing pollution attendant on the growth process.

This U-shaped relation, however, does not warrant complacency on environmental matters in poor countries. First of all, the relationship has been shown only for emissions of a few air and water pollutants (and not for dispersed, long-term pollutants like carbon dioxide), not generally for resource stocks (particularly of the kind that are important on the local commons) or stocks of waste. Second, a relation observed in cross-country data does not imply that for a given poor country the environment will automatically improve with income over time (just as the famous Kuznets U-shaped curve showing income inequality eventually declining with income does not warrant acquiescence at existing inequalities in poor countries). Third, more than in the case of the Kuznets curve, there are certain irreversibilities in environmental damage; the earth's resource base may not be able to recover if countries such as China or India now deplete and pollute at the same rate as countries like the United States did at their early stages of industrialization. On the positive side, there now exist technologies for pollution abatement (which were not available earlier), improved access to which (with international help, because these technologies are expensive) is imperative, so that the wait for the turning-point in the U-shaped curve is shortened for a poor country.

Environmental economics is a fast-growing subject with an already voluminous literature. In the rest of this brief chapter we shall focus on two primary issues—incentive design and property rights, and trade policy—issues that have given rise to a great deal of controversy in recent years.[3]

II

A major distinguishing feature of environmental economics is, of course, the predominance of externalities. The problem of the environment often arises

---

[3] In our discussion of the first issue, we have drawn upon the overview papers of Seabright (1993) and Dasgupta and Maler (1995), and for the second issue on the papers by Copeland and Taylor (1994, 1995).

from an institutional failure (on the part of the market, the state or the community) to cope with these externalities.

The standard prescription is that since, on account of externalities, market prices do not reflect social priorities and costs, they should be brought in line with the shadow prices of the environmental resources through appropriate taxes and subsidies. Sometimes quantitative restrictions on resource use (such as limits on effluent discharges or quotas on fishing) are preferred to price-based instruments like taxes. This may be partly because quotas are easier to administer in many cases, and partly because, as Weitzman (1974a) has emphasized, in a situation of uncertainty about how the control mechanism will work a quota may pose lower risks than a price mechanism. This is particularly important when one is near the threshold level beyond which the capacity for self-renewal for a resource can be seriously damaged. In general, as the literature on cost–benefit analysis makes clear, shadow prices cannot be relied upon if there are non-convexities (of which threshold effects provide an example) in the production technology.[4]

It should also be pointed out that the way shadow prices are usually computed, they reflect only the direct use-value of a resource. This leaves out the additional value of preserving the stock of a resource, from the point of view of both its non-commercial value (including indirect effects, such as forests' soil erosion prevention or recycling carbon dioxide) and its 'option value', when society may want to keep open the possibility of its future use-value and when there are irreversibilities in the process of depletion. (A major example is that of a varied genetic pool in tropical forests.)

A well-known case of environmental externality is that related to what is called 'the tragedy of the commons', where the private cost of using a resource being less than its social cost leads to over-exploitation in the (open-access) commons. A simple exercise will suffice to demonstrate this.

Suppose, in a common fishing ground of a given size, each fisherman uses a single private input, a fishing boat, in catching fish. The fish production function is $C = F(K)$, which is increasing and strictly concave, where C is the total catch and K is the size of the total fishing fleet. The competitive price of a boat is p. The Pareto-optimal solution for K is given by K^* when

$$F'(K^*) = p. \qquad (1)$$

Suppose that the fish are evenly distributed in the fishing grounds so that each boat catches the same amount. At the Nash equilibrium, each fisherman will take the total size of the fleet of all the other fishermen, $\tilde{K}$, as given and will

---

[4] As Baumol and Bradford (1972) and Starrett (1972) have shown, with non-convexities associated with external diseconomies, what are called Lindahl equilibria (with competitive prices for externalities) typically do not exist even if property rights are well-defined and enforceable. For a full discussion of this problem in the context of resource economics, see Dasgupta (1982).

maximize the profits from his share of the catch, $\{[k/(k+\tilde{K})]F(k+\tilde{K}) - pk\}$, with respect to k, the fisherman's choice variable of the number of fishing boats. At a symmetric equilibrium with n fishermen $k/K = 1/n$, and the first-order condition for profit maximization yields

$$p = (1/n)F'(K) + [(n-1)/n]F(K)/K. \tag{2}$$

This means that the price of the boat is to be equated to a weighted sum of its marginal and average product. When access to the fishing grounds is free and the number of fishermen is very large, the price converges to the average product, profits approach zero, and the size of the fleet is larger than Pareto-optimal. This is the case of over-exploitation referred to in the literature on the tragedy of the (open-access) commons.

Some resource economists have rightly pointed out that the open-access case is not quite relevant for many of the local common property situations where a community or some other group has the right to exclude non-members from the use of the resource. Nevertheless, with major demographic and institutional changes often weakening the traditional rights of local communities and with some cases where the group is no longer very well-defined, it may be important to keep the open-access case as a benchmark.

Faced with the externalities inflicted by one user on another and the consequent overuse (and under-maintenance) of common resources, the conventional wisdom in mainstream economics is to favour the establishment of well-defined private property rights over them. This is to generate incentives for greater internalization of externalities and for careful husbanding of resources by private owners. For any remaining externalities, many would turn to the famous proposition of Coase (1960) whereby private parties can negotiate their way to efficiency with appropriate side-payments, if necessary.

However, straightforward privatization of common property resources often has serious distributional consequences, particularly in the form of disenfranchizement of the poor. From the enclosure movement in eighteenth-century England to the current appropriations of forests and grazing lands in developing countries by timber merchants and cattle ranchers, it has been the same sad story. Even when resources are better managed under private ownership, many of their traditional users are not adequately compensated. In this context, Weitzman (1974b) raises the question of whether, with the increased efficiency under private management, the former common property users, now working as wage-earners for the private owners, can actually gain from privatization. He answers in the negative for the open-access resource; going back to equation (2) above, we can guess why. Instead of the fishing boat, suppose the variable factor is labour, which in the open-access case gets paid its average product. Under private management, labour use and hence equilibrium output will be less than in the open-access equilibrium, where the profits are driven down to zero. With positive profits and lower output under private manage-ment, the total wage payments are less than the total labour earnings (equal to output) under open access, even though the latter is the less efficient system.

In addition to this regressive distributional impact, privatization of the com-mons can create important problems even from the point of view of efficiency. Time discount rates of private owner-users may be higher (and therefore resource exploitation rates larger) than what is appropriate for the community as a whole. Besides, as Seabright (1993) has pointed out, when contracts are necessarily incomplete, attempts to enforce private property rights may weaken the mechanisms of cooperation that previously existed among the users, who may have shared implicit non-contractual rights in the common property resource, in two important ways. First, privatization typically shifts the bar-gaining power sufficiently in favour of those who acquire the property rights so that the parties may no longer share enough interdependence—or what Singleton and Taylor (1992) call 'mutual vulnerability'—to make cooperation credible. In fact when privatization is perceived as unfair by the dispossessed previous users, it can lead some of these users to irresponsible and destructive practices, and ultimately everyone, including the owner of the newly created property right, may be worse off. Second, a central characteristic of most private property rights is their tradability, and tradability may undermine the reliabil-ity of a long-term relationship among beneficiaries of a resource. Relationship-specific investments in the maintenance and preservation of a resource may thus be discouraged.[5]

As for the remaining externalities among private owners, there are, as we dis-cuss in Chapter 17, problems with the Coase solution, particularly when much information is privately held and when transaction costs are high (for example in the case of upstream deforestation resulting in floods and soil erosion in downstream communities). The difficulties of negotiation may be particularly acute when there are many parties involved or when there are non-convexities in the form of environmental damage thresholds. Then there are parties (e.g. future generations who may bear the brunt of the externalities) that are not in a position to negotiate.

Although privatization has its equity and efficiency problems, nationaliza-tion of a local common property resource and its management by a distant bureaucracy is rarely any better, and in some cases is actually much worse. The state may have superior technical expertise about the larger implications of some types of ecological processes at work or better ability to coordinate exter-nalities across local jurisdictions, but management from above often leads to

---

[5] Seabright (1993) is, however, careful to stress that the circumstances under which this problem occurs are somewhat special. Long-term implicit contracts are not weakened by the mere fact of trad-ability of property rights in assets; it is tradability plus a sufficient likelihood of the presence of potential new owners with different out-of-equilibrium payoffs that is the key factor.

insufficient utilization of local information and initiative. As ineffective or corrupt government supervision replaces traditional control structures, a common property resource can become a hunting ground for overexploitation and malfeasance by influential interest groups and an object of predation by even formerly responsible, now dispossessed, local users. The widespread depletion and degradation of the commons in many poor countries where they were taken over by the colonial and post-colonial governments bear testimony to the ravages of this system. Where state management has worked it has been usually through involving the local people whose livelihood depends on the resource (as in some of the joint forest management projects in parts of India or the wildlife management projects in southern Africa).

III

As an alternative to the polar opposites of private and state control (which dominate much of the public policy discussion), there exists the important possibility of local-level (mostly informal) community organizations managing resources and resolving conflicts and disputes (both on goals to be pursued and on the manner in which they are to be implemented). This places decision making in the hands of people who have the information and the motivation that outsiders lack and yet can avoid some of the pitfalls of privatization. There are several documented examples—see Ostrom (1990) and Baland and Platteau (1996)—of successful and autonomous local community-level cooperation in the management of common property resources in different parts of the world today. There are, of course, numerous cases of failures of such cooperation as well, making it important to understand the conditions for and against sustainability of local cooperation on the commons.[6]

While sociologists and anthropologists look at social norms and codes of conduct in understanding cooperative behaviour, economists usually emphasize incentives and penalties. In the literature on repeated Prisoners' Dilemma games, it is shown that cooperative equilibria can be spontaneously sustained by the long-run interests of foresighted self-interested individuals. The possibility of cooperation depends, of course, on the future payoffs not being discounted too heavily, and/or the short-run rewards to defection (like stealing water from a common irrigation system) not being too large. The latter, of course, will depend on the sanctions that other people can impose on the potential defector.

---

[6] For attempts at this, see Wade (1987), Ostrom (1990), Bardhan (1993), and Baland and Platteau (1996).

To put it in formal, but simple, terms, suppose there are two players. If both cooperate, they both receive x; if both defect, both receive 0. If one defects and one cooperates, the cooperator gets $(-z)$ while the defector gets y. Suppose, $y > x > 0$, that $z > 0$, and $2x > y - z$, and the discount factor is $\rho < 1$. Then we know that, provided $y - x < \rho x/(1 - \rho)$, there exists a retaliation strategy which consists of playing Defect for a finite number of periods in the event that the other player has played Defect after an agreement to cooperate, and which ensures that the other player is no better off from the defection.

Let T be the lowest integer such that

$$y - x \leq \rho x + \rho^2 x + \ldots + \rho^T x.$$

Then T is the smallest number of periods for which each player must threaten to retaliate in order for the threat credibly to sustain cooperation. If, on the other hand, it happens that $y - x \geq \rho x/(1 - \rho)$, then there exists no finite T, and consequently no retaliatory strategy that can sustain cooperation.

The retaliatory strategies should not merely make it sufficiently costly for the defector, but to be credible they should not be too costly for the punisher. But therein lies a second-order collective action problem, since punishment is costly to the punisher, while the benefits are distributed diffusely in the community.[7] The primary trick here is to devise strategies that punish players who fail to play their part in punishing the defector, i.e. rules of what can be called meta-punishment.[8] This may be a problem in very large groups, as sanctions may run out of steam at two or three removes from the original violation. But in a small community of resource users meta-punishments may not be unreasonable (but then, in small communities the social costs of punishment to the punisher as well as the punished may also be larger).

The benefits of cooperation in the future must themselves be sufficiently probable to act as an incentive to cooperation in the present. For this one may need the game to be infinitely repeated (to avoid the standard problem of breakdown of cooperation by backward induction in finite-period games), or there may be sufficient uncertainty about how many times it will be repeated. An alternative solution[9] is 'reputation': even a very small probability that the player

---

[7] In actual field settings, as Ostrom (1990) has noted, a community mitigates this problem by pre-committing to the appointment of collectively arranged and financed 'enforcers' of cooperative arrangements (like field-guards or nightwatchmen).

[8] Extending the theory of repeated games to the case of matching games (without 'common knowledge'), Kandori (1992) shows that a community can sustain cooperation, even when each agent knows nothing more than her personal experience, through what he calls the 'contagious equilibrium'. (Defection by a few spreads like an epidemic, and the threat of a complete breakdown may act as a deterrant to defection.)

[9] Other alternatives that have been tried in the literature are to assume 'bounded rationality', or a one-shot game that has multiple Nash equilibria with two or more different payoffs to each player. In the latter case, Benoit and Krishna (1985) have proved, under fairly general conditions, that the average

is of a type that intrinsically prefers to cooperate acts as an incentive to all types of player to behave cooperatively, so long as the game is sufficiently far from its final period for the loss of reputation for cooperation to be costly.

The theoretical models point to a potentially large number of equilibrium outcomes, facing which players may use observed past behaviours of others as a guide in their choice. In other words, even when costs and benefits of cooperation are otherwise identical, what degree of trust the players have in one another serves a crucial role. Seabright (1997) has in this context a model of trust where he shows that when many equilibria can exist in which the players' beliefs about each other's trustworthiness are confirmed by subsequent behaviour, there is a tendency of cooperative behaviour to enhance the prospects for successful further cooperation.

Many writers in the literature on the local commons have suggested that the constellation of the relevant costs and benefits of collective action are often of a kind that is more favourable to the possibility of cooperation than the Prisoners' Dilemma game. Even in a one-shot coordination game, for example, it is in the interest of the players to cooperate provided they can be assured (sometimes therefore it is called an assurance game) that others (or a sufficient number of others in a multi-person game) will do the same.

Suppose the payoff structure in a two-by-two one-period game is as follows:

Player II

		C	D
	C	$(2, 2)$	$(-1, 1)$
Player I			
	D	$(1, -1)$	$(0, 0)$

In this case each player cooperates when the other does, but defects when the other defects. This captures a widely observed phenomenon in the field studies: nobody wants to be 'suckered', but they want to be cooperative when the others are, something the static Prisoners' Dilemma game with its dominant strategy of defection for each player does not capture. The payoff structure above, of course, allows three possible equilibria (two in pure strategies and one in mixed strategy), and which equilibrium is selected will depend on the prior expectations of each individual's action. In the actual case of local commons mutual expectations of cooperation may be facilitated by pre-play communication and the opportunities for mutual reassurance.

In many cases coordination is effective only if the number of cooperators reaches a critical mass. For this we shall consider here an n-player assurance

---

payoffs in subgame-perfect equilibria of long, finitely repeated versions of this game are very close to any average payoffs attainable in the infinitely repeated versions of the game.

game discussed by Baland and Platteau (1996).[10] Suppose a given local public good (say, the maintenance and management of an irrigation system) yields individual benefits to each member of a group equal to $b(N)$, where N is the number of voluntary contributors. Each such contributor incurs a fixed cost of c, and so the total cost for the group is cN. The choice facing player i is then as follows:

	Payoff to player i if the number of other contributors is				
	$N-1$	$N-2$	$N-3$	$\ldots$	0
Player i					
contributes	$b(N)-c$	$b(N-1)-c$	$b(N-1)-c$	$\ldots$	$b(1)-c$
does not contribute	$b(N-1)$	$b(N-2)$	$b(N-3)$	$\ldots$	0

Suppose there are increasing returns in the provision of the public good, so that both the first and second derivatives of $b(N)$ are positive. Assume also that $b(1)$ is less than c, so that if no other player contributes to the public good, player i chooses not to contribute. Yet, there exists a critical size N^* such that $b(N) - c > b(N^* - 1)$, i.e., once a certain number, N^*, of other players agree to contribute, player i has an incentive to do the same, since the cost of individual contribution is less than the marginal individual benefit from that contribution. Since the second derivative of $b(N)$ is positive, if $b(N^*) - c > b(N^* - 1)$, then $b(j) > b(j-1) + c$ for all $j > N^*$. Therefore, as long as at least N^* other players contribute, player i prefers to cooperate rather than free-ride. In such games there is an important role for community leadership, i.e. to mobilize a sufficient number of contributors and set the assurance process rolling.

While game-theoretic models in general give us important insights into the sustainability of cooperation among self-interested agents in a situation of strategic interdependence in the management of common resources, it is at the same time useful to recognize that there are aspects of real-world cooperation with which the models are much too rigid and limited to be able to cope with any degree of subtlety. For example, they cannot usually handle the impact of ongoing interactions among agents in the updating and contingent modifications of the rules of the game. (The latter may include group dynamics in some real-world settings of community leadership, which through deliberation and persuasion may bring about endogenous preference changes and reorientation of values in a community, and thus may break pre-existing deadlocks.)

Both theoretical models and field studies, however, agree on the importance of group size for cooperation. Cooperation in general works better in small groups with similar resource needs and close interactions, shared norms (which

---

[10] Baland and Platteau (1996) also discuss interesting hybrid cases of payoff structures, where players with a payoff structure characteristic of the assurance game face players with a payoff structure characteristic of the Prisoners' Dilemma.

act as focal points and coordinate expectations), and patterns of reciprocity. In such communities monitoring is easier, the 'common knowledge' assumption of models of strategic decisions is likely to be more valid, incentive dilution is less of a problem, chances of pre-play communication and learning about one another's intended plans of action are better, and social sanctions are easier to implement through reputation mechanisms and multiplex relationships of face-to-face communities. Migration and mobility possibilities work against cooperation. Contact with outsiders and the exit option reduce the effectiveness of social norms, and prolonged repetition of the game also becomes more uncertain, raising incentives for short-run opportunism.

IV

In the previous two sections we have discussed issues of incentive systems of managing environmental resources on which there has been some controversy, and about which environmentalists (often suspicious of both the state and the market) have raised concerns regarding loss of local community control. In this section we address another of their concerns, namely the possible damaging effects of the international market integration process. Environmentalists and international trade economists have often been on opposite sides on the issue of trade liberalization (for example on recent international policy issues such as the North American Free Trade Agreement, or the proposals for adoption of environmental standards by the World Trade Organization). In our brief exploration of the issues, we shall point to the complexities involved and consider the possibility that the answers are less straightforward than may be implied by either side.

While environmentalists worry about the effect of the global market expansion process in accelerating the degradation of the fragile environment in poor countries and turning them into international 'pollution havens', they often overlook the fact that such expansion and economic growth may also increase the financial, technological, and organizational capability for (and public awareness of and demand for) pollution abatement. International trade economists, worried about 'green protectionism', are quick to point out that trade restrictions are not the first-best way of tackling environmental market failures. Such failures are better addressed by domestic regulations, price and tax-subsidy policies and infrastructural investments. Underpricing of natural resources (e.g. subsidized water in India or energy in Russia, or timber royalty concessions in public forests in Indonesia and the Philippines) and a lack of well-defined and enforced property rights lead to extensive depletion and to a distortion of production and trade. But if these domestic policies and regulations are not in place and are likely to take a long time to be established, it is not clear that the second-best policy is to go ahead with trade liberalization.

As Chichilnisky (1994) and Brander and Taylor (1995) have shown in a general equilibrium setting, trade tends to magnify the effects of market failure resulting from externalities and makes the misallocation worse. Going back to our discussion of the model of (open-access) commons in Section II, we have seen that the equilibrium tends to be characterized by over-exploitation; international trade induces the exporters of the resource-intensive good to exploit the resource even more. Ill-defined property rights and the associated under-pricing of common resources, with private costs lower than social costs of resource exploitation, create a motive for trade even with otherwise identical countries but with better enforced property rights (or better regulated common property). Chichilnisky gives the example of Honduras, with its scarce forest resources, exporting wood to the United States, which has some of the largest forests in the world.

Abstracting from the problem of property rights and underpricing, we shall now explore the income effects of trade on pollution and follow the model of Copeland and Taylor (1994). Suppose there are two countries, one rich and the other poor, (sharply) different only in their endowments of human capital or effective labour, which is the only primary input in production. There is a continuum of goods produced, indexed by $z \in [0, 1]$. Pollution discharge is a byproduct of this production process[11] and it requires labour to abate; so, for all practical purposes, pollution is like an input in production. We can therefore rank all the goods in terms of pollution intensity, ranged from left to right on a line as follows:

$$0 \qquad\qquad z^* \qquad\qquad 1$$

The cost of polluting is a pollution tax that one has to pay. The tax is part of an endogenous environmental policy, set equal to the marginal damage (in terms of consumer disutility) caused by pollution emissions.[12] The tax is increasing in income, since environmental quality is a 'normal' good. So it is costlier to produce pollution-intensive goods in the rich country. Trade is driven entirely by income-induced international differences in pollution policy.

The rich country has a higher pollution tax and the pollution-intensive goods are costlier there under autarky than in the poor country. So trade will drive the poor country to export pollution-intensive goods to the rich country and import (effective) labour-intensive goods. If z^* represents the equilibrium,

---

[11] We shall assume that pollution is confined to the country of emission and does not cross the international boundary.

[12] We assume that the government does not attempt to use the pollution tax policy to manipulate the country's terms of trade.

the rich country produces all goods, $z \in [0, z^*)$, and the poor country produces all goods, $z \in (z^*, 1]$. Comparing free-trade pollution levels with those in autarky, Copeland and Taylor decompose the effect of trade into a scale effect (an increase in pollution as the level of economic activity goes up), a technique effect (a change in aggregate pollution when higher taxes lead to the adoption of cleaner techniques of production), and an output composition effect (a change in the range of goods produced by a country). If z^*, the range of goods produced in the rich country, increases, pollution in both countries will increase: in the rich country the marginal goods added to its production range are more pollution-intensive than average, whereas the poor country will lose its cleanest industries.

The scale effect of trade (increasing pollution) following upon the income gains from trade is counteracted by the technique effect (decreasing pollution, as higher income leads to higher pollution tax and thus cleaner techniques) in both countries. But with the assumptions of the model (e.g. unit elasticity of substitution in production as well as consumption), Copeland and Taylor show that the output composition effect dominates. By this critical output composition effect, following from the poor country exporting pollution-intensive goods to the rich country and importing effective labour-intensive goods, the pattern of trade lowers the pollution level in the rich country and raises it in the poor country, compared with the situation under autarky.

The effect of economic growth (in the sense of human capital accumulation) in this model is also asymmetric. Suppose, first, that there is growth in the rich country but not in the poor country. In this case, as growth improves the effectiveness of labour in the rich country, z^* increases, and from the discussion of the output composition effect above, pollution increases in *both* countries. Take now the opposite case of growth in the poor country, but not in the rich country: as z^* falls, with the poor country graduating to relatively clean industries, pollution goes down in *both* countries.

In the above model consumers suffer from a direct disutility from pollution, but there are many cases where pollution discharge from one industry causes negative production externality for another (e.g. industrial effluents poisoning the water, which affects output in fisheries or agriculture). In such a situation the production set may be non-convex, and, as is familiar from the literature on international trade with production externality, trade may drive a country to complete specialization. Under autarky, a country may produce some of the clean products (say, fish) to satisfy domestic demand, but with trade this demand can be met by imports, and the country may specialize in dirty products, increasing the total pollution. Thus, as Copeland and Taylor (1995) show in a two-sector dynamic model (allowing for the regenerative capacity of environmental capital), the separation of the location of consumption and production eliminates the domestic market-driven check on the level of pollution. The opening of trade, even at world prices that are arbitrarily close to autarky prices, may thus cause a large discrete change in environmental quality. The terms of trade between dirty and clean products determine how the productivity gains created by spatial separation of their production will be shared across countries.

All this suggests that pushing for trade expansion without at the same time strengthening domestic environmental policies and their effective implementation may be harmful to the environment. With the threshold effects of environmental degradation (which we have talked about before) and, in general, the cost of cure being larger than the cost of prevention, we cannot afford to wait for the possible trade-induced gains (in income, access to abatement technology, and awareness) to work out their beneficial effects on the environment in the long run. At the same time many empirical studies suggest that one should not exaggerate the impact of inter-country differences in regulatory standards or pollution control costs on patterns of international trade and investment. Nor should we allow our concern with the costs of 'green protectionism' in rich countries to deflect our attention from the far more substantial costs imposed by their traditional trade barriers against labour-intensive manufactures and agricultural products of poor countries. The cost of compliance with reasonable environmental standards in commodity production (adopting the 'polluter pays' principle) in the exporting developing countries can be largely shifted to the consumers in rich countries (whose demand for many of these commodities is price-inelastic), provided the developing countries can work out agreements among themselves on these policies and effectively enforce these agreements. With adequate safeguards, the goals of trade liberalization and environmental improvement can be complementary in large measure.[13]

REFERENCES

Arrow, K., *et al.* (1996), 'Economic Growth, Carrying Capacity, and the Environment', *Environment and Development Economics*, 1.

Baland, J. M., and Platteau, J. P. (1996), *Halting Degradation of Natural Resources: Is There a Role for Rural Communities?* Rome: Food and Agriculture Organization of the United Nations.

Bardhan, P. (1993), 'Analytics of the Institutions of Informal Cooperation in Rural Development', *World Development*, 21.

Baumol, W. M., and Bradford, D. (1972),'Detrimental Externalities and Non-Convexity of the Production Set', *Economica*, 39.

Benoit, J. P., and Krishna, V. (1985), 'Finitely Repeated Games', *Econometrica*, 53.

---

[13] For a balanced discussion of some of the policy issues, see Repetto (1995).

Brander, J. A., and Taylor, M. S. (1995), 'International Trade and Open Access Renewable Resources: The Small Open Economy Case', NBER Working Paper no. 5021, February.

Chichilnisky, G. (1994), 'North–South Trade and the Global Environment', *American Economic Review*, 84.

Coase, R. (1960), 'The Problem of Social Cost', *Journal of Law and Economics*, 3.

Copeland, B. R., and Taylor, M. S. (1994), 'North–South Trade and the Environment', *Quarterly Journal of Economics*, 109.

—— and —— (1995), 'Trade, Spatial Separation, and the Environment', NBER Working Paper no. 5242, August.

Dasgupta, P. (1982), *The Control of Resources*. Oxford: Basil Blackwell.

—— and Mäler, K. G. (1995), 'Poverty, Institutions, and the Environmetal Resource Base', in J. Behrman and T. N. Srinivasan (eds.), *Handbook of Development Economics*, iiiA. Amsterdam: North-Holland.

Grossman, G. M., and Krueger, A. B. (1995), 'Economic Growth and the Environment', *Quarterly Journal of Economics*, 112.

Kandori, M. (1992), 'Social Norms and Community Enforcement', *Review of Economic Studies*, 59.

Ostrom, E. (1990), *Governing the Commons: The Evolution of Institutions for Collective Action*. New York: Cambridge University Press.

Repetto, R. (1995), 'Trade and Sustainable Development', in M. G. Quibria (ed.), *Critical Issues in Asian Development: Theories, Experiences and Policies*. New York: Oxford University Press.

Seabright, P. (1993), 'Managing Local Commons: Theoretical Issues in Incentive Design', *Journal of Economic Perspectives*, 7.

—— (1997), 'Is Cooperation Habit-Forming?' in P. Dasgupta and K. G. Maler (eds.), *The Environment and Emerging Development Issues*. Oxford: Clarendon Press.

Singleton, S., and Taylor, M. (1992), 'Common Property, Collective Action and Community', *Journal of Theoretical Politics*, 4.

Solorzano, R., et al. (1991), *Accounts Overdue: Natural Resource Depreciation in Costa Rica*. Washington: World Resources Institute.

Starrett, D. A. (1972), 'Fundamental Non-Convexities in the Theory of Externalities', *Journal of Economic Theory*, 4.

Wade, R. (1987), *Village Republics: Economic Conditions for Collective Action in South India*. Cambridge: Cambridge University Press.

Weitzman, M. L. (1974a), 'Prices vs. Quantities', *Review of Economic Studies*, 41.

—— (1974b), 'Free Access vs. Private Ownership as Alternative Systems for Managing Common Property', *Journal of Economic Theory*, 8.

World Bank (1992), *World Development Report*. New York: Oxford University Press.

14

Trade and Development

I

The literature on trade and development in economic theory is quite old, dating at least back to Adam Smith, who (for example) linked development with the role of trade as a 'vent for surplus'.[1] The postwar theoretical literature on the subject largely emanates from Hicks's famous Inaugural Lecture at Oxford (Hicks 1953): this particular strand deals with the comparative-static effects of economic expansion on terms of trade and balance of payments. A byproduct of this literature was the analysis of the determinants of terms of trade between rich and poor countries (the so-called North–South models, or what used to be called centre–periphery models) with differential demand structure, labour market conditions, and patterns of growth.

Then the literature on growth theory was duly extended to the case of an open economy (the old growth theory in the 1950s and the 1960s,[2] and then the 'new' growth theory in more recent years), and these extensions had obvious implications for trade and development. In particular, the old learning-by-doing literature which led to an analysis of the theory of infant-industry protection in the context of development was extended more recently to the important case of learning-driven movement up the quality ladder of goods and its impact on the international division of labour. In general, the endogenous growth theory of the 1960s as well as that of the 1980s put the focus of the literature on the effect of trade policy on the rate of growth. We shall see that the results here are not always as clear-cut as some policy economists are inclined to suggest; this is at least consistent with the ambiguous results on the relationship between trade and growth that careful examinations of the voluminous empirical literature on the subject indicate.[3]

[1] For an illuminating discussion on this see Myint (1958).
[2] For a review and extension of this literature in the context of trade and development, see Bardhan (1970) and Findlay (1973).
[3] For a review of this empirical literature with clear pointers to the serious methodological and econometric problems, see Harrison and Revenga (1995).

In this chapter we shall start with a simple comparative-static exercise to illustrate the effect of growth on the terms of trade between a rich and a poor country. Then in Section II we analyse the pro-competitive effect of trade liberalization on output expansion in the context of imperfect competition and a vertical industrial structure. Finally, in Section III we briefly assess the implications of the recent literature on endogenous growth in an open economy.

In order to concentrate on some specific determinants of the terms of trade between a rich and a poor country in a simple comparative-static framework, we abstract from many other aspects[4] and assume that both countries are completely specialized, the poor country producing and exporting only a primary product m and the rich country only a manufactured product c (the numeraire good). The trade deficit, D, for the poor country is then given by

$$D = L z_c(y, 1/p) - \bar{L} p x_m(\bar{y}, p) \geq 0, \tag{1}$$

where z_c is per capita import of c in the poor country, x_m is export of m by the poor country *per person in the rich country*, L and y are the population and per capita income, respectively, in the poor country, the same variables with overbars represent those for the rich country, and p is the commodity terms of trade for the poor country. The demand for imports in each country (the import in the rich country is what the poor country exports) depends on per capita income in that country, and on the relative price of the relevant good. We take, not unrealistically in most cases, the trade deficit of the poor country to be non-negative.

Using a circumflex over a variable to represent percentage change in it, we can now get

$$\hat{D} = a\hat{p} + b, \tag{2}$$

where $a = M\eta - N(1 - \bar{\eta})$, with $M = L z_c/D$, $N = \bar{L} p x_m/D$, $M \geq N$, and η is the (positively defined) price elasticity of demand for import in the poor country (with an overbar for the rich country); and

$$b = M e_c\hat{y} - N \bar{e}_m \hat{\bar{y}} + M\hat{L} - N\hat{\bar{L}},$$

with e as the income elasticity of demand for the good denoted by the subscript.

With the standard Marshall–Lerner stability condition for international equilibrium, $(\eta + \bar{\eta})$ is larger than unity, and thus a is positive. With Engel's law, i.e. that the income elasticity of demand is larger for the manufactured good c than for the primary product m in either country, b is positive if the population grows at a faster rate in the poor country than in the rich country (which we can safely assume) and if per capita income grows in the poor country at a rate no less than that in the rich country (which we shall call the growth objective).

---

[4] For a more comprehensive review (to date) of North–South models, see Ocampo (1986).

From (2), if a poor country does not want its trade deficit to grow,

$$\hat{p} \le -b/a. \tag{3}$$

This means when b is positive, $\hat{p}$ is negative. In other words, the terms of trade will decline for the poor country if the latter has what we have called the growth objective (not a very ambitious objective, we may note) and at the same time does not want its trade deficit to grow. This in some sense captures the spirit of a large part of the early development economics literature on an allegedly secular downward trend in the terms of trade of a primary-goods-exporting poor country. In the model, this is driven largely by the demand structure (as incorporated in the Engel's law). Of course, a decline in terms of trade with economic growth is not necessarily bad for a country's real income, but with a low price elasticity of demand for primary exports (at least for the poor countries all together), it is a matter of some concern.

If foreign debt and/or foreign capital inflow are not forthcoming or have problems of their own, so that not allowing the trade deficit to grow is a reasonable objective, and if the poor country wants to grow at least as fast as the rich country, the only major way to avoid the decline in terms of trade with reference to the analytical framework is to go out of the restrictive confines of complete specialization in the above model; in particular, to follow a policy of import substitution (producing the income-elastic manufactures at home) or even export substitution (switching from primary exports to those of manufactures), presumably after a sufficient industrial base has been built at home. Of course, the history of poor countries over the last few decades is littered with instances of prolonged high-cost import substitution regimes, crippling economic growth and export competitiveness. The success stories, such as those in East Asia in the 1980s and early 1990s, where a country has graduated swiftly from import substitution to an expansion of exports of increasingly complex manufactures, are few and far between.

II

One of the ways in which the import substitution regime is supposed to hurt the economy in poor countries is by blocking the discipline of international markets on domestic production efficiency. Although there are not too many theoretical models spelling out the exact analytical mechanism, the pro-competitive effect of trade liberalization on output expansion is part of the conventional wisdom of the trade literature. In the industrial economics literature, however, the relationship between competition and incentives for cost reduction at the firm level is often found to be rather ambiguous (see e.g. Schmidt 1994): on the one hand, there is the 'Darwinian' force putting pressure on the managers to cut costs in order to avoid bankruptcy; on the other hand, there is the 'Schumpeterian' argument that competition, by reducing the expected market share of the firm, may deter the profit-maximizing owner from investing in cost-reducing innovations.

In the context of developing countries, where the domestic market in the industrial sector is often highly imperfect and fixed costs are significant, and where much of the imports provide the vital industrial inputs, one can make a special case for the beneficial pro-competitive effects of trade liberalization in those inputs. The following model, based on Venables (1996), is meant to illustrate this.

We focus on two industries: an upstream industry, X, which supplies an intermediate good that is used in the downstream industry, Y, producing final output. In the downstream industry the returns to scale are constant and firms are price-takers in both output and input markets. The total output of the industry is denoted by Y, and its domestic price by q. The good is tradable in the world market, and we shall take q as a constant, consisting of a constant world price plus any domestic taxes or tariffs. This industry uses as inputs labour, with wage w, and the intermediate good X which has a price p. Taking a Cobb–Douglas form for simplicity, and μ as the share of the intermediate good in the total value of final output, we get q as equal to the unit cost function in industry Y; i.e.,

$$q = p^{\mu} w^{1-\mu} \tag{4}$$

At the output level Y, the demand for the intermediate good X is given by $(\mu q Y/p)$. It can be supplied from two sources: from the domestic (X) industry, and the other is by imports at tariff-inclusive price $\bar{p}$. The domestic upstream industry is composed of (an endogenously determined number of) Cournot-oligopolistic firms, each with a technology that uses labour alone and has increasing returns to scale. If the fixed cost is f in terms of labour and the marginal cost is b per unit of firm output x, the profits of a single representative firm in this industry are given by

$$\pi = px - w(f + bx) \tag{5}$$

Suppose for the time being that the import price, $\bar{p}$, is prohibitively high, and there are n identical domestic firms operating. Then $X = nx$, and with equality of marginal revenue to marginal cost, we get

$$p(1 - 1/n\epsilon] = bw, \tag{6}$$

where ϵ is the elasticity of demand for upstream output. The value of this elasticity, of course, depends on the game being played between upstream and downstream firms. For simplification, we assume that upstream and downstream firms choose output levels simultaneously.

With the number of firms, n, in the upstream industry determined by free entry and exit in response to profits, and with n as a continuous variable (as a simplification device), we get average-cost pricing in equilibrium:

$$p = w[b + f/x] \qquad (7)$$

If demand for intermediates ($\mu qY/p$) is met solely by domestic supply, we can use (6) and (7) to get the equilibrium number of upstream firms and price as a function of the value of downstream output:

$$n = \sqrt{\frac{\mu qY}{wf\varepsilon}} \qquad (8)$$

$$p = wb \left(1 - \frac{1}{\varepsilon}\sqrt{\frac{wf\varepsilon}{\mu qY}}\right). \qquad (9)$$

A higher value of downstream output, qY, raises demand for the upstream industry, thus attracting entry as indicated by (8), and thereby making the upstream industry more competitive and lowering its average cost and price, as indicated by (9). This feedback effect plays an important role in this model.

Equation (9) gives the price on the assumption that the import price of the upstream good is prohibitive. The availability of imports puts an upper bound on prices charged by domestic firms, so $p \leq \bar{p}$. If the price constraint provided by imports is binding, then domestic firms will sell at just less than $\bar{p}$, undercutting imports and taking the entire domestic market.

Combining the labour demand from the upstream and downstream industries we get

$$L^d = (1 - \mu)qY/w + n(f + bx) = qY/w. \qquad (10)$$

If L is the economy's given labour endowment, $(L - L^d)$ is employed in the rest of the economy, the tradable output of which is used as the numeraire. This sector has a diminishing marginal product of labour which is equal to w. As L^d is given by (10), we can easily see that w is an increasing function of qY.

The equilibrium of the model is illustrated in Figure 14.1, with the upstream price, p, on the vertical axis and the value of downstream output, qY, on the horizontal. The curve DD traces out the demand price for the intermediate good as a function of downstream output, as can be derived from (4):

$$p = q^{1-\mu}[w(qY)]^{(\mu-1)/\mu} \qquad (11)$$

The curve DD is downward-sloping because increasing qY raises industrial employment and the wage, reducing the price that the downstream industry can pay for the intermediate good.

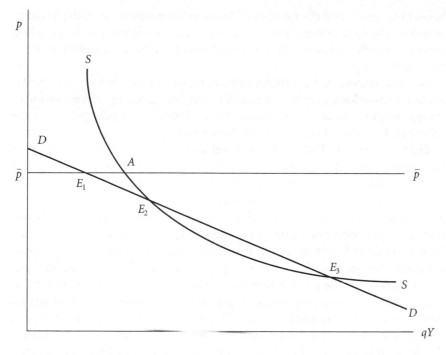

Figure 14.1

The curve SS represents the supply price of the intermediate good from the upstream industry (in the absence of import competition) as a function of downstream output, as can be derived from (9), only now taking w as a function of qY. If n, the number of upstream firms, were fixed, the SS curve would have a positive slope, as increasing qY raises wages and marginal costs. However, growth of downstream demand, qY, also increases n, thus increasing competition and pulling down the price. These opposing effects contribute to the U shape of the curve in the figure.

The horizontal line $\bar{p}\bar{p}$ represents the price of imports of the intermediate good. At downstream output levels to the left of point A, the import threat creates a discipline on domestic industry, so the actual price is the lower of $\bar{p}$ and that given by SS. At output levels to the right of A, domestic competition is sufficient to give a price less than $\bar{p}$.

Figure 14.1 suggests three equilibria. Point E_3 is an equilibrium in which competition between domestic firms is intense enough to result in a price lower than the import price. This low upstream price supports a high volume of downstream output, in turn supporting sufficiently many upstream firms to generate intense competition. Equilibrium E_1 has price $\bar{p}$ and, as a consequence, a small downstream industry. Domestic upstream firms sell at (or marginally below) this price, and the number of firms in the upstream industry is determined by the requirement that they cover fixed costs at price $\bar{p}$. As qY is low, there are insufficient domestic upstream firms to create competition to drive the price below $\bar{p}$.

We shall assume that upstream firms enter or exit in response to instantaneous profits or losses. Equilibria E_1 and E_3 are then stable; an increase in downstream output, qY, drives the demand price below the supply price. On the other hand, E_2, the third equilibrium, is unstable.

The level of the $\bar{p}\bar{p}$ line can be changed with trade policy. Protection of the upstream industry increases $\bar{p}$. This has no effect on the DD and SS curves, but shifts line $\bar{p}\bar{p}$ upward. Of course, protection is relevant only if the economy is at equilibrium E_1, i.e. if it is facing effective import competition. This equilibrium will now be shifted to the left, reducing output in the downstream industry, this then leads to a reduction in output in the upstream industry, so the protected industry ends up in a contraction. Trade liberalization obviously has the opposite effect, moving E_1 to the right and expanding production. This becomes discontinuous when the tariff is reduced to the point where $\bar{p}$ lies below E_2, at which point there is an expansion of industry to equilibrium E_3. At point E_2, downstream output reaches the critical level at which the upstream industry is large enough for competition within the industry to result in a price less than the demand price from the downstream industry. Passing this point triggers expansion: with the simple entry dynamics we have assumed, output in both the downstream and upstream industries expands until rising wages reduce profits to zero at point E_3. Upstream trade liberalization therefore expands the domestic production of both the upstream and the downstream good.

Downstream protection, however, will have a different effect. If the downstream good, Y, is also an importable, protection will raise its price, q. The SS curve is unaffected by changes in q (since q enters its determining equation only in the form qY, which is the unit of measurement of the horizontal axis), and the DD curve is shifted upwards by an increase in q. Thus, downstream protection expands production in both industries, shifting stable equilibria E_1 and E_3 to the right. Furthermore, if the economy is initially in equilibrium E_1 and the shift in the DD curve moved E_1 to point A, then it will trigger expansion to equilibrium E_3. The downstream industry reaches a scale at which it can support an upstream industry with sufficiently many firms to give a price less than $\bar{p}$.

In general, this model of Venables (1996) shows that, in an environment of increasing returns to scale and imperfect competition, intermediate goods create pecuniary externalities between firms. There are 'demand linkages', as an increase in the scale of operation of the downstream industry benefits upstream firms, and 'cost linkages', as expansion of the upstream industry may lead to lower prices, bestowing benefits on the downstream industry. These externalities create the possibility of multiple equilibria (of a kind similar to those discussed in Chapter 16, except that the intermediate products are now tradable). There may be a stable equilibrium at a low level of output (with a high-cost and highly concentrated upstream industry), and another at a high level of output (with a low-cost and less concentrated industry). Protection of the upstream industry may lock in the economy at a low-level equilibrium. Trade liberalization, on the other hand, may dislodge the economy from this equilibrium, triggering an expansion to the higher-output equilibrium; in fact, in this model it may even enable the domestic upstream industry to undercut the import price and reduce imports.

This may be an extreme form of the pro-competitive effect of international trade, but it points our attention to the importance of taking advantage of international competition in traded inputs in the actual process of development. Many of the inefficient and protracted import substitution regimes of poor countries have missed this. It is also a major lesson of the successful East Asian experience, where trade liberalization in imported inputs came much earlier than that in final consumer goods.

III

We shall now briefly assess the effects of trade policy on the rate of growth as analysed in endogenous growth theory, both old and new. Arrow's (1962) celebrated learning-by-doing model has led to applications—as in Bardhan (1970)—providing a formal rationale for an old argument for infant-industry protection: i.e. that dynamic learning spillovers (intra-industry or inter-industry) accruing from production experience measured, say, by cumulated domestic output may call for policy intervention in favour of some firms and industries, producing import substitutes or new exports. Krugman (1987) emphasized the self-reinforcing nature of initial specialization which results from the learning process, as an economy becomes better at producing the same thing; he also stressed how a deliberate policy intervention may be needed to pry the economy loose from an historical 'lock-in' with respect to specialization in a slower-growing sector. Of course, trade policy is not the first-best way of resolving this market failure. (A credit market intervention enabling a nascent firm or industry to tide over temporary losses may be more appropriate.) Besides, in a world of imperfect information, the learning function is not common knowledge, and this may create severe problems for policy intervention (including in the credit market) on the part of an imperfectly informed government. On the other hand, as Hoff (1995) has suggested, the experience gained by each entrant to a new industry may be viewed as an experiment that reveals information about the production function to later entrants; and, in the context of such learning by experimentation, industrial policy can improve on the competitive equilibrium. There is, of course, a time inconsistency problem that afflicts such policies in most countries: once protected, the infant sometimes refuses to grow and face competition, and instead concentrates on lobbying for prolonged protection.

Lucas (1993) points our attention to another aspect of the learning process which has been ignored in the earlier literature: for learning, particularly on-the-job learning, to occur in an economy on a sustained basis, it is necessary that workers and managers continue to take on tasks that are new to them, so as to continue to move up the quality ladder in goods. The major formulations that try to capture this in the context of an open economy are those of Young (1991) and Stokey (1991). Stokey has a model of so-called North–South trade, based on vertical product differentiation and international differences in labour quality; the South produces a low-quality spectrum of goods and the North, a high-quality spectrum. If human capital is acquired through learning-by-doing and so is stimulated by the production of high-quality goods, free trade (as opposed to autarky) will speed up human capital accumulation in the North and slow it down in the South. A similar result is obtained by Young (1991). The country that begins with a technological lead tends to widen the lead over time.

On the basis of learning effects that spill over across industries (but not across nations), and are bounded in each industry, Young's model endogenizes the movement of goods out of the learning sector into a mature sector in which learning no longer occurs, and thus gives a plausible account of an evolving trade structure. In his model, both the North and the South are endowed with a single primary factor of production, i.e. skilled labour, and both may produce any one of an infinite number of goods $s \in [0, \infty]$, where goods are indexed in terms of technological sophistication. Technologies differ in terms of unit labour requirements. More sophisticated goods (produced on more recent product lines) are assumed to be characterized by lower *potential* unit labour requirements, but by higher *actual* unit labour requirements when first introduced. Actual unit labour requirements fall over time owing to learning-by-doing, but there is a lower bound to the potential unit labour requirements for each good. Young considers a special case in which potential unit labour requirements $\bar{a}(s)$ are exponentially decreasing in the degree of technological sophistication s, so that

$$\bar{a}(s) = \bar{a}\, e^{-s}. \tag{12}$$

For all goods for which the potential for learning-by-doing has not yet been exhausted, *actual* unit labour requirements at time t, i.e. $a(s, t)$, are assumed to be increasing in s. Specifically,

$$a(s, t) = \bar{a}\, e^{-s} \text{ for all } s \leq S(t)$$

and

$$\bar{a}\, e^{-s(t)}\, e^{s-S(t)} \text{ for all } s > S(t) \qquad (13)$$

where $S(t)$ denotes the most sophisticated good for which all potential for learning-by-doing has been exhausted, and characterizes the stock of technical knowledge. With externalities in learning across industries, $S(t)$ rises at a rate that depends on the economy-wide flow of skilled labour devoted to the production of goods where learning potential still exists:

$$\dot{S}(t) = \int_{s(t)}^{\infty} L(s,\, t)\mathrm{d}s, \qquad (14)$$

where $L(s,\, t)$ is the amount of labour employed in the sector producing good s. Young then compares the autarky equilibria of the North and the South, the former characterized by a higher initial value of $S(0)$, with the equilibria where trade (but not international spillover of technology) is allowed for. The higher $S(t)$ in the North implies that the unit labour requirement $a(s,\, t)$ in the North relative to that in the South will be lower in more sophisticated goods, where it has had greater opportunity to benefit from learning-by-doing, whereas the relative unit labour requirement in the South will be lower in less sophisticated goods. So under free trade, comparative advantage will imply that the North will reallocate resources towards more sophisticated goods where learning-by-doing may still occur, whereas the South will reallocate resources towards the least sophisticated goods where no potential for learning exists. This means that the free-trade growth rate in the North is greater than under autarky, while in the South it is lower than under autarky. Of course, it does not follow that the southern consumers will be necessarily better off under autarky: the result will depend on a comparison of the static gains from trade with the dynamic losses.

From equation (14), the larger an economy's supply of skilled labour, the greater the rate at which learning-by-doing occurs and the faster $S(t)$ rises over time. Initial conditions thus play an important role in this model. Comparative advantage is endogenously determined by country-specific stocks of technical knowledge. The past history of technical change shapes current patterns of comparative advantage and international specialization; at the same time, current patterns of comparative advantage play an important role in determining the rate of technological change. These self-reinforcing effects also suggest the possible scope for using trade and industrial policies in the South to induce specialization in goods with greater potential for further learning-by-doing.

One limitation of the Young–Stokey story is the presumption that all imports substitute for domestic production. But, as Wan (1996) has emphasized, when imported inputs are complementary with domestic production,[5] there may be

---

[5] Lee (1995) has a growth model in which the efficiency of capital accumulation is helped by imported capital goods which are essential in the production of domestic capital goods. In the transitional

a lot of scope for learning in the assembly and processing of imported industrial inputs, as the early stages of East Asian industrialization seem to indicate (e.g. imported Mitsubishi engines in Hyundai cars in Korea, imported petrochemicals in toys and plastic flowers in Hong Kong). Trade may be crucial for development in (*a*) providing the means to import an essential ingredient for a production process that gives the opportunity to continuously upgrade domestic skills, and (*b*) providing an external market for the output thus produced, which many consumers at home still cannot afford. Of course, one needs an adequate supply of basic skills and education in the labour force to utilize this trade-related learning.

In the recent literature on endogenous technical progress and trade, for example the works of Grossman and Helpman (1991), Rivera-Batiz and Romer (1991), and others, a major result is to show how economic integration in the world market, compared with isolation, helps long-run growth by avoiding unnecessary duplication of research and thus increases aggregate productivity of resources employed in the R&D sector (characterized by economies of scale, both internal and external). International competition gives incentives to entrepreneurs in each of the trading countries to invent products that are unique in the world economy. R&D expenditures create new intermediate goods which are different from (in the horizontally differentiated inputs model) or better than (in the quality ladder model) those already existing, and as these goods enter international trade the importing country's productivity improves through the R&D efforts of its trade partner. Trade also directly helps the transmission of useful ideas in production engineering and information about changing product patterns.

If, however, spillovers from research activity are largely localized, as in the learning-by-doing models discussed above, initial conditions and country size influence the long-run patterns of trade in this literature. For example, if the poor country has a low accumulated knowledge capital stock (which determines research effectiveness) and a smaller (economic) size, then in the evolution of the world economy the rich country will capture a growing market share of the total number of differentiated varieties (of goods or inputs). The entrepreneurs in the poor country, foreseeing capital losses, may then innovate less rapidly in the long-run equilibrium with international trade than under autarky, and resources may be driven to specialization in slower-growing sectors, and more often in production than in research. Thus, as in the Young–Stokey models of learning, a country that begins with a technological disadvantage may find that international competition slows its technological progress further. Grossman and Helpman (1991) also discuss the effect of trade

---

dynamics of his model, he shows how the imported proportion of total investment affects the growth rate in the transitional period over which the economy approaches the steady state.

policy on the rate of innovation, which depends on whether the sector that is helped is a substitute or a complement for R&D in the general equilibrium production structure.

It should be pointed out that much of this literature, with its emphasis on the trade-induced general equilibrium type reallocation of resources between production and the R&D sector as a primary determinant of the rate of innovation, is not particularly relevant for poor countries. In most poor countries, even the only relevant type of R&D (which is technological adaptation of products and processes invented abroad and in imitation) is so small that it does not warrant such a major role for these general equilibrium effects of trade on growth.

Imitation, particularly in the context of imperfectly enforced intellectual property rights,[6] provides a major source of trade competition from poor countries in some products. In the usual model of the innovating North and the imitating South, as in Grossman and Helpman (1991), labour costs form the only component of the cost of entry into the imitative–adaptive activity in the South. So, armed with cheaper labour, the southern firms can relentlessly keep on targeting northern products for imitation, unhampered by many of the formidable real-world non-labour constraints on entry (e.g. those posed by the lack of a viable physical, social, and educational infrastructure, or of organizational know-how in a poor country). In a related vein, Keller (1996) has pointed out in a formal model of trade and growth how absorptive capacity in terms of basic skills can constrain the implementation of the new technology that trade liberalization may make available. In his model, without an acceleration in the rate of domestic human capital accumulation, the benefits from trade liberalization in terms of faster technological transformation cannot be sustained.

In general, the new growth literature focuses welcome attention on fixed costs and non-convexities in the process of diffusion and adoption of new goods and technologies in a developing country, provides a tractable imperfect competition framework for analysing these issues, and yields some ambiguous results on the relationship between trade and growth. But, of course, its domain is rather narrow in terms of understanding the development process. It does not

---

[6] Protection of intellectual property rights (IPR) is a divisive issue between rich and poor countries, increasingly so as knowledge-intensive goods become more important in international trade. Rich countries often claim that a tighter IPR regime encourages innovations (by expanding the duration of the innovator's monopoly) from which all countries benefit. Poor countries often counter this by pointing to their losses following upon increased monopoly power of the larger companies of rich countries. Since the poor countries in any case form a very small part of the world market for many industrial products (with exceptions in cases like drugs for tropical diseases), the disincentive effects of lax patent protection in those countries may be marginal on the rate of innovation in rich countries, and as such attempts at free-riding by the poor countries may make sense. For a partial equilibrium treatment of the theoretical issues, see Deardorff (1992), and for a general equilibrium treatment in terms of endogenous growth theory, see Helpman (1993).

attempt to provide any new insights for the abiding concerns of development economists with the problems of structural transformation, nor with the institutional transition from traditional sectors to other sectors with different organizational and technological dynamics.

REFERENCES

Arrow, K. J. (1962), 'The Economic Implications of Learning by Doing', *Review of Economic Studies*, 29.

Bardhan, P. (1970), *Economic Growth, Development, and Foreign Trade: A Study in Pure Theory*. New York: Wiley Interscience.

Deardorff, A. (1992), 'Welfare Effects of Global Patent Protection', *Economica*, 59.

Findlay, R. (1973), *International Trade and Development Theory*. New York: Columbia University Press.

Grossman, G. M., and Helpman, E. (1991), *Innovation and Growth in the Global Economy*. Cambridge, Mass.: MIT Press.

Harrison, A., and Revenga, A. (1995), 'The Effects of Trade Policy Reform: What Do We Really Know?' NBER Working Paper no. 5225, August.

Helpman, E. (1993), 'Innovation, Imitation, and Intellectual Property Rights', *Econometrica*, 61.

Hicks, J. R. (1953), 'An Inaugural Lecture', *Oxford Economic Papers*, 5.

Hoff, K. (1995), 'Bayesian Learning in a Model of Infant Industries', unpublished paper, University of Maryland.

Keller, W. (1996), 'Absorptive Capacity: On the Creation and Acquisition of Technology in Development', *Journal of Development Economics*, 49.

Krugman, P. (1987), 'The Narrow Moving Band, the Dutch Disease, and the Competitive Consequences of Mrs. Thatcher: Notes of Trade in the Presence of Dynamic Scale Economies', *Journal of Development Economics*, 27.

Lee, J.-W. (1995), 'Capital Good Imports and Long-run Growth', *Journal of Development Economics*, 48.

Lucas, R. E. (1993), 'Making a Miracle', *Econometrica*, 61.

Myint, H. (1958), 'The Classical Theory of International Trade and the Underdeveloped Countries', *Economic Journal*, 68.

Ocampo, J. A. (1986), 'New Developments in Trade Theory and LDCs', *Journal of Development Economics*, 22.

Rivera-Batiz, L. A., and Romer, P. M. (1991), 'Economic Integration and Endogenous Growth', *Quarterly Journal of Economics*, 106.

Schmidt, A. (1994), 'Managerial Incentives and Product Market Competition', unpublished paper, University of Bonn.

Stokey, N. (1991), 'The Volume and Composition of Trade between Rich and Poor Countries', *Review of Economic Studies*, 58.

Venables, A. J. (1996), 'Trade Policy, Cumulative Causation, and Industrial Development', *Journal of Development Economics*, 49.

Wan, H. (1996), 'Why Trade Matters', unpublished paper, Cornell University.
Young, A. (1991), 'Learning by Doing and the Dynamic Effects of International Trade',
    Quarterly Journal of Economics, 106.

15

The Dual Economy

I

The well-known model of Arthur Lewis (1954) (to which we have already referred in Chapter 4), drawing upon the ideas of classical economists about the process of industrial transformation in the early stages of capitalist development in Europe, focused on agriculture–industry relationships in a two-sector formalization of the economy. This and the subsequent models on the 'dual economy' differed from the standard two-sector models of mainstream economics in at least two kinds of asymmetry between the sectors. First, the produce of the agricultural sector is used primarily for consumption, whereas that of the industrial sector can be used both for consumption and capital accumulation. As sustained growth thus depends on industrial expansion, the needs of industrial investment acquired some salience in this class of models.

Second, and more important, from the point of differentiation from the standard two-sector models, the organization of production and the associated labour market conditions are qualitatively different between the two sectors. While the industrial sector is organized on capitalist (or state-capitalist) lines with agents maximizing profits (or investible surplus), the agricultural sector is composed primarily of family farmers who may not be full participants in commodity or labour markets. In particular, Lewis emphasized the large numbers of underemployed and virtually unemployed workers living off the family farms, working at low marginal productivity, and available for transfer at some point to the industrial sector. Three decades before Lewis wrote, Preobrazhensky (1926), probably the earliest formulator of the dual economy model, emphasized another aspect of this organizational asymmetry of the two sectors. Given the nature of organization of relatively small-scale family farms and their limited participation in markets, it may be more difficult to tax (and mobilize the surplus from) the agricultural sector, whereas the state may have more control over the industrial sector. This asymmetry in the power of the state over the two sectors was a matter of great concern and debate among the planners and politicians in the 1920s in the Soviet Union, and Preobrazhensky was one of the best known participants in that debate.

In this chapter we start with a model focusing on the relation between labour transfer from the agricultural to the industrial sector and the resultant pressure on food prices, and on what this implies for the industrial wage rate. In Section II we discuss the impact of agricultural productivity improvements on industrial growth, and in Section III we trace the effect of growth on income distribution in the development process of a dual economy.

There are two sectors in the economy, agriculture (denoted by subscript a) and manufacturing (denoted by subscript m). Suppose employment in the two sectors, denoted by L_i ($i = a, m$), adds up to unity. (We ignore growth in population or in the labour force.) Given the capital stocks, output Q_i in sector i depends on labour alone, so that the production function is indicated by $Q_i = F_i(L_i)$, with average product of labour denoted by V_i, and marginal product of labour by M_i. The labour elasticity of output in sector i is given by $(EQ_i, L_i) = M_i / V_i$, which lies between 0 and 1. (From here on, the elasticity of any x with respect to z will be represented by the notation $(E x, z)$.)

Suppose that the manufacturing product m is the numeraire good, and that the absolute as well as the relative price of a is p. The industrial wage rate paid in terms of m is W. The industrial worker has to be compensated for the forgone average earning at the family farm, so that

$$W = pV_a. \tag{1V}$$

This is the standard Lewis assumption; it presumes that, once the peasant leaves the village, she has no claim on the family farm output. For cases where she does retain some claim, we shall assume an alternative wage determination, given by value marginal productivity, i.e.,

$$W = pM_a. \tag{1M}$$

For more realistic cases, the industrial wage may be some weighted average of the marginal and average product in agriculture, with a mark-up for higher costs of living in the urban sector, a larger degree of unionization in the industrial sector, some discount factor for the uncertainty of getting a job, and so on, all of which we ignore here.

If y is labour income (earnings on the family farm plus in the factory), then for the two alternative cases we have

$$y = WL_m + pQ_a = WL_m + pV_aL_a = W(L_m + L_a) = W \tag{2V}$$

and

$$y = WL_m + pQ_a = WL_m + pM_aL_a + pQ_a[1 - (EQ_a, L_a)]$$
$$= W + pQ_a[1 - (EQ_a, L_a)]. \tag{2M}$$

Suppose the peasant and the industrial worker have the same demand function and spend all of their income on consumption. The demand function for a is given by

$$C_a = f(y, p), \qquad (3)$$

where C_i is consumption of good i ($i = a, m$). The budget constraint is given by

$$y = pC_a + C_m. \qquad (4)$$

If the economy is closed, the equilibrium in the market for the agricultural good a is given by

$$Q_a = f(y, p). \qquad (5)$$

Consumption of m and investment add up to the total output of m, Q_m.

Now to comparative statics. First, let us take the case when the industrial wage is equal to the value of average product in agriculture. From (1V), (2V), and the definition of average product in sector a,

$$(EW, L_a) = (Ep, L_a) - [1 - (EQ_a, L_a)]. \qquad (6V)$$

From (5),

$$(EQ_a, L_a) = e_a (EW, L_a) - \eta_a (Ep, L_a), \qquad (7V)$$

where e_a and η_a are the income elasticity and price elasticity (positively defined) demand for the agricultural product a.

We shall assume that $\eta_a > e_a$. Under this condition the marketed surplus of a is an increasing function of its price.[1]

Solving the simultaneous equations (6V) and (7V), we get

$$(EW, L_a) = -\{(EQ_a, L_a) + \eta_a [1 - (EQ_a, L_a)]\} / (\eta_a - e_a) < 0 \qquad (8V)$$

and

$$(Ep, L_a) = -\{(EQ_a, L_a) + e_a [1 - (EQ_a, L_a)]\} / (\eta_a - e_a) < 0. \qquad (9V)$$

Equations (8V) and (9V) suggest that a decline in L_a, with the transfer of labour from the agricultural to the industrial sector in the process of industrialization, will raise the price of the agricultural product (say, food) and also the industrial wage. In fact, the denominator in both equations is likely to be a very small fraction, whereas the numerators are weighted averages of 1 and either the price

[1] When p goes up, the usual price effect lowers consumption of a, but the increase in p also redistributes income in favour of peasants, which tends to push up their consumption of a. The condition $\eta_a > e_a$ is to ensure that the usual price effect dominates, and so the supply curve of 'exports' of a from the agricultural sector is upward-sloping in the standard way. If one looks at the 'balance of trade' between the two sectors and considers p to be the agricultural sector's 'terms of trade', one can show that the condition $\eta_a > e_a$ is somewhat like what is known as the Marshall–Lerner stability condition of international trade.

elasticity of demand (for, say, food) or the income elasticity (which in poor peasant economies is often quite high); under the circumstances, the absolute values of the elasticity of both the industrial wage and the agricultural product price with respect to intersectoral labour transfer is likely to be large. This is quite contrary to the horizontal supply curve of labour made familiar by the Lewis (1954) model, where the industrial wage rate is not sensitive to the labour transfer until quite late in the the process of industrialization, even though we have kept the Lewis assumption of the industrial wage rate equalling the *average* product in agriculture.

One may also point out that, if the numerator in (8V) is a weighted average of 1 and η_a (which, even when it is below unity, cannot be be very much below, since it has to be larger than the income elasticity of demand for, say, food, which, as we have noted above, can be high in poor peasant economies), the elasticity of the industrial wage rate to the intersectoral labour transfer is not likely to be very sensitive to the value of labour elasticity of output, contrary to the implication of the Lewis-inspired early development literature where a great deal of discussion was on the plausible value of the marginal product of labour in agriculture. For the pressure on the industrial wage rate and food prices in the process of industrialization, the properties of the agricultural production function seem to matter much less than the properties of the demand function of the agricultural product.[2] For example, if we take η_a to be 0.9, and e_a to be 0.7, the absolute value of (EW, L_a) in (8V) varies only from 4.5 to 4.75 to 5.0 as the labour elasticity of agricultural output varies all the way from the extreme of 0 to the value of 0.5 to the other extreme of 1. On the other hand, the absolute value of (EW, L_a) nearly doubles when one reduces the value of η_a from 0.9 to 0.8, keeping everything else the same.

For the alternative wage determination case (1M), where the industrial wage is equal to the value of the marginal product of labour in agriculture, the derivation of (EW, L_a) and (Ep, L_a) is similar, though slightly more cumbersome. Leaving the derivation as an exercise for the reader, we set out the results for the specific case of a constant-elasticity production function in the agriculture sector:

$$(EW, L_a) = -\{(EQ_a, L_a) + \eta_a [1 - (EQ_a, L_a)] - e_a \theta\} / (\{\eta_a - e_a\}, \text{(10M)}$$

and

$$(Ep, L_a) = -\{(EQ_a, L_a) + e_a [1 - (EQ_a, L_a)] - e_a \theta\} / (\eta_a - e_a), \quad \text{(11M)}$$

where

$$\theta = L_a[1 - (EQ_a, L_a)] / \{L_a[1 - (EQ_a, L_a)] + (EQ_a, L_a)\} \leq 1.$$

---

[2]   This was well emphasized in the work of Dixit (1973) on the dual economy.

In this case, going back to our numerical examples, if η_a is 0.9, e_a is 0.7, the labour elasticity of agricultural output is 0.5, and if the proportion of the labour force that is in the agricultural sector is 80 per cent, we can see that the absolute value of (EW, L_a) is 3.2—which is lower than 4.75 for the case of (8V), but still substantial—and the absolute value of (Ep, L_a) is 2.7. Once again, both (EW, L_a) and (Ep, L_a) are very sensitive to the demand parameters for the agricultural product, nearly doubling in value if the value of η_a is reduced from 0.9 to 0.8, other things remaining the same.

II

In the preceding section we have concentrated on the comparative-static results on the pressure generated in the labour and food markets by the process of intersectoral labour transfer at early stages of industrialization. In this section we shall illustrate the effect of productivity changes in agriculture on the industrial growth rate in terms of a simple formal model due to Matsuyama (1992). The purpose is formally to depict the general idea that, historically, a technological revolution in agriculture may be a precondition of the industrial revolution; it may also illustrate the impact of the so-called green revolution in recent years.

Once again, we have two sectors, a and m, with m as the numeraire good, and the labour employed in the two sectors, L_i ($i = a, m$), adds up to unity. We shall abstract from population growth or capital accumulation: the only source of growth is technical progress.

The output in each sector is given by

$$Q_i = A_i F_i(L_i), \tag{12}$$

where labour has a positive but diminishing marginal product, with $F_i(0) = 0$, and A_i is a technical progress parameter. Suppose productivity growth in the industrial sector is endogenously determined by learning-by-doing, i.e.

$$\dot{A}_m = \delta\, Q_m, \delta > 0. \tag{13}$$

This means that technical knowledge capital in manufacturing accumulates as a byproduct of the current production experience in that sector; this effect is external to the individual firms but internal to the industry.

Assuming that there is no wage gap between the two sectors, labour allocation in the two sectors will be determined by competition between them until in equilibrium we get

$$pA_c F'_c (L_c) = AmF'_m(L_m). \tag{14}$$

On the demand side, p should be equal to the marginal rate of substitution in consumption. Suppose the utility function takes the following specific 'addilog' form:

$$U = \ln(C_a - \underline{C}) + \ln C_m, \tag{15}$$

where $\underline{C}$ is a subsistence level. (Thus preferences are non-homothetic and the income elasticity of demand for a is less than unity.) So, for all above-subsistence consumption of good a,

$$p = C_m / (C_a - \underline{C}) = Q_m / (Q_a - \underline{C}) \tag{16}$$

The second equality in (16) follows from our continued assumption of a closed economy. From (14) and (16),

$$\frac{\underline{C}}{A_a} = F_a(L_a) - F_m(L_m)\frac{F_a'(L_a)}{F_m'(L_m)} = \phi(L_m), \tag{17}$$

with

$$\phi(0) = F_a(1); \phi(1) < 0; \phi'(L_m) < 0.$$

Figure 15.1 depicts the $\phi(L_m)$ curve and the equilibrium value of L_m as determined by the parameter A_a. One can see that productivity improvements in the

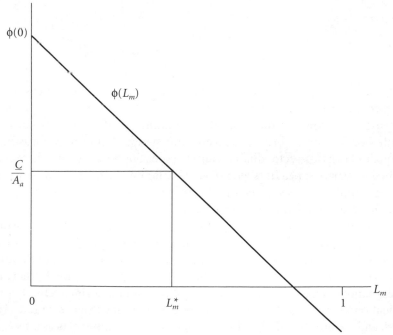

Figure 15.1

agricultural sector increase the employment share in manufacturing. In the figure we have assumed that $A_a F_a(1) > \underline{C}$, i.e. that the agricultural sector is productive enough to provide subsistence to everybody if all of labour is devoted to that sector.

From (13), given the parameter A_a, the growth rate in the manufacturing sector is given by

$$\hat{Q}_m = \hat{A}_m = \delta F_m(L_m(A_a)), \tag{18}$$

where a circumflex above a variable indicates the percentage growth rate of that variable. It is clear that in this model productivity improvements in the agricultural sector raise the growth rate in the industrial sector.

This result will change if we have an open economy. In such an economy, if the country starts with a comparative advantage in the agricultural product, productivity improvements in that sector with trade may induce the drawing of resources away from the manufacturing sector, thus lowering the industrial growth rate in this model (leading to a process of 'deindustrialization' over time). This model, of course, concentrates on the effects of the two sectors competing on the labour market and ignores all kinds of possible complementarities in the two sectors. (For example, when products of one sector can be used as inputs in the other sector, productivity improvements in either sector can help both sectors.)

III

In this section we go back to the model of Section I (with some changes) and try to trace the impact of growth (capital accumulation) on inequality. For this purpose we follow the model of Bourguignon (1990), who introduces the whole Lorenz curve (instead of using the standard summary measures of inequality) in a two-sector dual economy model. Suppose there are three classes of income-earners: peasants who have their family farms in sector a, workers who are employed in sector m, and the capitalists who employ them. Also suppose that there is a hierarchy of income of these three classes: capitalists have a per capita income π, which is larger than the workers' per capita income or the wage rate, W, which in turn is larger than the per capita income y_a of self-employed peasants on the family farms. Since workers earn more than their opportunity income on the farm (unlike in our model of Section I), there is an excess supply of labour willing to come to the manufacturing sector. For simplification we shall take the non-market-clearing industrial wage rate, W, as fixed, and the number of capitalists, n, as given. The number of peasants, L_a, the number of workers, L_m, and the number of capitalists, n, add up to the total labour force which is normalized to one, as before. The manufactured good is again the numeraire and the economy is closed.

With fixed W and constant returns to scale in sector m, capital and labour coefficients in that sector are constant, so that output $Q_m = AK$, and employment $L_m = BK$, where A and B are constant coefficients and K is the capital stock in manufacturing. The income of capitalists is given by

$$\pi = (Q_m - WL_m)/n = (A - BW)K/n. \tag{19}$$

The per capita income of peasants, y_a, is given by pV_a, where, as before, p is the price of the agricultural product and V_a is the (fixed) average product in agriculture. L_a, the number of peasants left on the farm are those not absorbed elsewhere, and thus is given by $(1 - n - BK)$. The overall mean income, $\bar{y}$, for all classes together is given by $(Q_m + pL_aV_a)$.

Let C_a^i be the consumption demand for product a for an individual in each class i (with $i = 1$ for peasants, 2 for workers, and 3 for capitalists), which will be determined by p and the per capita income for each class. We can now write the market equilibrium condition for a as when the excess demand for a, $X_a(p, K)$, is zero, or

$$X_a(p, K) = (1 - n - BK)C_a^1(p, pV_a) + BKC_a^2(p, W) + nC_a^3[p, (A - BW)K/n]$$
$$- (1 - n - BK)V_a$$
$$= 0. \tag{20}$$

Differentiating in (20) we can get (Ep, K), the elasticity of p with respect to K:

$$(Ep, K) = \left[\gamma^2 + (1 - \gamma^1)\frac{L_m}{L_a} + \gamma^3 e_a^3 \right] \bigg/ (\bar{\eta}_a - \gamma^1 e_a^1), \tag{21}$$

where γ^i is the share of class i in the total demand for the agricultural product, $\bar{\eta}_a$ is the weighted average (across the three classes) price elasticity of demand (positively defined) for a, and e_a^1 is the peasants' income elasticity of demand for a. In the denominator on the right-hand side of (21), the price elasticity of demand has to be larger than income elasticity as a sufficient condition for stability in this model. (We have made a somewhat similar assumption in Section I.) Under this condition, capital accumulation turns the terms of trade in favour of the agricultural sector. Since this helps the poorest class, the peasants, this factor works in favour of equality, even when other factors (such as the enlargement of the higher-income manufacturing sector) may not.

Given the structural and behavioural parameters, we can now trace the effect of capital accumulation on income distribution in this dual economy, by looking at shifts in the Lorenz curve with comparative-static changes in K. Consider the Lorenz curve in Figure 15.2, which has two kinks. The horizontal coordinate of the first kink, $L_a = 1 - n - BK$, decreases with K, but that of the second kink is constant at $1 - n$. If $f(y)$ is the density of income distribution, the coordinates

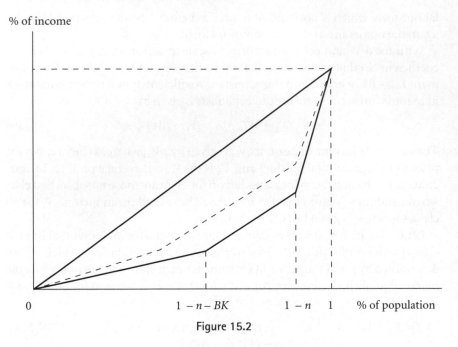

% of income

0      $1-n-BK$ $1-n$ 1   % of population

Figure 15.2

of the Lorenz curve are given by $\int_0^x f(y)\,dy$ and $\int_0^x yf(y)\,dy/\bar{y}$, so that the slope of the curve obtained by differentiating with respect to x is $x/\bar{y}$. In other words, the slope of the Lorenz curve at a given point is equal to the ratio of the income of the corresponding fractile of the distribution to the mean income of the whole population. This means if the Lorenz curve were to shift upward (i.e. if the distribution were to become unambiguously more equal), the following necessary and sufficient conditions have to be satisfied:

$$\frac{\mathrm{d}(y_a/\bar{y})}{\mathrm{d}K} \geq 0; \quad \frac{\mathrm{d}(\pi/\bar{y})}{\mathrm{d}K} \leq 0.$$

Let β_a be the share of sector a in national income, so that

$$\frac{y_a}{\bar{y}} = \frac{\beta_a}{1-n-BK} \tag{22}$$

and

$$\frac{\pi}{\bar{y}} = \frac{\alpha_m(1-\beta_a)}{n} \tag{23}$$

where α_m is the profit share in sector m, which is constant, since it is equal to $(1 - BW/A)$. If β_a increases with K, it can be checked from (22) and (23) that $\pi/\bar{y}$

decreases and $y_a/\bar{y}$ increases with K. But, historically, the share of agriculture in national income usually *declines* with economic growth. So the unambiguous upward shift in the Lorenz curve is unlikely.

If β_a declines with an increase in K, then from (23) $\pi/\bar{y}$ increases, and if the decline in β_a is faster than that in L_a (which is often historically the case), then $y_a/\bar{y}$ falls. These slope changes in the Lorenz curve, however, imply that we cannot be unambiguous about an increase in inequality with capital accumulation. With similar slope changes, Figure 15.3 shows the ambiguous case with intersecting Lorenz curves, while Figure 15.4 shows an unambiguous increase in inequality. In the model above, the industrial wage rate, W, has been kept constant. But if instead W were to grow with capital accumulation, that would lower the profit share (if the elasticity of substitution in the industrial production function were less than unity). This might make an egalitarian upward shift in the Lorenz curve possible even if the share of agriculture in national income were to decline with economic growth.

This chapter started with a simple model of agriculture and manufacturing in a poor country and formally demonstrated the pressure that industrialization, with its attendant intersectoral movement of labour, puts on the food price and the industrial wage rate. Section III showed how capital accumulation in this kind of context has an ambiguous effect on income inequality. The focus on food price also underlines the need for improvements in agricultural

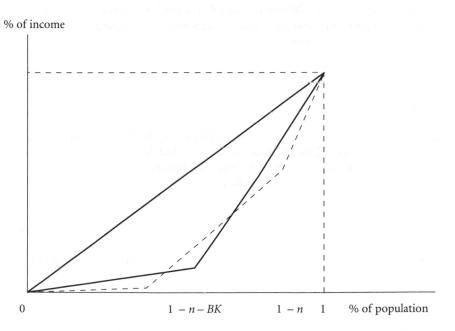

Figure 15.3

% of income

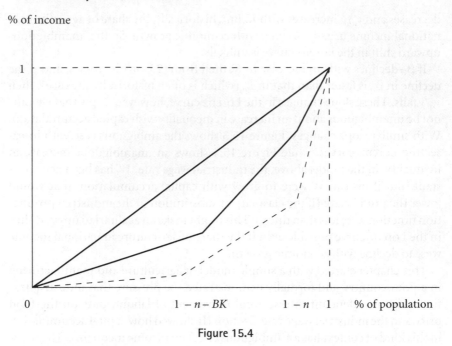

Figure 15.4

productivity: Section II showed in a simple model how agricultural productivity improvement can boost industrial growth, thus suggesting interdependence of growth in the two sectors.

REFERENCES

Bourguignon, F. (1990), 'Growth and Inequality in the Dual Model of Development: The Role of Demand Factors', *Review of Economic Studies*, 57.

Dixit, A. (1973), 'Models of Dual Economies', in J. Mirrlees and N. Stern (eds.), *Models of Economic Growth*. London: Macmillan.

Lewis W. A. (1954), 'Economic Development with Unlimited Supplies of Labour', *Manchester School*, 28.

Matsuyama, K. (1992), 'Agricultural Productivity, Comparative Advantage, and Economic Growth', *Journal of Economic Theory*, 58.

Preobrazhensky, E. (1926), *The New Economics*. Oxford: Clarendon Press, 1965 edn.

16

Intersectoral Complementarities and Coordination Failures

I

In the immediate postwar fluorescence of development economics, one idea that was particularly prominent was that of how a coordination of investments across sectors is essential for industrialization. The literature that grew out of the famous paper of Rosenstein-Rodan (1943) emphasized that when domestic markets are small, a simultaneous expansion of many sectors can be self-sustaining through mutual demand support, even if by itself no sector can break even (primarily because firms in a sector may not by themselves be able to generate enough sales to render the adoption of modern increasing-returns technologies with large fixed costs profitable). The models start with a presumption of multiple equilibria and pose the essential problem as one of escaping a 'low-level equilibrium trap' to a higher-income equilibrium with industrialization. (A major difference in the more recent models from the earlier ones is that in the former complementarities arise through the nature of equilibrium interactions.)

Most models in the literature focus on the effect of a firm's investment on the size of the markets for output in other sectors. One common objection to this is that, in an open economy where an industry faces the world market, the size of the domestic market cannot plausibly limit the adoption of increasing returns technologies. Such objections usually overstate the importance of the tradables sector in most economies and underestimate how the size of the domestic market matters even in an open economy.[1] Nevertheless, keeping the objection in mind, we shall in this chapter illustrate the idea of intersectoral

[1] Krugman (1992) in this connection refers to a study of the Massachusetts economy by the Federal Reserve Bank of Boston. The study shows that even perfectly open economies like that of the state of Massachusetts are engaged primarily in producing for the local market, and less than 30% of employment was in what one would consider tradables.

complementarities in investment with the help of two models which are (or can be) consistent with an open economy with tradable final outputs.

The first model, originally due to Murphy, *et al.* (1989), shows how, in the case of shared infrastructure (e.g. roads, railways, power stations, training facilities) each industrializing firm that uses the infrastructure contributes to the large fixed cost of building it, and thereby indirectly helps other users and makes their industrialization more likely. In an extremely simplified version of the model, let us suppose there is only one factor of production, labour, whose supply is fixed at L; all consumption is over two periods but there is no discounting; the total number of consumer goods produced in the economy is N, all of which are symmetric in consumption; consumers all have similar preferences and each spends a constant fraction of income on each commodity in both periods so that $C_i^j = y^j / N p_i$, where $j = 1, 2$ refers to the two periods, $i = 1, \ldots, N$ refers to the consumer goods, C_i^j is the amount consumed of good i in period j, y^j is income in period j, and p_i is the price of good i. Each commodity can be produced with two types of technology, one traditional and one modern. The first one is a constant returns-to-scale 'cottage-industry' technology, which allows one unit of output for every unit of labour input, so that $Q_{ic} = L_{ic}$, where Q_{ic} and L_{ic} are output produced and labour used in the ith sector with the 'cottage' technology. It is assumed that this technology does not need the infrastructure. The firms using this technology are competitive, so that the price charged by each firm is equal to the marginal cost, which is equal to the wage rate, which in turn is equal to one, taking the wage rate as numeraire.

The second technology available is an increasing-returns-to-scale (IRS) technology, which can be operated only by one firm in each sector. To adopt that technology, however, the firm has to invest a fixed cost F in the first period; then in the second period this yields $b > 1$ units of output per unit of labour. For the IRS technology, infrastructure is essential.

Let us suppose the IRS technology comes in two types. A fraction N_1, of sectors (type 1 firms) requires a fixed cost F_1 to be incurred in the first period to build a factory, whereas the fraction $N_2 = N - N_1$ (type 2 firms) requires a fixed cost $F_2 > F_1$. In the second period all fixed-cost firms have labour productivity b, so that $Q_{im} = bL_{im}$, where Q_{im} and L_{im} are the output produced and labour used by the ith industry using the 'modern' (IRS) technology. The price that both types of modern firms will charge in the second period is always one, since they face the potential competition from the competitive fringe of cottage firms who charge the price of one for all i.

Let us assume that it takes a fixed cost of R units of labour in the first period to build the infrastructure and that the marginal cost of using it is zero. Let us also assume that the low fixed-cost type 1 firms cannot generate enough surplus to pay for the infrastructure, even if they could profitably industrialize alone. Since type 1 firms have higher profits than type 2 firms, this assumption implies that *both* types of firms must industrialize in order to pay for the infrastructure. This assumption means that

$$R > \left(\frac{(b-1)L}{bN - (b-1)N_1} - F_1 \right) N_1. \tag{1}$$

The right-hand side in inequality (1) represents the total profits of the low fixed-cost type 1 firms if they were to industrialize alone. To see why that is so, one has to work through the following steps. If type 1 firms industrialize alone, they will have to invest F_1 in the first period and in the second period will produce Q_m using the IRS technology. For each firm the total revenue is equal to Q_{im}, and total cost is $L_{im} = Q_{im}/b$, as the price and the wage rate are both equal to unity. Since income in the second period is equally allocated among all goods, $Q_{im} = y^2/N$. So profits in the second period for each firm are equal to $(b-1)y^2/bn$. But income in the second period y^2 is equal to the sum of wage income L and profits aggregated over all firms, from which we can solve $y_2 = bLN/[bN - (b-1)N_1]$. Summing up the profits of the two periods aggregated for type 1 firms, we get the right-hand side of (1).

Using Figure 16.1, adapted from Krugman (1992), we can study what the economy would produce in the second period if all labour were allocated either

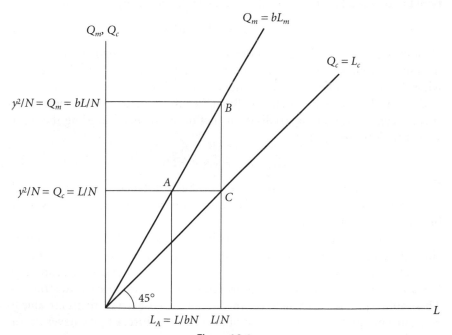

Figure 16.1

to the modern or the traditional sector. The 45° line describes the traditional technology, $Q_c = L_c$. The line with slope $b > 1$ describes the IRS technology, $Q_m = bL_m$. If in the second period all workers were used either in the 'cottage' production sector or in the 'modern' IRS sector, by symmetry, L/N workers would be employed in the production of each good. If all goods were produced using the traditional technology, each good would have an output of $Q_c = L/N$ (point C in the figure). Since, with equal allocation of income among all goods, Q_c is also equal to y^2/N, we can say that the second period income in the equilibrium without industrialization would be $y^2 = L$. But if all goods in the second period were produced using the IRS technology, each good would have an output of $Q_m = bL/N$ (point B in the figure). Again with equal allocation of income among all goods, the second-period income in the industrialized equilibrium would be $y^2 = bL$; and the second-period profits that production of each good would yield would be equal to $(b-1)L/N$. Since each firm had to incur the fixed cost in the first period, total profits (summing up over two periods) for the low fixed-cost type 1 firms will be, $\pi_1 = (b-1)L/N F_1$, while those for high fixed-cost type 2 firms will be $\pi_2 = (b-1)L/N - F_2$. Since $F_1 < F_2, \pi_1 > \pi_2$.

The infrastructure builder (the builder for short) cannot price-discriminate between the firms of two types, as the former does not observe the fixed cost of firms. For an equilibrium to exist in which the infrastructure gets built and both type 1 and type 2 firms industrialize, we need the following condition:

$$(b-1)L/N - F_2 > R/N. \tag{2}$$

Condition (2) implies that the builder can cover his costs when he charges each firm the amount equal to the profit of the type 2 firm; the latter breaks even while the type 1 firm earns a profit equal to $(F_2 - F_1)$.

Of course, it is socially efficient to build the infrastructure whenever the total surplus generated by industrialization (net of the costs of building the infrastructure) is positive, i.e. if

$$(b-1)L - N_1 F_1 - (N - N1)F_2 > R. \tag{3}$$

Since condition (3) is less stringent than (2), the infrastructure may not get built even when it is socially efficient. This is essentially because of the inability of the builder to price-discriminate.

Thus, there are potentially three equilibria in this model. In the first equilibrium, the economy never industrializes because the surplus generated by industrialization is not enough to cover the costs of the infrastructure, i.e., condition (3) is violated. In the second equilibrium, the economy always industrializes. This equilibrium occurs whenever the high fixed-cost type 2 firms are able to generate enough to pay for the cost of the infrastructure, i.e. whenever condition (2) holds.

In the third equilibrium, it does not pay a single type 1 firm to invest when expected income is L. But if many type 1 firms invest simultaneously, then the economy's income will rise and thus it will be profitable to adopt the IRS technology. This equilibrium will occur whenever conditions (2) and (3) hold and also if profits of the low fixed-cost firms when income is L are negative. In Figure 16.1, when expected income is L, a type 1 firm will be producing at point A. At that point, second period profits would be $(b-1)L_A$, and total profits would be $\pi_1 = (b-1)L_A - F_1$. From the figure, $L_A = L/bN$. Therefore, this third equilibrium, requires, in addition to conditions (2) and (3),

$$\frac{(b-1)L}{bN} - F_1 < 0. \tag{4}$$

Under these conditions, in this third equilibrium the infrastructure will make money on its first-period investment if the economy industrializes, but will incur a large loss if no industrialization takes place and there are no users of its services. The investment R might then not be made for fear of this possibility. Thus, the infrastructure might not be built lest an insufficient number of firms industrialize, and the fact that it isn't built in turn could ensure that firms will not make the large-scale investments needed to industrialize. This is an under-development trap caused by a coordination failure. What seems called for if the infrastructure is to be built ahead of demand is, apart from public subsidies towards the construction of the infrastructure, an attempt at coordination of investments by enough private users of the infrastructure to get to the equilibrium with industrialization.

II

In this section we introduce another example of multiple equilibria arising from sectoral complementarity and cumulative processes generated by increasing returns in the production of support services and inputs.[2] In our model, the tradable final goods require such (non-traded) intermediate inputs and services as repair and maintenance, some parts and components, and financial, transport, communication, and distribution services to be readily available in close proximity. The domestic availability of a wide variety of such specialized inputs enhances the productive efficiency of the manufacturing sector, but the extent of input specialization (or division of labour in their production) is limited by the extent of the market. In such a situation the economy may get stuck in an equilibrium where the division of labour in the input-producing sector is

---

[2] The basic model is due to Rodríguez (1996), though our exposition here is somewhat different and is influenced by Matsuyama (1993).

shallow and the final goods production remains confined to the use of low-productivity techniques that do not require a wide variety of inputs. Similar stories of what are called agglomeration economies causing uneven regional development have also been seen to be important in the literature on economic geography of developed countries.[3]

Suppose there are two tradable final goods, c and m, produced under competition, and one primary factor of production, labour. The production functions are given by

$$Q_c = L_c, \tag{5}$$

$$Q_m = H, \tag{6}$$

where Q_i is output of the ith good ($i = c, m$), L_c is the amount of labour employed in the traditional sector c where one unit of labour produces one unit of output, and H is a composite of specialized intermediate inputs which, without the help of any labour (for simplification), produce output m. The specialized inputs are aggregated in a way familiar from Ethier (1982):

$$H = \left(\int_0^n x^\alpha(i)\mathrm{d}i \right)^{1/\alpha}, \quad 1 > \alpha > 0, \tag{7}$$

where $x(i)$ is the output of intermediate good i, and n is the number of varieties of the differentiated intermediate inputs available in the economy. Since all varieties enter symmetrically in H and production costs of all varieties are the same, in equilibrium $x(i) = x$ for all i. This implies that

$$H = xn^{1/\alpha}. \tag{8}$$

This suggests how the degree of specialization in the intermediate inputs sector, indexed by n, affects productive efficiency in m.

Now suppose that production of x of each variety requires $(ax + F)$ units of labour, where F is the fixed cost and a is the marginal labour requirement. If L is the total amount of labour in the economy, labour market equilibrium is given by:

$$n(ax + F) + L_c = L. \tag{9}$$

The differentiated intermediate goods are produced under monopolistic competition. From (6) and (7), we can see that the price elasticity of demand for $x(i)$ is $1/(1 - \alpha)$, whereby the marginal revenue of each firm in the intermediate goods sector is $\alpha p(i)$ where $p(i)$ is price of variety i. Since marginal cost is equal to aW, where W is the wage rate and $p(i) = p$ is the same for all varieties, we get

[3] For a simple exposition of the recent results in this literature, see Krugman(1995: app.).

$$p = \frac{aW}{\alpha}. \tag{10}$$

Since, $p_H H = \int_0^n p(i)x(i)\mathrm{d}i = npx$, where p_H is the price of the composite input H, we can write

$$p_H = pn^{-\gamma}, \tag{11}$$

where $\gamma \equiv (1-\alpha)/\alpha$. But then, as $p_c = W$ and $p_m = p_H$, where p_c and p_m are the prices of the final goods c and m, we get from (10) and (11) the domestic relative price $\tilde{P}$ of c and m:

$$\tilde{P} = p_c/p_m = (\alpha/a)n^\gamma. \tag{12}$$

From (5), (6), (8), (9), and (12), and assuming that a constant fraction β of income is spent on m, under autarky we get

$$x = \frac{\alpha\beta[(L/n) - F]}{a(\alpha\beta + 1 - \beta)}. \tag{13}$$

Gross profits under autarky are $\pi = (p - aW)x$. Substituting (10) and (13) in this, we get

$$\pi/W = \frac{(1-\alpha)\beta[(L/n) - F]}{(\alpha\beta + 1 - \beta)}. \tag{14}$$

As shown in Figure 16.2, the gross profit equation may be represented by a downward sloping curve. With free entry into the intermediate goods sector, in the long run each firm makes zero net profits so that $\tilde{\pi} = WF$. Now equating (14) to F, we can solve for $\tilde{n}$, the number of firms each producing a differentiated intermediate good under autarky:

$$\tilde{n} = \beta(1 - \alpha)L/F. \tag{15}$$

Thus, if fixed costs are very large, $\tilde{n}$ would be small and consequently the productivity level in the production of final goods m would be low.

Now suppose that the economy trades final goods in the world market. If it is a small open economy, let us take the world relative prices of c and m as equal to one. In that case, if $P < 1$, the economy specializes in the production of the labour-intensive traditional good c, whereas if $\tilde{P} > 1$, the economy specializes in the production of m. From (12), this means that if $n < \tilde{n}$, where $\tilde{n} \equiv (a/\alpha)^{1/\gamma}$, m is not produced and obviously gross profits are zero. But if $n > \tilde{n}$, c is not produced, $L_c = 0$ in equation (9), and gross profits in the open economy, π^*, are given by:

$$\frac{\pi^*}{W} = \gamma\left(\frac{L}{n} - F\right). \tag{16}$$

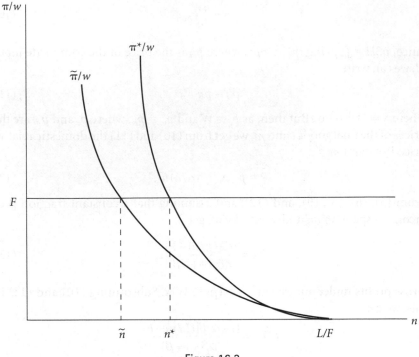

Figure 16.2

In Figure 16.2, (16) is represented by a downward-sloping curve that lies entirely above the corresponding curve under autarky defined by (14); this is because $\beta < 1$.

In the long run, when net profits are zero, so that (16) is equal to F, we obtain the equilibrium number of firms n^* producing intermediate inputs in the open economy when the economy specializes in the production of final good m:

$$n^* = (1-\alpha)\frac{L}{F}. \tag{17}$$

Comparing (15) and (17), it is clear that $n^* > \tilde{n}$.

Note that in the open economy there can be two equilibria: $n = 0$ and $n = n^*$, with $n = \tilde{n}$ being the threshold level. If the fixed costs F are sufficiently large and/or if the labour coefficient in the intermediate goods sector is larger than the degree of substitutability between every pair of varieties (i.e. if $a > \alpha$), then the open economy can be trapped in a low-level equilibrium ($n = 0$).[4]

[4] This also implies that if the parameters, α, β, L, and F are such that $\tilde{n} > \bar{n}$, a temporary isolation would help the economy to escape the low-level equilibrium; as the economy opens after a period of isolation n^* would exceed $\tilde{n}$ and therefore $\bar{n}$, and the open economy would specialize in the production of good m.

In the models of both sections, we have multiple equilibria with underdevelopment traps. In the model of this section, we have a country that may get trapped in an historical pattern of low-productivity specialization; the task of development policy here is to compensate for an historical handicap, either by trade policy, or by a policy of subsidization of fixed costs, or by other ways of encouraging appropriate linkages between the final goods sector and the intermediate inputs sector. In the third equilibrium of the model of Section I, on the other hand, coordination of investments between sectors is the key, and the role of expectations (about investment by other firms) and self-fulfilling prophecy become more important. The task of development policy is to coordinate expectations around high investment. This 'history versus expectations' dichotomy in the dynamic processes of how a particular equilibrium gets established has been further analysed by Krugman (1991) and Matsuyama (1991), and the relative importance of the past and expected future is shown to depend on some parameters of the economy (such as the discount rate and the speed of adjustment). Expectations play a more important role in breaking coordination failures, particularly when there is some kind of a first-mover advantage.

Multiplicity of equilibria with complementarity gives rise to the possibility that in a dynamic model a small difference in the initial conditions may be magnified over time to generate marked differences in the long run. This may give us some clue to the path-dependent diversity in the history of development, even among countries otherwise not very dissimilar in their initial conditions. While this suggests some scope for policy activism, it also raises serious questions about the replicability of successful cases, particularly if we do not have a good understanding of the mechanisms that worked in the latter cases, and most models to date are not very satisfactory in this respect.

The idea of strategic complementarities between sectors generated by increasing returns must be one of the early examples in the flowering of the general literature on coordination failures in economics. It was so central to the development economics of the 1950s; yet it lost much of its intellectual force in the subsequent decades, not so much because it lacked, until recently, a firm anchoring in a formal model using tools of imperfect markets equilibrium analysis, as Krugman (1995) suggests, but more because at the policy level the difficulties of aggregate coordination (and of inferring how expectations are formed and how they react to government policies) were underestimated, particularly at the existing levels of administrative capacity and political coherence in the developing countries. In addition, the difficulty of identifying firms generating positive feedbacks and the incentive and organizational issues of micro management of capital were underappreciated. The resulting government failures diverted the profession's attention from what nevertheless remains an important source of market failure discovered by early development economics.

REFERENCES

Ethier, W. (1982), 'National and International Returns to Scale in the Modern Theory of International Trade', *American Economic Review*, 72.

Krugman, P. (1991), 'History versus Expectations', *Quarterly Journal of Economics*, 106.

——(1992), 'Toward a Counter-Counterrevolution in Development Theory', *Proceedings of the World Bank Annual Conference on Development Economics*. Washington: World Bank.

——(1995), *Development, Geography, and Economic Theory*. Cambridge, Mass.: MIT Press.

Matsuyama, K. (1991), 'Increasing Returns, Industrialization and Indeterminacy of Equilibrium', *Quarterly Journal of Economics*, 106.

——(1993), 'Modelling Complementarity in Monopolistic Competition', *Bank of Japan Monetary Economics Studies*, 11.

Murphy, K., Shleifer, A., and Vishny, R. (1989), 'Industrialization and the Big Push', *Journal of Political Economy*, 97.

Rodríguez, A. (1996), 'The Division of Labor and Economic Development', *Journal of Development Economics*, 49.

Rosenstein-Rodan, P. (1943), 'Problems of Industrialization of Eastern and Southeastern Europe', *Economic Journal*, 53.

17

Institutional Economics and the State in Economic Development

I

With the decline of the pervasive influence of Walrasian models in economics in recent years, it is now generally recognized that 'institutions matter', and that the associated incentive structures substantially influence economic performance. But beyond this general agreement there are still many differences among reasonable people concerning which institutions affect the process of development and how. In particular, different institutional economists emphasize different institutional impediments to development. The purpose of this chapter is to bring some of these contrasting positions into the open, and to focus on underdevelopment as an institutional failure and on the persistence of dysfunctional institutions. For our present purpose we define 'institutions' very generally (and vaguely) as social rules, conventions, and other elements of the structural framework of social interaction.

The New Institutional Economics literature points to some very important features of institutional failures that cause or prolong underdevelopment. This particularly refers to legal and contractual structures and rules of third-party enforcement which are necessary for most arms'-length market transactions. Let us follow a by now well-known account, as in North (1981, 1990). In a small, closed, face-to-face peasant community, transaction costs are low, but production costs are high, because specialization and division of labour are severely limited by the extent of market defined by the personalized exchange process of the small community. In a large-scale complex economy, as the network of interdependence widens the impersonal exchange process gives considerable scope for all kinds of opportunistic behaviour and the costs of transacting can be high. In Western societies, over time, complex institutional structures have been devised to constrain the participants, to reduce the uncertainty of social interaction, and in general to prevent the transactions from being too costly, and thereby to allow the productivity gains of larger-scale and improved technology to be realized. These institutions include elaborately defined and effectively enforced property rights, formal contracts and guarantees, trademarks, limited liability, bankruptcy laws, and large corporate organizations with governance structures to limit problems of agency and, as Williamson (1985) has emphasized, of incomplete contracting and *ex post* opportunism. Some of these institutional structures are non-existent or weak or poorly devised and implemented in less developed countries.

In particular, this literature emphasizes the institutions that a society, as it evolves beyond the face-to-face village community, develops (or fails to develop) for long-distance trade, credit, and other intertemporal and inter-spatial markets where the transactions are not self-enforcing. In this context, the analysis of North (1990), Greif *et al.* (1994), and Greif (1994) have pointed to the importance of institutions such as the Merchants' Guilds (for example those in Italian city-states, or inter-city guilds like the German Hansa), the Law Merchant system (of private judges recording institutionalized public memory at the Champagne fairs, which provided an important nexus of trade between northern and southern Europe), the Maghribi traders' coalition, and the Community Responsibility System in the Mediterranean and European trade during the late medieval commercial revolution in the period between the eleventh and the fourteenth centuries. These institutions facilitated economic growth by reducing opportunism in transactions among people largely unknown to one another and providing a multilateral reputation mechanism supported by frameworks of credible commitment, enforcement, and coordination.

In the informal enforcement of mercantile contracts, bilateral reputation mechanisms (i.e. where the cheater is punished only by the party that is cheated) are usually more costly than multilateral reputation mechanisms (where punishment is inflicted by a whole community to which the party that is cheated belongs) or a community responsibility system (in which a whole community is jointly liable if one of its members cheats). In the case of bilateral reputation mechanisms simple efficiency–wage considerations suggest that in order to keep a long-distance trading agent honest, the agent has to be paid by the merchant (the principal) a wage higher than the agent's reservation income, whereas in more 'collectivist' forms of enforcement this wage need not be as high, as the penalty for cheating is higher or else peer monitoring makes cheating more difficult. However, in a world with information asymmetry, slow communication, and plausibly different interpretations of facts in a dispute, an uncoordinated multilateral reputation mechanism may not always work, and it may need to be supplemented by a more formal organization in order to co-ordinate the expectations and responses of different members of the collectivity and to enforce transactions. In medieval Europe the merchant guilds provided such an organization. In governing relations between merchants and their various towns and the foreign towns with which they traded, the guilds had the ability to coordinate merchants' responses to abuses against any merchant and to force them to participate in trade embargoes. This credible threat of collective action from the guilds enabled the medieval rulers to commit to respecting the property rights of alien merchants, and thus facilitated exchange and market integration.[1] Of course, the strategic considerations involved in such coordination and commitment give rise to multiple equilibria in theoretical frameworks, which suggest the historical context specificity of such institutional arrangements and the path dependence of their evolution.

Many developing countries have a long history of indigenous mercantile institutions of trust and commitment (based on multilateral reputation mechanisms and informal codes of conduct and enforcement)—examples of such institutions of long-distance trade and credit abound among mercantile families and groups in pre-colonial India, Chinese traders in South-east Asia, Arab 'trading diasporas' in West Africa, and so on. But these traditional institutions of exchange often did not evolve into more complex (impersonal, open, legal–rational) rules or institutions as occurred in early modern Europe. Economists do not yet have good clues about this evolutionary process, and it is clear that social structures, political environment, and cultural belief systems (that coordinate expectations) play an important role here. The New Institutional Economics literature emphasizes the need for the evolution of the more formal (legal–contractual) institutions of enforcement. But the dramatic success story of rapid industrial progress in South-east Asia in the recent past, often under the leadership of Chinese business families, suggests that more 'collectivist' organizations can be reshaped in particular social–historical contexts to facilitate industrial progress, and that clan-based or other particularistic networks can sometimes provide a viable alternative to contract law and impersonal ownership. In a study of seventy-two Chinese entrepreneurs in Hong Kong, Taiwan, Singapore, and Indonesia, Redding (1990) shows how, through specific social networks of direct relationship or clan or regional connection, the entrepreneurs build a system dependent on patrimonial control by key individuals, personal obligation bonds, relational contracting, and interlocking directorships.[2] As Ouchi (1980) had noted some years back, when ambiguity of

---

[1] As Greif *et al.* (1994) point out, the usual interpretation of merchant guilds as mere cartels presents a puzzle: 'If the purpose of the guilds was to create monopoly power for the merchants and to increase their bargaining power with the rulers, why did *powerful* rulers during the late medieval period cooperate with alien merchants to establish guilds in the first place? What offsetting advantages did the rulers enjoy? The puzzle is resolved if the guild's power enabled trade to expand to the benefit of the merchants and rulers alike.'

[2] As Redding (1990) points out, 'Many transactions which in other countries would require contracts, lawyers, guarantees, investigators, wide opinion-seeking, and delays are among the overseas Chinese dealt with reliably and quickly by telephone, by a handshake, over a cup of tea. Some of the most

performance evaluation is high and goal incongruence is low, the clan-based organization may have advantages over market relations or bureaucratic organizations. In clan-based organizations goal congruence (and thus low opportunism) is achieved through various processes of socialization; performance evaluation takes place through the kind of subtle reading of signals, observable by other clan members but not verifiable by a third-party authority. Of course, as may be expected, the arrangements in the Chinese business families are somewhat constrained by too much reliance on centralized decision-taking and control, internal finance, too small a pool of managerial talent to draw upon, a relatively small scale of operations, and, in the case of large organizations, a tendency to subdivide into more or less separate units, each with its own products and markets. A major problem of 'collectivist' systems of enforcement is that the boundaries of the collectivity within which rewards and punishment are practised may not be the most efficient ones and may inhibit potentially profitable transactions with people outside the collectivity.

II

The literature on the New Institutional Economics is often marked by a kind of functionalism and social Darwinism (a belief in the survival-of-the-fittest institution): more efficient institutions and governance structures evolve as the parties involved come to appreciate the new benefit–cost possibilities. But an institution's mere function of serving the potential beneficiaries is clearly inadequate in *explaining* it[3] (just as it is an incompetent detective who tries to explain a murder mystery only by looking for the beneficiary and, on that basis alone, proceeds to arrest the heir of the murdered rich man).

The basic source of institutional change that is usually emphasized in the literature on institutional history is fundamental and persistent changes in relative prices, which change with population growth or decline and with improvements in production or military technology. This acts as a main motive force for institutional changes in history, primarily by inducing the development of property rights to the benefit of the owners of the more expensive factor of production. For example, demographic changes altering the relative price of labour to land led to the incentive to redefine property rights on land and rearrange labour relations. North (1981) and Hayami and Ruttan (1985) give

massive property deals in Hong Kong are concluded with a small note locked in the top drawer of a chief executive's desk, after a two-man meeting.' (One hears similar stories about the Hasidic diamond traders of New York and about firms in industrial districts in northern Italy).

[3] One should, of course, distinguish between explaining the origin of an institution and that of its sustenance: the former may come about unintended, but then the beneficiaries may eventually become aware of the function an institution serves for them and strive to maintain it.

several examples from European and recent Asian history, respectively. But from Brenner's (1976) analysis of the contrasting experiences of different parts of Europe on the transition from feudalism (those between Western and Eastern Europe and those between the English and the French cases even within Western Europe), we know that changes in demography, market conditions, and relative prices are not sufficient to explain the contrasts. Changes in relative prices may at most change the costs and benefits of collective action for different social groups (creating new opportunities for political entrepreneurs), but they cannot predetermine the balance of class forces or the outcome of social conflicts. Brenner shows that much depends, for example, on the cohesiveness of the landlords and peasants as contending groups and on their ability to resist encroachments on each other's rights and to form coalitions with other groups in society. Hayami and Ruttan (1985) refer to the case of mid-nineteenth century Thailand, where the expansion of international trade triggered a rise in rice prices which led to a major transformation of property rights: traditional rights in human property (corvee and slavery) were replaced by more precise private property rights in land. But one should not forget that the expansion of grain trade in the sixteenth and seventeenth century Poland (the rise in grain prices fuelled particularly by expansion of Dutch demand) was quite compatible with the *relapse* into serfdom. There are other examples of institutional stagnation or retrogression following an expansion of trade in more recent colonial history. Even in the United States Wright (1987) has pointed to the adverse effects of product market integration on development in the post-bellum South.

The 'old' institutional economists (including Marxists) often used to point out how a given institutional arrangement serving the interests of some powerful group or class acts as a long-lasting block to economic progress. In contrast, the property rights school as well as the transaction cost theorists often underestimate the tenacity of vested interests and the consequent persistence of dysfunctional institutions. One cannot get away from the enormity of the collective action problem that limits the ability of potential gainers to get their act together in bringing about institutional changes. There are two kinds of collective action problem involved here: the well-known free-rider problem about sharing the costs of bringing about change, and a bargaining problem, in which disputes about sharing the potential benefits from the change may lead to a breakdown of the necessary coordination. The costs of collective action may be too high, particularly when, as we know from Olson (1965), the losses of the potential losers are concentrated and transparent, while the gains of the potential gainers are diffuse[4] (or uncertain for a given individual, even though not for the group, as suggested by Fernandez and Rodrik 1991). It is also difficult for the

---

[4] As Machiavelli wrote in 1513 in *The Prince*, 'the reformer has enemies in all those who profit by the old order, and only lukewarm defenders in all those who would profit by the new'.

potential gainers to credibly commit to compensate the losers *ex post*, which makes the potential losers particularly recalcitrant in matters of institutional change.

One can also formalize the obstruction by vested interests in terms of a simple bargaining model, where the institutional innovation may shift the bargaining frontier outward (thereby creating the potential for all parties to gain), but in the process the disagreement payoff of the weaker party may also go up (often owing to better options of 'exit' and 'voice'), and it is possible for the erstwhile stronger party to end up losing in the new bargaining equilibrium. (How likely this is will, of course, depend on the nature of shift in the bargaining frontier and the extent of change in the disagreement payoffs.) The classic example is provided by the violent and tortuous history of land reform in many countries, which points to the numerous road blocks on the way to a more efficient reallocation of land rights put up by vested interests for generations. In general, given the differential capacity of different groups in mobilization and coordination, institutional arrangements are more often the outcome of strategic distributive conflicts, in which groups with disproportionate resources and power try to constrain the actions of others, rather than the outcome of a society's decentralized attempt to realign property rights and contracts in the light of new collective benefit–cost possibilities, as is the presumption in much of the New Institutional Economics.

III

We have so far ignored the role of the state in building the institutional base of an economy. There is a general consensus that a successful package of development policy has to contain as a minimum some policies towards macroeconomic stability and fiscal discipline, and on the microeconomic front policies that secure property rights and provide a predictable and reliable legal and contractual structure. The prevailing view in the New Institutional Economics is that the state has to be strong enough to be able to ensure this minimum policy package, and yet has to credibly commit to not making confiscatory demands on the private sector. The recommendation is for a 'strong but limited' government. It has to be strong enough to resist the inevitable political pressures for market intervention (this is far from the minimal state of classical liberalism), and at the same time it has to constrain itself from interfering with market-led growth. This is a major dilemma of political governance, as strong states often become interventionist and confiscatory. Very few states succeed in fully resolving this dilemma.

First, some qualifications about the microeconomic components of the minimum policy package. The legal and contractual structure is, to some extent, dependent on the level of economic development itself.[5] Courts in many poor countries do not have the manpower or the resources, and are hopelessly clogged with a large backlog; lack of education and information makes access to the legal process very difficult and costly to the clients; the formal legal process, disrupting traditional arbitration procedures and norms, creates new uncertainties; and so on. Even in terms of theoretical models, in the context of incomplete contracts it is not always clear that making one market (say, the credit market through legal enforcement of debt contracts) more complete, while other markets (like insurance) remain highly incomplete or non-existent on account of information problems is necessarily efficiency-enhancing. Kranton and Swamy (1997) provide an example from the Bombay Deccan in colonial India, where the introduction of civil courts to facilitate contract enforcement and increased entry in agricultural credit markets led to increased competition among lenders, but resulted in lower consumption-smoothing opportunities for the poor borrowers (who previously were accustomed to having more of their loans forgiven in bad years by the monopolistic village moneylenders).

Beyond the minimum policy package cited above, there is much less agreement about the role of the state. Standard welfare economics used to ascribe some positive role for the state in the case of public goods, merit goods (like education), and general cases of market failures with externalities. After about four decades of state activism in developing countries, the literature is now full of gory accounts of the failures and disasters of regulatory, interventionist states. The state is now more often presumed to be captured by special-interest groups, patronage machines, and plundering bureaucrats and politicians; it has neither the capacity nor the motivation to play the positive role envisaged for it by early development economics.

The recent theoretical literature on imperfect information and incomplete contracts takes a more agnostic position on the role of the state (see e.g. Stiglitz *et al.* 1989). Under imperfect information, the market equilibrium is in general not Pareto-efficient. But many of the information problems are no less acute for the regulatory or planning authorities than for the private sector. While some private markets (like credit or insurance) are severely afflicted by moral hazard, adverse selection, and enforcement problems, the state, of course, has the advantage of coercive powers and compulsory, universal membership (so that, for example, some of the good risks cannot opt out of a risk-pooling arrangement); on the other hand, it is difficult for the state to credibly commit not to bail out in case of failures (the soft budget constraint), which gives out wrong incentives. In the provision of public and merit goods the bureaucrats may not have enough incentive to reduce costs, compared with a private contractor

---

[5] Thus, 'institutional quality' which is sometimes used as an explanatory variable for statistical analysis of development performance, may itself be an endogenous variable.

(who is the residual claimant in any profits from cost-cutting); but, as Hart *et al.* (1997) point out, if quality of services is important and non-contractible (for example, the imperfectly measurable quality of education, or the hard-to-spell-out special needs or characteristics of disadvantaged customers), the case for public provision of these services is stronger.[6]

In the case of externalities, the celebrated Coase (1960) result has suggested that if property rights are well defined voluntary negotiation and bargaining can be a way out, without government intervention, provided the costs of nego-tiating and transacting are not high. These costs, however, are often quite high, making agreements difficult to secure and costly to enforce. Besides, in a world of imperfect information, Farrell (1987) has shown that, in a mechanism design setup, the outcome of an assignment of property rights followed by Coasean bargaining may be inferior to the outcome achieved by even an 'uninformed and bumbling bureaucrat'.[7] This, of course, leaves out the case of the rapacious bureaucrat. A mechanism design approach, as Farrell himself mentions in pass-ing, generally overlooks the fact that the bureaucrat may not be able to credibly precommit to the designed incentive scheme, which then opens the door for all kinds of lobbying and rent-seeking by private agents (to which we return later).

The major (positive) externality problem under imperfect information and incomplete markets that arises in the early stages of industrialization relates to a possible coordination failure in decision-making. In Chapter 16 we discussed some examples of this. The essential structure of a coordination game can be represented in a simple two-player, two-strategy payoff matrix as described in Chapter 13, Section III. In such a game, in one equilibrium both players select Defection as a strategy, and in the other, both select Cooperation. The former equilibrium is Pareto-dominated by the latter, but the players may get stuck in the inferior equilibrium because of a failure to coordinate their strategies. When there are many parties, the coordination problem in multilateral negoti-ations can be quite complex.

This coordination problem is particularly acute in the capital market and makes the all-important leap from the mercantile to the industrial economy difficult in the history of many countries. Even when mercantile family firms thrived in their network of multilateral reputation and enforcement mecha-nisms, the latter often were not adequate for supporting the larger risks of

---

[6] For example, private schools, even when students are paid by the government through vouchers, may reject children with learning or behavioural problems who would be more expensive to educate; or private hospitals would find ways of rejecting the extremely sick (and typically poor) patients. Similarly, private institutions (schools, prisons) may not spend enough resources on some difficult-to-measure aspects (e.g. imparting civicness in education, or following some standards of humane treatment of prisoners).

[7] Farrell's detailed example is that of a bilateral externality problem with private information. Maskin (1994) shows how the result is dependent on the assumptions of a small number of agents and on the non-excludability of externalities (i.e., no one can be excluded from their effects).

longer-horizon industrial investment. These firms, by and large, had a limited capacity to pool risks and mobilize the capital of the society at large in high-risk, high-return, long-gestation industrial ventures. The usual imperfections of the credit and equity markets emphasized in the literature on imperfect information and the 'strategic complementarities' emphasized in the macroeconomic literature are crucial in these early stages of industrial development. The investment in learning-by-doing is not easily collateralizable and therefore is particularly subject to the high costs of information imperfections. Learning by experimentation gives rise to externalities for other firms. The role of the government can become very important here, as Gerschenkron (1962) emphasized for the late industrializers of Europe.

There are, of course, scattered cases in some developing countries of coordination and mutual support among merchant families helping the transition to the industrial economy without much assistance from the government. For example, for India in the nineteenth century Bayly cites an important case:

In Ahmedabad, the one case of a 'traditional' merchant city which industrialised from inside, it was several of the leading families who controlled resources and status within the trade guilds who went into the cotton mill ventures. No small man could go it alone. But if the leaders of the community who could themselves call on a wide range of security and information made the initial move, then others would follow. (Bayly 1983: 424)

More often, such coordination in investment and risk-taking on the part of the merchant families was missing. This issue becomes particularly important when externalities of information and the need for a network of proximate suppliers of components, services, and infrastructural facilities with economies of scale make investment decisions highly interdependent and the raising of capital from the market for the whole complex of activities particularly difficult. In East Asia the state has played an important role in resolving this kind of coordination problem, a role that is arguably much beyond that of the 'strong but limited government' prescribed in the New Institutional Economics.[8] The recent failures in the East Asian financial markets should not blind us to the positive role the state played in the early stages of industrial transformation.

In the successful cases of East Asian development (including that of Japan), the state has often actively intervened in the capital market, at times in subtle but decisive ways, using regulated credit allocation (sometimes threatening the withdrawal of credit in not-so-subtle ways) in promoting and channelling industrial investment, underwriting risks and guaranteeing loans, establishing public development banks and other financial institutions, encouraging the development of the nascent parts of financial markets, and nudging existing firms to upgrade their technology and to move into sectors that fall in line with

---

[8] For some of the major studies of the lessons of the East Asian success story in development, see World Bank (1993), Fishlow *et al.* (1994), Aoki *et al.* (1996), and Campos and Root (1996).

an overall vision of strategic developmental goals. In this process, as Aoki *et al.* (1996) have emphasized, the state has enhanced the market instead of supplanting it; it has induced private coordination by providing various kinds of cooperation-contingent rents. In the early stages of industrialization, when private financial and other related institutions were underdeveloped and coordination was not self-enforcing, the East Asian state created opportunities for rents conditional on performance or outcome (in the mobilization of savings, commercialization of inventions, export 'contests', and so on) and facilitated institutional development by influencing the strategic incentives facing private agents through an alteration of the relative returns to cooperation in comparison with the adversarial equilibrium.

One should not, of course, underestimate the administrative difficulties of such aggregate coordination, and the issues of micro management of capital may be much too intricate for the institutional capacity and information-processing abilities of many a state in Africa, Latin America, South Asia, and even East Asia (for example the Philippines). One should also be wary, as the recent East Asian financial crashes warn us, about the moral hazard problems and the political pressures for bail-out and for throwing good money after bad (i.e. already sunk investment in large projects that are doing badly) that a state-supported financial system inevitably faces. This is the 'soft budget constraint' problem of refinancing in centralized credit systems, formally analysed by Dewatripont and Maskin (1993). While government-supported development banks (e.g the Credit Mobilier in the nineteenth century or later the Credit National in France, the Kredintaltanlt für Weidarufban in Germany, the Japan Development Bank, and the Korea Development Bank) have played a crucial role in long-term industrial finance in past and recent history, their experience in other developing countries (say, in India or Mexico) has been mixed at best. Armendariz de Aghion (1995) has suggested that the efficiency of government sponsorship can be enhanced if conditions such as targeting development bank intervention (thus helping the acquisition of specialized expertise in financing projects in particular sectors), co-financing arrangements (thus helping risk diversification and dissemination of expertise) and/or co-ownership with private financial institutions are attached to government sponsorship.

It is also worth emphasizing that in the final analysis there can be no clear-cut answer to the abstract question of the appropriate role of the state. The state is an institution embedded in a web of other institutions, and the role it can play depends on the interactions of these institutions. Thus, the extent and characteristics of the moral hazard and political pressures involved in bail-outs, financial market interventions, and coordination efforts will vary dramatically across states, even if the formal institutions involved in these efforts are identical.

IV

We have discussed above the importance of the role of the state as a coordinator and have hinted at some of the administrative and political difficulties of playing that role. But a prior question is, why would the state leadership be interested in playing such a positive role in the development process? What's in it for them? Wouldn't they be interested instead in maximizing their loot? Wouldn't rent-seeking groups try to influence them to lay their hands on the rents generated by state policies and regulations? The public choice literature has drawn pointed attention to how the regulatory, interventionist state spawns an enormous waste of resources in such rent-seeking activities, over and above the standard economic losses arising from the misallocation effects of policy-induced distortions.

Suppose there are n firms competing for a given rent, R. The ith firm spends resources amounting to x_i in a contest to win the rent, and decides on the amount by maximizing expected profits:

$$E\Pi_i = p_i(R - x_i) + (1 - p_i)(- x_i), \tag{1}$$

where p_i is the probability of winning the rent $= x_i/X$,

$$X = x_1 + x_2 + \ldots + x_n,$$

and there are n (number of) such symmetric rent-seeking firms.

In Nash equilibrium, each firm takes the decisions of the other $(n-1)$ firms as given. If $\bar{x}$ denotes the average spending of the other $(n-1)$ firms, we can write $p_i = x_i/[(n-1)\bar{x} + x_i]$

Maximizing (1) with respect to x_i, assuming symmetry so that $x = x_i = x$, we get

$$X = nx = R(n-1)/n. \tag{2}$$

The total amount of resources spent by rent-seekers is X, while the winner gets R. The larger is the number of firms, the more is the dissipation of the contested rent. In the rent-seeking literature there are now several models of barriers to entry in the rent-seeking sector (including models of dynamic games of moves and countermoves of the contending rent-seekers) and of the various transaction costs and risks that the rent-seekers have to face.[9]

The fragmented rent-seeking special-interest groups and lobbies do not have what Olson (1982) calls an 'encompassing interest' in the productivity of the society as a whole. But what prevents the ruler or the state leadership from having such an 'encompassing interest'? In fact, McGuire and Olson (1996) have argued that a rational autocrat (if he has security of tenure and a long horizon)

---

[9] For a survey of the rent-seeking literature, see Hillman (1989).

will take into account the deadweight losses from unduly onerous impositions on society's productive capacity. They compare this with the usually smaller distortionary effects of the exactions of a 'stationary bandit' as opposed to that of a 'roving bandit'. They also show that a majoritarian democracy (even one with no scruples about robbing the minority but with a stake in the market economy) will similarly have an encompassing interest in non-confiscatory policies.

Let us pursue this rational ruler model with some changes to make it structurally similar to the principal–agent model of sharecropping discussed in Chapter 6. Suppose the ruler provides a public input G (say, some infrastructural facility), which, along with L, the labour put in by the ruled or the citizens, produces the national output. The ruler maximizes his net revenue $[\tau F(G, L) - G]$, where τ is (for simplification) a linear tax rate and F is a production function with the usual properties. But the principal/ruler cannot observe or control the labour effort put in by the agent/ruled. The latter decides on L, taking τ and G as given, to maximize $[(1 - \tau) F(G, L) + W(1 - L)]$, where let us suppose the agent has the opportunity to use part of her labour effort in the underground economy (which the long arm of the ruler does not reach) at a given compensation rate of W.[10] The first-order maximizing condition for the agent is then given by

$$(1 - \tau)F_2(G, L) - W = 0, \tag{3}$$

which defines an implicit function, $L^*(\tau, G)$. Equation (3) suggests the usual distortion on labour supply as a result of the tax imposition: the marginal product of labour, F_2, is larger than the opportunity cost of labour.

We can now write the principal/ruler's objective as

Max $[\tau F(G, L) - G]$ with respect to τ and G, subject to $L = L^*(\tau, G)$. (4)

The first-order condition with respect to τ can be rewritten as

$$F_2\left(-\frac{\partial L^*}{\partial \tau}\right)\bigg/ F = 1/\tau. \tag{5}$$

This means that the distortionary effect as a proportion of actual output is equal to the reciprocal of the chosen tax rate. (This is like the reciprocal relationship that characterizes all redistributive taxation in the models of McGuire and Olson.) One can easily check that with diminishing marginal productivity $\partial L^*/\partial \tau$ is negative. One can also see that, since the ruler takes into account the distortionary effect of the tax rate on labour supply, his chosen tax rate is less than the maximum possible rate.

---

[10] In this partial equilibrium model, we are ignoring the effect of the ruler's action on W.

If the cross-partial F_{21} is positive, i.e. if the marginal product of labour increases in G, then $\partial L^*/\partial G$ is positive. This means that the ruler will in this case provide more of the public input G than if he were to take L as a parameter and did not take into account the complementarity between G and L.

Thus, in this model the ruler maximizes his own objective function subject to the reaction function of the ruled and in the process internalizes the economic costs and benefits of his actions in accordance with that reaction function. In other words, the ruler is taken to be a Stackelberg leader. In contrast, one can say that the weak or the 'soft' state is a Stackelberg follower: it cannot commit to a particular policy and merely reacts to the independent actions of the private actors such as special-interest groups. Thus, we can now say that, compared with the 'strong' state ('strength' defined as ability to credibly precommit), the 'soft' state will have too much of undesirable interventions (creating distortions in the process of generating rent for the lobbying groups), and by the same logic, will have *too little* of the desirable interventions (as in the case of market failures or the kind of coordination failures we have alluded to in the preceding section), since the state does not take into account or internalize the effects of its own policies.[11] So the distinction between a 'strong' state (as in much of East Asia) and a 'soft' state (as would be the case in much of Africa or South Asia) lies not in the *extent* of intervention, but in its *quality*. This also means that the benefi cial effects of a 'strong' state go beyond the ideal of 'strong but limited government' of the New Institutional Economics.

An important example of the strong state's ability to precommit like the Stackelberg leader arises in the case of the popular infant-industry argument for protection. When such protection is initiated, by the very nature of the argument for temporary protection, it is granted for a short period –until the industrial infant can stand on its feet. But in most countries infant-industry protection inevitably faces the time inconsistency problem: when the initial period of protection nears its completion, the political pressures for its renewal become inexorable, and so the infant industry soon degenerates into a geriatric protection lobby. In the recent history of the strong states of East Asia, however, there have been some remarkable instances where the government has withdrawn protection from an industry after the lapse of a pre-announced duration, letting it sink or swim in international competition.[12]

Another important aspect of the quality of state intervention in East Asia has to do with the use, by and large, of clear, well-defined, pre-announced rules of performance criteria. In South Korea, for example, the heavy involvement of the state in directing investment through credit allocation has been successful

---

[11] For a similar result, see Rodrik (1992).

[12] For an example of how the government in Taiwan imposed an import ban on VCRs in 1982 to help out two of the main domestic electronic companies, and withdrew it after 18 months when they failed to shape up to meet international standards, see Wade (1990).

largely because of its strict adherence to the criterion of export performance. Through this precommitment device, the strong South Korean state has used the vital disciplining function of foreign competition to encourage quick learning and the development of cost and quality consciousness among domestic enterprises, something that has been conspicuously absent in many other interventionist regimes (even though South Korea, at least until the 1980s, shared with the latter regimes many of the restrictive policies on imports and foreign investment).

The difficulty lies in determining the factors that predispose a state or a political coalition to have an 'encompassing interest' in the economic performance of the country as a whole. There is an important collective action problem here, the resolution of which has eluded many developing countries outside East Asia: that is to formulate cohesive developmental goals with clear priorities and to avoid prisoners'-dilemma-type deadlocks in the pursuit of even commonly agreed-upon goals. There are obviously many social and political factors that have facilitated the process in East Asia (e.g. social norms of rule obedience and organizational loyalty, meritocratic rather than political recruitments in bureaucracy, dense networks of government–business relations, geopolitical exigencies), but it is also important to keep in mind the influence of the policy of broad-based or shared growth. When wealth distribution is relatively egalitarian, as in large parts of East Asia (particularly through land reforms and widespread expansion of education and basic health services), it is easier to enlist the support of most social groups (and to isolate the radical wings of the labour movement and the petty bourgeoisie) in making short-run sacrifices and coordinating on growth-promoting policies.[13] There is some cross-country evidence (see Keefer and Knack 1997) that inequality and other forms of polarization make it more difficult to build a consensus about policy changes in response to crises and hence result in an instability of policy outcomes and an insecurity of property and contractual rights.

The general theory of bureaucracy[14] suggests that it is difficult to devise high-powered incentive contracts for civil servants, primarily because of what is called a 'common agency' problem (i.e., the civil servant has to be the agent of multiple principals, none of whom can fully internalize the spillover effects of any high-powered incentives offered) or a multi-task problem (where she has to pursue multiple goals, many of which are hard to measure and therefore prone to be neglected in favour of goals with measurable performance yardsticks

---

[13] Campos and Root (1996) emphasize this point: 'In contrast with Latin America and Africa, East Asian regimes established their legitimacy by promising shared growth so that demands of narrowly conceived groups for regulations that would have long-term deleterious consequences for growth were resisted. In particular, broad-based social support allowed their governments to avoid having to make concessions to radical demands of organized labor.'

[14] See Wilson (1989); Tirole (1994); Dixit (1995).

under incentive payment systems). With low-powered incentives for civil servants, their 'capture' by interest groups is considered very likely,[15] and this is usually taken into account in structuring bureaucratic organizations in the form of checks and balances in the allocation of control rights and some kind of multiple veto power systems. But these institutional devices create their own opportunities for a kind of inefficient corruption. A multiple veto power system makes centralized collection of bribes in exchange for guaranteed favours very difficult. In general, centralized corruption (as in South Korea or Taiwan) has less adverse consequences for efficiency than decentralized bribe-taking, since in the former case the bribee will internalize some of the distortionary effects of corruption. Shleifer and Vishny (1993) have used a similar argument in explaining the increase in inefficient corruption in post-Communist Russia compared with the earlier regime of centralized bribe collection by the Communist Party. In the public choice literature, it is the regulatory state that is at the root of the inefficiency owing to corruption spawned by the regulations.[16] But for the economic consequences of corruption, the extent of centralization in the rent-collection machinery is particularly important: a weak and fragmented government (even under authoritarian rulers), with its inability to stop the setting up of independent corruption rackets (a kind of economic warlordism), as is not uncommon in parts of Africa, makes the problem of inefficiency particularly acute.

We do not yet have a satisfactory and comprehensive explanation of why the incidence of corruption is so palpably different in different countries, and why in some cases corruption is so persistent.[17] But the idea of multiple equilibria recurs in the theoretical literature on these questions. The basic idea is that corruption represents an example of what are called frequency-dependent equilibria, with our expected gain from corruption depending crucially on the number of other people we expect to be corrupt. At a very simple level, the idea may be illustrated, as in Andvig (1991), with a so-called Schelling diagram, shown in Figure 17.1. The distance between the origin and any point on the horizontal

[15] Within any large centralized organization, including a private firm, there are what Milgrom and Roberts (1990) call 'influence costs' incurred by insider lobbies; these are akin to the rent-seeking costs in the public sector, but in most situations, particularly in developing countries, they are likely to be more costly in the public sector.

[16] The simple policy prescription is thus to get rid of those regulations. But the matter is a little more complicated, as many regulations are there to serve some valued social objective (like controlling pollution or distributing rationed food to the very poor), and there may be a trade-off between these objectives and that of reducing corruption through deregulation. For an example of the complexities involved in deciding on a suitable compensation policy for corruptible enforcers of a regulation like pollution standards, see the principal–agent model with a double moral hazard problem (one between the regulator and the pollution inspector and the other between the regulator and the polluting factory) in Mookherjee and Png (1995).

[17] For a survey of some of the relevant issues and the policy questions they raise, see Bardhan (1997).

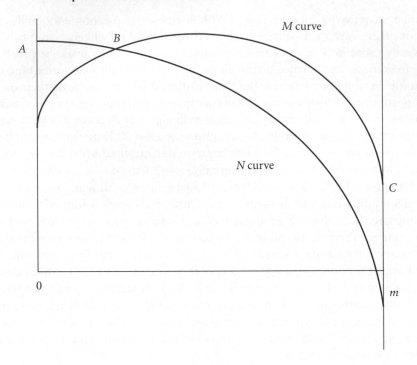

Figure 17.1

axis represents the proportion of a given total number of officials (or transactions) that is known to be corrupt, so that the point of origin is when no one is corrupt, and the end-point m is when everyone is corrupt. The curves M and N represent the marginal benefit for a corrupt and a non-corrupt official, respectively, for all different allocations of the remaining officials in the two categories. The way the curve N is drawn, the benefit of a non-corrupt official is higher than that of a corrupt official when very few officials are corrupt, but it declines as the proportion of corrupt officials increases and ultimately becomes even negative when almost all others are corrupt. The M curve goes up at the beginning when more and more officials are corrupt (for the marginal corrupt official, lower reputation loss when detected, lower chance of detection, lower search cost in finding a briber, etc.), but ultimately declines (e.g. when the size of bribe is bid down by too many competing bribers), even though at the endpoint the payoff for a corrupt official remains positive. In the figure there are three equilibrium points, A, B, and C. A and C are stable, but B is not. At point A all are non-corrupt, and it does not pay anyone to be corrupt. At C all are corrupt, and it does not pay anyone to be non-corrupt. At B, any given official is indifferent between being corrupt and non-corrupt, but if only one more official is corrupt it pays to become corrupt; on the other hand, if one fewer is corrupt, the marginal official will choose to be non-corrupt. So initial conditions are important: if the economy starts with (or gets jolted into) a high average level of corruption, it will move towards the high-corruption stable equilibrium C; if the initial average corruption is low, the economy will gravitate towards the honest equilibrium A. The diagram illustrates in an elementary way how two otherwise similar countries (both in socioeconomic structures and in moral attitudes) may end up with two very different equilibrium levels of corruption; also, how small changes may have a large impact on corruption if one starts out at points close to B.

V

In much of the discussion in the preceding section we have emphasized the importance of credible commitment and coordination, but, as Laffont and Tirole (1994) remind us, the commitment of the ruler, for all its credibility, may not always be to a socially beneficial policy. In a multi-period model, if the state actors, who behave like a Stackelberg leader with a presumed encompassing interest, have some chance of being thrown out of office (in future elections or otherwise), commitment may act as a rent-perpetuating device. Thus, the 'strength' of a state in the sense of its ability to credibly commit itself to developmental goals is clearly not sufficient to ensure the pursuit of those goals. It may not even be necessary: the remarkable economic success of Italy over three decades (until very recently), albeit with a notoriously weak and corrupt government heavily involved in the economy, is an obvious counterexample. Nevertheless, the correlation between growth performance and state 'strength' is probably quite robust. It is of course possible, that economies in their most successful phases have less political conflict (most groups are doing well without political exertion, and the few losing groups are bribed) and therefore that their governments have an appearance of 'strength'; their commitments are not challenged or reversed by political action. This may give rise to a selection bias. This is an important issue that needs to be examined with detailed historical data. The determined way the South Korean state handled various macroeconomic crises in the 1970s (the two oil shocks, massive foreign debt, inflation, etc.) suggests that the South Korean state's 'strength' at that time was not just a reflection of the success of the economy.

In most situations, the state is neither a Stackelberg leader nor a Stackelberg follower. Neither the state actors nor the private interest groups usually have the power to define unilaterally the parameters of their action. Both may be strategic actors with some power to influence the terms, and the outcome of the bargaining game will depend on their varying bargaining strengths in different situations. This points to a major inadequacy of the model of the principal–agent ruler–ruled model of the previous section. In that model, the power of the ruler to collect taxes or rents is invariant with respect to policies to promote productivity. But some of the latter policies may change the disagreement payoffs of the ruled if one thinks of it as a bargaining game (so that an increase in G may end up weakening the power of the ruler to impose τ). As Robinson (1996) has emphasized, it may not be rational for an autocrat to carry out institutional changes that safeguard property rights, law enforcement, and other economically beneficial structures if in the process his rent extraction machinery has a chance of being damaged or weakened, as protests and other forms of collective action on the part of the citizens are thereby rendered less difficult. He may not risk upsetting the current arrangement for the uncertain prospect of a share in a larger pie. For some of the 'stationary bandits' in this century (the Duvaliers in Haiti, Trujillo in the Dominican Republic, Somoza in Nicaragua, Mobutu in Zaire etc.), who systematically plundered and wrecked their economies for excruciatingly long periods, this may have been a serious consideration.

When state leadership and the private interest groups in democratic and semi-democratic countries are pitted against one another in a bargaining setup, it is important to strengthen the accountability mechanisms on both sides, as Przeworski (1995) emphasizes. On the one hand, credible commitment devices and rules (including constitutional safeguards) may be necessary to insulate some of the economic decision-making processes from the marauding lobbies of special-interest groups; on the other hand, institutional arrangements such as an independent office of public accounting and auditing, an election commission with powers to limit (and enforce rules on) campaign contributions and to conduct fair elections, citizens' watchdog committees providing information and monitoring services, or an office of local ombudsman with some control over the local bureaucracy can help in limiting the abuse of executive power and providing a system of punishments for undesirable government interventions in the economy and rewards for desirable interventions. In poor agrarian countries, where most of the economy is still in the informal sector and is dispersed in far-flung villages, such accountability mechanisms would have to be reinforced by informal institutions at the local community level, an issue discussed in Chapter 13.

REFERENCES

Andvig, J. C. (1991), 'The Economics of Corruption: A Survey', *Studi Economici*, 43.
Aoki, M., Murdock, K., and Okuno-Fujiwara M. (1996), 'Beyond the East Asian Miracle: Introducing the Market Enhancing View', in M. Aoki, H. Kim, and

M. Okuno-Fujiwara (eds.), *The Role of Government in East Asian Economic Development: Comparative Institutional Analysis*. New York: Oxford University Press.

Armendariz de Aghion, B. (1995), 'Development Banking', Discussion Paper no. 64, London School of Economics.

Bardhan, P. (1997), 'Corruption and Development: A Review of Issues', *Journal of Economic Literature*, 35.

Bayly, C. A. (1983) *Rulers, Townsmen and Bazaar: North Indian Society in the Age of British Expansion 1770–1870*. Cambridge: Cambridge University Press.

Brenner, R. (1976), 'Agrarian Class Structure and Economic Development in Pre-industrial Europe', *Past and Present*, 70.

Campos, E., and Root, H. L. (1996), *The Key to the East Asian Miracle: Making Shared Growth Credible*. Washington: Brookings Institution.

Coase, R. (1960), 'The Problem of Social Cost', *Journal of Law and Economics*, 3.

Dewatripont, M., and Maskin, E. (1993), 'Centralization of Credit and Long-Term Investment', in P. Bardhan and J. Roemer (eds.), *Market Socialism: The Current Debate*. New York: Oxford University Press.

Dixit, A. (1995), *The Making of Economic Policy: A Transaction Cost Politics Perspective*. Cambridge, Mass.: MIT Press.

Farrell, J. (1987), 'Information and the Coase Theorem', *Journal of Economic Perspectives*, 1.

Fernandez, R., and Rodrik, D. (1991), 'Resistance to Reform: Status Quo Bias in the Presence of Individual-Specific Uncertainty', *American Economic Review*, 81.

Fishlow, A., Gwin, C., Haggard, S., Rodrik, D., and Wade, R. (1994), *Miracle or Design? Lessons from the East Asian Experience*. Washington: Overseas Development Council.

Gerschenkron, A. (1962), *Economic Backwardness in Historical Perspective*. Cambridge, Mass.: Belknap Press.

Greif, A. (1994), 'Trading Institutions and the Commercial Revolution in Medieval Europe', in A. Aganbegyan, O. Bogomolov, and M. Kaser (eds.), *Economics in a Changing World*, i. London: Macmillan.

Greif, A., Milgrom, P., and Weingast, B. (1994), 'Coordination, Commitment, and Enforcement: The Case of the Merchant Guild', *Journal of Political Economy*.

Hart, O., Shleifer, A., and Vishny, R. W. (1997), 'The Proper Scope of Government: Theory and an Application to Prisons', *Quarterly Journal of Economics*, 112.

Hayami, Y., and Ruttan, V. (1985), *Agricultural Development: An International Perspective*. Baltimore: Johns Hopkins University Press.

Hillman, A. (1989), *The Political Economy of Protection*. New York: Harwood Academic Publishers.

Keefer, P., and Knack, S. (1997), 'Does Social Capital Have an Economic Payoff? A Cross-Country Investigation', *Quarterly Journal of Economics*, 112.

Kranton, R. E., and Swamy, A. V. (1997), 'The Hazards of Piecemeal Reform: British Civil Courts and the Credit Market in Colonial India', unpublished paper, University of Maryland.

Laffont, J. J., and Tirole, J. (1994), *A Theory of Incentives in Procurement and Regulation*. Cambridge, Mass.: MIT Press.

Maskin, E., (1994), 'The Invisible Hand and Externalities', *American Economic Review*, May.

McGuire, M. C., and Olson, M. (1996), 'The Economics of Autocracy and Majority Rule', *Journal of Economic Literature*, 34.

Milgrom, P., and Roberts, J. (1990), 'Bargaining Costs, Influence Costs, and the Organization of Economic Activity', in J. E. Alt and K. A. Shepsle, *Perspectives on Positive Political Economy*. New York: Cambridge University Press.

Mookherjee, D., and Png, I. P. L. (1995), 'Corruptible Law Enforcers: How Should They be Compensated?' *Economic Journal*, 105.

North, D.C. (1981), *Structure and Change in Economic History*. New York: W. W. Norton.

—— (1990), *Institutions, Institutional Change and Economic Performance*. New York: Cambridge University Press.

Olson, M. (1965), *The Logic of Collective Action: Public Goods and the Theory of Groups*. Cambridge, Mass.: Harvard University Press.

—— (1982), *The Rise and Decline of Nations: Economic Growth, Stagflation, and Social Rigidities*. New Haven: Yale University Press.

Ouchi, W. G. (1980), 'Markets, Bureaucracies, and Clans', *Administrative Science Quarterly*, 25.

Przeworski, A. (1995), 'Reforming the State: Political Accountability and Economic Intervention', unpublished paper, New York University.

Redding, S. G. (1990), *The Spirit of Chinese Capitalism*. New York: Walter de Gruyter.

Robinson, J. A. (1996), 'Theories of "Bad Policy"', unpublished paper, University of Southern California.

Rodrik, D. (1992), 'Political Economy and Development Policy', *European Economic Review*, 36.

Shleifer, A., and Vishny, R. (1993), 'Corruption', *Quarterly Journal of Economics*, 108.

Stiglitz, J. E. *et al.* (1989), *The Economic Role of the State*. Oxford: Blackwell.

Tirole, J. (1994), 'The Internal Organization of Government', *Oxford Economic Papers*, 46.

Wade, R. (1990), *Governing the Market: Economic Theory and the Role of the Government in East Asian Industrialization*. Princeton: Princeton University Press.

Williamson, O. (1985), *The Economic Institutions of Capitalism*. New York: Free Press.

Wilson, J. Q. (1989), *Bureaucracy: What Government Agencies Do and Why They Do It*. New York: Basic Books.

World Bank (1993), *The East Asian Miracle: Economic Growth and Public Policy*. New York: Oxford University Press.

Wright, G. (1987), 'The Economic Revolution in the American South', *Journal of Economic Perspectives*, 1.

Index

Index 241